ESTATE PLANNING
A Guide for Advisors and Their Clients

About the Authors

D. Larry Crumbley, CPA, is Deborah D. Shelton Taxation Professor at Texas A&M University. A former trustee and president of the American Taxation Association, he is author or coauthor of 15 books, including 3 books in the estate and gift tax area. He is editor of the *Oil and Gas Tax Quarterly* and coeditor of the *Texas Tax Service*. Professor Crumbley currently serves on the editorial advisory board of the *Journal of the American Taxation Association,* the Energy Taxation Subcommittee of the American Institute of Certified Public Accountants, and the State Sales and Use Taxation Committee of the National Taxation Association. Dr. Crumbley is the author or coauthor of more than 200 articles in tax, accounting, and business publications.

   Edward E. Milam, CPA, is Dean and Professor of the School of Accountancy at the University of Mississippi. He is currently serving as Treasurer of the Federation of Schools of Accountancy and is on the Board of Trustees of the Mississippi Tax Institute. Dr. Milam is a charter member of the American Taxation Association and has served as secretary-treasurer of that organization. He has also been vice chairman of the Taxation Committee of the Mississippi Society of Certified Public Accountants and has participated in the Northeast Chapter of the Mississippi Estate Planning Association. Dr. Milam is active in numerous other professional activities and programs. He has published several books and articles in the area of taxation, including *Estate Planning in the '80s, A Practical Guide to Preparing a Tax Return for a Closely-Held Corporation,* "The CPA's Responsibility in Estate Planning" in *Estate Planning,* and "The Estate Planning Process" in *Trusts and Estates.*

ESTATE PLANNING
A Guide for Advisors and Their Clients

D. Larry Crumbley, CPA

Edward E. Milam, CPA

DOW JONES-IRWIN
Homewood, Illinois 60430

ISBN 0-87094-686-2
Library of Congress Catalog Card No. 85–71435

Printed in the United States of America

1 2 3 4 5 6 7 8 9 0 K 3 2 1 0 9 8 7 6

Preface

Everyone needs an estate plan—male or female, rich or poor, single or married, parent or child. Estate planning is a necessity not only for most business owners and employees but also for persons of more modest means. With the inflation of the last decade, many middle-class Americans who own their own homes and have life insurance policies often have a net worth approaching the estate tax threshold. This important book familiarizes readers with the important provisions of the estate, gift, and income laws so that they can realistically assess their personal financial situations.

A will is vital for everyone. Stories are legion about the disastrous consequences of dying without a will. Where there is no will the state court will appoint an administrator, and the law will determine how assets are to be distributed. Single people living together are especially vulnerable. Assets may go to distant nephews and nieces or even to enemies. The estate process can drag on for years. Who will take care of the children in case of a common disaster?

This helpful book provides a step-by-step process of evaluating an estate, investigating the utility of deferrals and gifts and trusts, assessing tax liabilities, and formulating a realistic plan suited to one's personal situation. This material also is helpful for reviewing older estate plans and wills. These plans and documents should be brought into compliance with the latest laws. Out-of-date plans should be altered in order to take advantage of various planning techniques. Otherwise, an estate tax liability may greatly exceed the amount that would be payable if some simple estate planning had been done.

Even though recent law changes have been far-reaching, the effect on any taxpayer depends entirely on his/her own specific circumstances. To be in the best possible position, taxpayers should be aware of all property owned. Second, they should resolve in their mind how the property might best be distributed among future heirs. As soon as these steps have been taken, expert estate and gift planning advice should be sought in order to ensure that these wishes will be fulfilled at the minimum tax costs.

This practical, easy-to-read guidebook spells out:

- What steps to take in order to protect your family now and in the future.
- How to make sure the government does not become your main beneficiary.
- How to plan for a common disaster in the form of custody agreements.
- How to work productively with tax pros to create an ironclad estate plan that keeps taxes to a bare minimum.
- How to create equitable treatment for children.
- How to plan for the enjoyment, management, and disposition of what you own and what you hope to accumulate.
- How to use trusts to manage assets and decrease liabilities.
- Tax-saving techniques to provide for the education of your children, the care of your spouse, and much more.

Give less to the IRS—legally.

D. Larry Crumbley
Edward E. Milam

Contents

1

The Estate Planning Process

Estate planning is social work among the rich.

—*Robert Brosterman*

Estate planning has been defined as the art of designing a program for the effective enjoyment, management, and disposition of property at the minimum possible tax cost.[1] It is more than just planning for death. Estate planning tries to encourage a wealth-building approach. Estate planning looks at the income tax, the fiduciary tax, the estate tax, and the gift tax in order to minimize the overall tax burden of the family unit. Building an estate throughout life should be part of estate planning.

Anyone with income or property must be concerned with estate planning. It may be even more important to the owner of a medium-sized estate than to the owner of a large estate, because the waste of a single asset in such an estate could prevent the accomplishment of objectives and bring hardship to the family. In other words, everyone who owns assets needs an estate plan. The estate plan might be reflected by a simple will or by a complex arrangement consisting of several of the estate planning devices or tools available to the estate owner. The massive changes in the estate tax area by the Economic Recovery Tax Act of 1981 and Tax Reform Act of 1984 make it imperative that all taxpayers review their current estate plans.

Because there are differences in people's objectives, attitudes, temperaments, and net assets, the estate plans of different people should be designed to meet their specific needs and satisfy their specific objectives. Moreover, each plan must reflect the responsibilities of the person for whom it is drawn. Estate planning is different in details for every individual, but the process is basically the same for everyone. It can be broken down conveniently into four steps:

1. Gathering the facts.
2. Evaluating the obstacles.
3. Designing the plan.
4. Implementing and reviewing the plan.

GATHERING THE FACTS

The facts themselves serve as the basis for all other procedures. Obtaining the facts may seem to be a simple task, but in many cases this is the most challenging part of the estate planning process. The facts needed can be classified into four categories: (1) domicile, (2) property, (3) beneficiaries, and (4) the individual's objectives.

Domicile

Domicile is important because it determines the law that will govern the validity of the will and its provisions. Domicile determines how title to property is held: community property versus separate property and joint tenancy versus a tenancy in common. Because the differences that exist between real property laws of differing states are significant, the domicile of the estate owner must be determined before plans are formulated.

Property

A complete inventory of a taxpayer's assets and liabilities should be gathered. Detailed information should be obtained with regard to all business and personal assets and liabilities. Such data would include insurance policies, powers of appointment, property owned separately and jointly, business interests, retirement and death benefits, claims under wills and trusts, and rights in future interests. In addition to these data, full information about the estate owner's obligations must be secured. These details include information about personal debts, business debts, accrued taxes, mortgages, leases, installment contracts, and all other debts, including contingent liabilities.

Special problems concerning an estate owner's business interests often arise in the analysis of his/her property, especially when these interests amount to a large portion of the estate. These business interests may be held in the form of sole propietorships, partnerships, stock in a closely held corporation or S corporation, or any combination of these.* Business ownership causes a problem of valuation. These interests must be properly valued for estate tax purposes in accordance with the Internal Revenue Code and Regulations. Another problem is the determination and the ability of the business to produce income for the benefit of the taxpayer's heirs after his/her death or retirement. Even when a business is the chief source of its owner's income and wealth and will continue to be so as long as it is actively managed by the owner, it may not continue to be profitable after the owner leaves or dies. Upon the death of the owner, the business interest becomes an investment of an estate, and it is valuable only if it continues to be profitable. Thus, care must be used in an evaluation of a person's business interests.

Beneficiaries

Facts concerning the beneficiaries of the estate owner must be gathered and accumulated by the estate owner or the estate planning team.† These facts should include the names and birthdates of the estate owner and all of his/her beneficiaries. An evaluation should be made of the estate owner's responsibility to the family. Such personal information as the character of the estate owner's spouse and other heirs and their busi-

---

*A corporation's stockholders may elect to be an S corporation, which allows the corporation to avoid the corporate tax.

†An estate planning team is often composed of an attorney, a certified public accountant (CPA), a trust officer, and a life insurance underwriter. This estate planning team can help in the selection of an executor or executrix.

ness abilities should be considered. A taxpayer's state of health, the wealth now available to his/her heirs, their financial needs, and the attitudes of individual beneficiaries toward each other are important. In summary, estate owners should obtain data about the health, wealth, education, character, and living needs of all their beneficiaries.[2]

Objectives

Finally, the objectives of the estate owner—his/her attitude and intentions toward the financial maintenance and security of the family—must be formulated. Many people feel that their heirs should have complete and unrestricted freedom to use the assets left to them while others have a fear of entrusting substantial amounts of money in lump sums to their beneficiaries. Family and human considerations may take precedence over tax considerations. For example, one of the authors heard one person state his estate objectives as follows: "I have told my children that if there is one thin dime left when I die, then that was a mistake on my part." Although few people will have such an attitude, making a determination of an estate owner's objectives is critical in the development of an estate plan. It is very often the most difficult phase of gathering the facts.

In addition to gathering the facts, an estate owner must determine and evaluate his/her existing estate plan. Whether estate owners are aware of it or not, they have an estate plan that may have been developed consciously or accidentally. Therefore, taxpayers must accumulate information concerning all gifts, trusts, wills, and reversionary interests they create or possess.[3]

This task of gathering the facts may appear to be tedious and dull, but it is often the most challenging and important part of the estate planning process. Many estate owners who have not made such a thorough analysis of their estates have been surprised at the results. Such an analysis is necessary to lay a firm foundation for the remainder of the estate planning process.

EVALUATING THE OBSTACLES

The second phase of the estate planning process is an evaluation of the obstacles that could impair the value of the estate.

An estate owner and the members of the estate planning team must be aware of the many forces that can shrink the value of the estate and deny the attainment of the owner's objectives. Some of the more obvious of these impairments are the cost of the last illness, funeral expenses, estate administration expenses, and federal estate tax. Consideration must be given to all debts of great magnitude and long duration, such as mortgages, installment contracts, and business obligations. Attention must also be directed toward unpaid income and property taxes as well as state inheritance taxes.

According to Pfeffer, there are four classes of risk encountered in estate conservation problems. These classes are business, investment, legal, and tax risks.[4]

Business Risks

The management of any business is subject to a wide spectrum of risks, and competent managerial personnel must have the ability to successfully operate the firm. Some relevant questions for estate planning are (1) whether or not the management has the technical ability and training to continue profitable operation of the firm; (2) whether or not there are any heirs or key employees who have the aptitude, temperament, and capacity to be potential successors to the management; and (3) whether or not additional capital contributions will be necessary to maintain the current level of earnings.[5] Moreover, any evaluation of business risks must include an analysis of the current and future economic climate and its influences on the business. In addition there are some important insurable business hazards that must be considered. These include legal liability; property damage; theft; surety bonds; and life, accident, and health risks.

If a taxpayer's business interests are closely held, special problems arise. These include problems of valuation and liquidity. To effectively analyze the business risks of a closely held firm, the estate owner and the estate planning team should be knowledgeable of the taxpayer's particular business as well as the economy in general. In valuing the business interests for estate planning purposes, several factors must be considered. These factors include the nature and history of the business, conditions in the specific industry as well as the general economic outlook, the financial condition of the organization, the book value of the taxpayer's interests, past earnings, current earnings as well as potential earning ability, dividend policy, and the value of goodwill and other intangibles. To determine whether the business can serve as a source of liquidity for the estate, an analysis of the firm's cash flow must be conducted.

Investment Risks

Portfolio management is concerned with investment risks, which are usually classified as purchasing-power risks, interest-rate risks, business risks, and market risks.[6] When the estate owner has significant investments, some member of the estate planning team must analyze these holdings with respect to the investment risks and take steps to prevent impairment of the estate if they are considered detrimental. Such steps would include diversification of various kinds and the selection of securities on the basis of their relative invulnerability to depreciation.[7]

Legal Risks

Another type of risk in estate planning, as pointed out by Pfeffer, is lack of legal documentation. Legal risk arises from the failure of the estate owner and the estate planning team to properly execute the appropriate documents essential to carry out the objectives of the estate owner. All wills, trusts, contracts, and titles to property must be valid and properly executed. These instruments should be prepared by a competent lawyer and then reviewed periodically to ensure that they are still in accordance with the desires of the individual. Estate plans that are developed in an atmosphere of ill-defined objectives, procrastination, poorly drawn legal documents, and uncoordinated planning result in unstable designs and legal vulnerability. Much of the ultimate frustration relevant to the legal aspects of estate planning can be avoided by consulting an attorney who is well versed in preventive law.[8]

Tax Risks

Estate owners frequently seek planning assistance because they are primarily concerned with estate conservation and the effect of taxes on it. Poor or no tax planning can seriously deplete the value of an estate. Many factors having significant tax consequences must be evaluated. These include the differential tax treatment of ordinary versus capital gains income, the two different effective tax rates under the single unified rate structure, devolution of community versus separate property, estates held in joint tenancy rather than in common, and gifts in contemplation of death versus valid gifts. Another factor having significant tax consequences is the successive taxation of estates when surviving heirs die shortly after the decease of the estate owner.[9]

An evaluation of these tax risks calls for a high degree of skill in the estate planning process. In order for the estate planning team to be effective, at least one member must be knowledgeable of the basic provisions of the federal estate and gift tax laws and must have an understanding of the sections of the Internal Revenue Code that govern the taxing of income of fiduciaries. Such knowledge is necessary so that protective tax planning can be carried out during the taxpayer's lifetime and can be applicable throughout the administration of the estate after his/her death.

Some member of the estate planning team should be familiar with the interrelationships among the federal estate and fiduciary income tax laws. When properly executed, many of these interrelationships allow the administrator to make tax elections that can result in significant overall tax savings to the beneficiaries of the estate. For instance, the value of the assets as shown on the estate tax return may determine the basis of these assets to the beneficiaries for income tax purposes under the step-up-in-basis rules. Many other interrelationships between the two taxes must be considered by the administrator (executor or executrix) and the tax advisor.

The inclusion in the decedent's gross estate of a comprehensive range of property and property interests along with the high estate tax rates magnifies the need for estate planning. Tax planning is not only very important in estate planning but is also necessary in postmortem planning. During this time, many decisions have significant effects on the conservation of the estate, and a proper analysis of available alternatives can result in significant tax savings and help preserve the taxpayer's estate.

Postmortem Conservation of Liquid Assets

Several other factors that cause impairment of the estate should be considered by the members of the estate planning team. One of the most important of these factors is the liquidity of the assets. Many estates are burdened with debts and obligations; the estate must pay the cost of the last illness, funeral expenses, estate-administration expenses, federal and state taxes, and it must also honor the cash bequests of the decedent. Since there must be a sufficient amount of liquid assets to meet these needs, the liquidity needs of the taxpayer's estate should be determined. Using the information obtained during the fact-gathering stage as a guide, the members of the estate planning team should be able to make rough estimates of these costs. These estimates will help determine the cash requirements of estate disbursements and serve as additional background information for the preparation of the estate plan. If the estate is burdened with a shortage of liquid assets, income-producing assets might have to be sold, possibly for less than their real value, to meet these needs. The dilution of the income-producing assets may have significant adverse effects on the survivors of the decedent.

Another source of impairment that demands consideration is the instability of the property values of the estate. Changes in consumer preference, obsolescence, or improper management of the estate's assets could cause a severe shrinkage in the value of the estate. It is important to consider the possibility of prolonged and expensive illness or disability, loss of income, and legal liability of the estate owner. Insurance should be acquired to help reduce the burden in case one or more of these possibilities occurs.[10]

Certainly, the members of the estate planning team must analyze all factors that could shrink or deplete the value of the taxpayer's estate. However, this evaluation of risks is only one step in the estate planning process. There are several other steps that are just as important.

DESIGNING THE PLAN

Designing the plan is the next step in the estate planning process. No meaningful design can be adopted until all the facts have been gathered and the objectives of the estate owner have been determined. It is on these facts and objectives that the plan must be based. To be worthwhile, the plan must be capable of accomplishing the objectives of the estate owner. This requisite increases the importance of the estate planning team, for the members of the team, having played the role of investigators, now must use their creative skills and abilities to create an effective plan, one that is as simple and flexible as possible while still accomplishing its objectives.[11]

A variety of methods exist to help accomplish the objectives of the estate owner. Through an analysis of various combinations of these transfers of assets, the ultimate plan is developed. The plan should be tested and the consequences evaluated. No attempt is made in this chapter to mention all the available vehicles of transfer, but the following strategies may be appropriate:

1. Equalize both spouses' estate tax brackets to take advantage of the progressive tax structure.
2. Make full use of the unified credit in the estate of both spouses.
3. Delay the payment of the estate tax liability until the death of the surviving spouse.
4. Defer the payment of current tax liability until more liberal features of the law come into effect.

The Estate Owner's Will

The will is a key vehicle of transfer, and its preparation is often the first step taken by estate owners in planning the disposition of their estates. *Everybody needs a will.* Stories are legion about the disastrous consequences of dying intestate. Dying intestate refers to dying without a will. In such a case, the state laws tell how the assets will be distributed—a will by default. The state court will appoint an administrator (who may not be qualified to manage your estate). Assets, therefore, might go to children of a previous marriage, to distant nephews and nieces, or even to enemies. The estate process can drag on for many years. The lawyer(s) may get the bulk of the estate assets.

Without a will, an estate owner agrees to allow the state to draft a will for the decedent. Most state laws assume that family members (and not friends) are the natural objects of one's bounty. For the nearly 2 million unmarried couples living together, dying without a will can have catastrophic consequences. Most state laws do not recognize a "living together" relationship. Certainly the law on intestate succession is especially problematic for homosexuals. Young people do not necessarily live to old age.

Wills and estate plans become outdated and must be reviewed and revised. Thus, people outgrow their initial wills, and new laws make revisions of wills essential. Estate planning is a lifelong process.

If a person runs a business, mention should be made in the will about operation of the business after the decedent's death. In some states an executor cannot lawfully continue a business without a specific authorization. The business operations may come to a halt, buildings may deteriorate, or the business may have to liquidate if proper authority is not given.

The will is used to designate heirs, identify the property they are to receive, indicate the person (or institution) who will act as administrator of the estate, and clarify similar details. Some useful provisions attached to this document are the marital deduction and the marital deduction trusts. The basic advantage of using the marital deduction is the favorable tax consequences. The cost of this tax savings, however, may be the compromise of the estate owner's objectives, the possible deferred increase in transfer costs, or the loss of control of an asset.[12]

Under certain conditions and limitations, the estates of citizens and residents of the United States are allowed an unlimited marital deduction. The purpose of the marital deduction is to eliminate the tax advantages held by those persons domiciled in community-property states. These statutes provide all taxpayers with the same tax treatment as were previously available only to residents of community-property states.

Trusts

Trusts are another means of transfer. Inter vivos and testamentary, revocable and irrevocable, and funded and unfunded trusts may be used by the estate planner. Some of the important advantages of trusts are that they are based on the concepts of property arrangement and property settlement. The main purpose of the trust device is to serve as a means of preserving and administering property for the benefit of the beneficiaries.

Because it permits considerable flexibility in the disposition of property, the trust is one of the most valuable tools in estate planning. It provides the flexibility needed to achieve nontax objectives, such as relieving other family members of responsibility, obtaining competent management of the property, providing discretion in income and principal distributions, and many others. Also advantageous, and perhaps equally significant in many instances, are the income and estate tax economies obtainable through the use of trusts.

Trusts are formed for many purposes. A trust may be created to achieve any desired objective, as long as the objective is not illegal or contrary to any policy or rule of law. Some of the more common types of trusts, classified as to purpose, include insurance trusts, educational trusts, support trusts, charitable trusts, exemption-equivalent trusts, and marital-deduction trusts.

When a trust is created, it is only natural and proper that the grantor and the estate planning team should construct it in a way that maximizes the use of the available favorable tax provisions. However, the purpose of a trust's establishment is ordinarily not just to save taxes. The saving of taxes is one reason for the creation of trusts, but the process of carrying out an orderly and sensible disposition of the trust property according to the desires of the estate owner should be the primary reason for its establishment. The generation-skipping tax must be considered when a trust is established, however.

Life Insurance

Another means of transfer is life insurance, which is often the only practical way of guaranteeing that sufficient cash will be available to meet the financial costs of death. Life insurance has many advantages. In many states its use provides savings in estate taxes. Also, insurance proceeds can be removed from the probate estate (by giving up all incidents of ownership), thus reducing probate and administrative costs. In many instances, the greatest advantage of life insurance in estate planning is that it can satisfy the obligations of the estate, thus preventing the forced sale of income-producing assets. In essence, the inclusion of life insurance in the estate plan should be determined by the needs for liquidity, flexibility, tax minimization, investment, and the requirements of family income.[13]

As with other devices of transfer, estate owners and their advisors should carefully consider the tax consequences of the use of life insurance, which provides many tax advantages.

Annuities

Private annuities represent another important vehicle of transfer. However, careful consideration must be given to the risks involved. In such a contract, the annuitant transfers property other than cash to the obligor in return for the obligor's unsecured promise to make periodic payments of money to the annuitant for a specific period of time. The period of time is usually for the life of the annuitant. Thus, the major risk to the annuitant is the obligor's failure to make the required payments.

Fortunately, the private annuity offers several tax advantages. First, since this is a valid sales contract, the property is removed from the estate of the obligor. Second, Section 72 (of the Internal Revenue Code) governs the income taxability of the annuity payments. Thus, each payment is broken into three portions: an excluded portion, an ordinary income portion, and a capital gain or loss portion. This gives the annuitant the additional advantage of spreading any gain from the sale of such property over a period of several years for income tax purposes. In essence, it gives the annuitant a deferment for payment of income taxes associated with the transfer.

A new set of 10 percent actuarial tables are used in valuation of annuities and life estates. These new tables require higher payments to be made in retained-income transactions and generate interest income to the annuitant, with a nondeductible basis to the obligor. Thus, an alternative to a private annuity is a self-canceling installment note (SCIN). Essentially, an SCIN works as follows. A person sells an asset to someone (such as a relative) and receives an installment note. The installment note is paid in full over the actuarial life expectancy of the seller. Since the installment note is canceled automatically in the event of the seller's death, a "risk premium" is added to the sale price of the asset to compensate the seller for a possible early death. An SCIN may be superior to a private annuity.

Lifetime Gifts

Another effective vehicle of transfer in estate planning is the lifetime gift, which eliminates all probate and administration expenses on the property transferred. Gifts may reduce estate taxes because the amount of income that would have been accumulated from the property is removed from the transferor's gross estate. Often the use of a gift provides savings in income taxes because the income is shifted from the high-income tax bracket of the transferor into the low income tax bracket of the transferee. Of course, the use of gifts produces many advantages other than taxes. They may be used to continue control of a business within the family or to serve specific desires the estate owner has for his children. Gifts, like all other devices, have their costs; the most significant cost of making a gift is the complete loss of control of the asset. Of course, with the unified tax structure, the use of gifts as an estate planning tool has lost some of its glamour.

Before making lifetime gifts, it must be remembered that, under certain circumstances, the gift property may later be included in the donor's gross estate along with a gross-up of the gift taxes even though they were made during the donor's lifetime. Without adequate and full consideration of this tax risk, any transfers of certain types of property made by the decedent within three years of death are interpreted as having been made in contemplation of death; thus, such property and gift tax gross-ups are included in the donor's gross estate. Likewise, the relinquishment of a power over property transferred during lifetime, or the exercise or release of a power of appointment, within three years before death is deemed to have been made in contemplation of death.

The vehicles of transfer discussed in the preceding paragraphs are only some of those available to the estate owner. During the design and before the implementation of an estate plan, the members of the estate planning team must evaluate the advantages and disadvantages of these methods of transfer. The vehicles that aid in the accomplishment of the estate owner's objectives should be incorporated into the estate plan.

IMPLEMENTING AND REVIEWING THE PLAN

Before the estate plan becomes effective, the appropriate legal documents must be executed. The necessity for careful planning and execution of the legal documents cannot be overemphasized, for faulty execution is a sure way of invalidating the entire efforts of any estate plan. Thus, these legal instruments must be drafted by a competent attorney who is well versed in estate planning techniques.

These documents must be reviewed periodically to ascertain that they continue to express the objectives of the estate owner. A periodic review of the financial status and other family relationships should be conducted to determine if there have been any changes that necessitate a revision of the estate plan. Also, the plan should be reviewed in the light of any changes or potential changes in the relevant legal or tax aspects. Such a review could bring about a modification in the plan that would produce significant benefits to the estate owner, while the neglect of such a review could be very costly.

As can be seen from the preceding discussion of the estate planning process, many professional skills are required to effectively perform such a service. Usually, a team effort is utilized during the process. The attorney, the accountant (CPA), the trust officer, and the life insurance underwriter are the professionals most often associated with the team.

THE ESTATE PLANNING TEAM

By virtue of his/her tendency toward salesmanship, the life insurance underwriter is often the prime motivator in interesting prospects in an estate plan that will eventually involve the orchestration of the other members of the estate planning team. Unlike the lawyer and the accountant, the insurance salesperson has a license to sell and has a special skill to seek out and solicit new insurance business. Often the life insurance underwriter uncovers situations where only a properly executed estate plan can save a taxpayer's estate from erosion.

Also, the insurance underwriter has a specialized knowledge of the many forms of life insurance and knows what various policies can and cannot do.

The attorney's participation is most essential in determining the legal and tax consequences of every phase in the process of developing an estate plan. The lawyer must determine whether certain recommendations and phases in the formulation of the plan have legal substance and merit. Only a competent attorney can draft the legal documents that provide the framework for the execution of the estate plan.

Estate planning is the trust officer's prime concern not only because it is a device for developing new business but also because it constitutes the bulk of the trust department's activities. The trust officer, who is essentially an instrument of estate conservation and management, can lend advice on the practicalities of the plan and play a major role in the administration of the estate. Under a specific agreement, he/she accepts custody of the property, manages and invests it, and distributes it to the beneficiaries according to the stipulations of the trust instrument.

Normally, the accountant (CPA) is considered to be the member of the estate planning team who is intimately acquainted with the financial affairs of the taxpayer and is knowledgeable about income and estate tax laws. In addition, the CPA is to advise on valuation problems and to determine the existing and potential earning power of a business. Otherwise, the accountant's role as a member of the estate planning team is not so easily ascertained or clearly defined as the roles of the other members; but because accountants know their clients' affairs, they should recognize each client's need for estate planning services. Therefore, the accountant is often the person on the team who has the responsibility to initiate the estate planning process.

NOTES

1. W. C. Clay, Jr., *Estate Planning* (Homewood, Ill.: Dow-Jones Irwin, 1982), p. 1.
2. W. H. Hoffman, Jr., *Effective Estate Planning Procedures for Minimizing Taxes* (Englewood Cliffs, N.J.: Prentice-Hall, 1968), p. 3.
3. L. J. Ackerman, "Estate Planning Principles," in *Life and*

Health Insurance Handbook, ed. D. W. Gregg (Homewood, Ill.: Richard D. Irwin, 1959), p. 498.

4. Irving Pfeffer, "The Nature and Scope of Estate Planning," *California Management Review* 9 (Fall 1966), p. 26.
5. Ackerman, "Estate Planning Principles," pp. 497–98.
6. Donald E. Vaughn, *Survey of Investments* (New York: Holt, Rinehart & Winston, 1967), p. 49.
7. Pfeffer, "The Nature and Scope of Estate Planning," pp. 26–27.
8. Ibid., p. 27.
9. Ibid.
10. Ackerman, "Estate Planning Principles," pp. 494–95.
11. Ibid., p. 498.
12. Ibid., p. 499.
13. Ibid., pp. 499–500.

2

What Is Included in Gross Estate?

The legal right of a taxpayer to decrease the amount of what otherwise would be his taxes, or altogether avoid them, by means which the law permits, cannot be doubted.

—Justice George Sutherland

The federal estate tax is an excise tax on the privilege of transferring property at the time of a person's death. This levy is not a property tax or a tax on the right of the beneficiary to receive the property. Unlike a state inheritance tax, the rates are not dependent upon the relationship of the beneficiaries to the decedent. Note that the same unified rate structure also applies to lifetime gifts after 1976.

Since the federal estate tax (like any other liability) dilutes the amount of assets passing to the heirs, many people seek effective ways to reduce this tax burden. However, before an individual can evaluate the diluting effects of federal taxes on assets, he/she must have some familiarity with the basic provisions of the estate tax laws. These laws apply not only to every citizen and resident of this country but also to any nonresident alien who dies and leaves property located within the United States. However, the federal estate tax laws differ between citizens and residents and those who are nonresidents and not citizens. This chapter is concerned only with the statutes that apply to citizens and/or residents of the United States.

OVERVIEW OF THE ESTATE TAX LAWS

Basically, the gross estate includes all property owned in whole or in part by the decedent at the time of death. The value of such property is limited to the extent of the decedent's interest in it. Also, the gross estate may include assets that may not be in the probated will. These assets may include property in which the decedent had a general power of appointment, certain gifts made within three years of death, jointly owned property, dower or curtesy rights of a surviving spouse, revocable transfers made by the decedent, proceeds of certain life insurance policies, and annuities.

In order to determine the decedent's taxable estate, certain deductions are subtracted from the gross estate. Some of the allowable deductions include funeral and administrative expenses, debts of the decedent, taxes, casualty losses, charitable contributions, and a marital deduction for bequests to the spouse.

The appropriate unified estate tax rates are applied to the taxable estate to obtain the gross estate tax. However, in order to determine the net estate tax that is payable, certain authorized credits are subtracted from the gross estate tax. These credits include a credit for state death taxes paid, a credit for tax on prior transfers, a credit for foreign death taxes, and a unified estate and gift tax credit. A credit is a dollar-for-dollar offset against the tax.

The unified credit for both the estate tax and the gift tax will be increased gradually from $47,000 to $192,800 over a six-year period, as shown in Table 1. Each unified credit is approximately equivalent to an exemption (that is, deduction) as listed in the last column of the table.

Since the unified credit is increased gradually, inflation will erode the impact of these increases. For example, with an average inflation rate of 10 percent, this $600,000 equivalent exemption in 1987 will be only about $300,000 in terms of 1981 dollars (10 percent $\times$ 5 years = 50 percent). Thus, the need for estate planning has not been eliminated.

The estate tax filing requirements have been revised to reflect the increased unified credits. In 1987 and thereafter, an estate tax return will have to be filed if the gross estate exceeds $600,000. In the interim the threshold filing requirement will be $225,000 in 1982, $275,000 in 1983, $325,000 in

TABLE 1 Increase in Unified Credit for the Estate
Tax and the Gift Tax from 1981 to 1987

Year	Unified Credit	Equivalent Exemption
1981	$ 47,000	$175,625
1982	62,800	225,000
1983	79,300	275,000
1984	96,300	325,000
1985	121,800	400,000
1986	155,800	500,000
1987 and after	192,800	600,000

1984, $400,000 in 1985, and $500,000 in 1986. Of course, these filing requirements are reduced (not below zero) by the sum of (1) any adjusted taxable gifts made by the decedent after December 31, 1976, and (2) any specific gift tax exemption that may have been used by the decedent for gifts and made between September 8, 1976, and January 1, 1977. (Obviously, in order to obtain the full reduction in the rates and the maximum unified credit, a person should wait until 1987 to die.)

GROSS ESTATE

Before any estimate can project the amount of estate tax to be paid on the death of an individual, one must know what assets are included in the gross estate and also the value to be placed on them. Without knowledge of these two things, the estate planner is helpless in estimating the potential estate tax.

All property, including real or personal, tangible or intangible, owned in whole or in part by the decedent at the time of death is included in gross estate to the extent of the value of any interest in such property.[1] Until July 1, 1964, the gross estate did not include any real property located outside the United States; however, the law was amended to include such property of all decedents who died after that date. Since the gross estate includes the value of the decedent's interest in all property owned at his/her death, ownership is an important factor in determining the gross estate. Normally, local property law controls the issue of ownership for tax purposes.

The decedent's gross estate is composed of a wide variety of "owned" property. The gross estate also includes certain other assets in which the interest of the decedent is considered to be substantially equivalent to ownership, although the decedent held no legal interest in the property at the time of death. Items in this category are discussed below.

A remainder interest or other future interest in property is pulled into gross estate by Section 2033 unless the interest is a contingent remainder or some other future interest that terminates upon the death of a decedent.[2] A contingent remainder is an interest that does not come into enjoyment and possession unless a certain condition or contingency occurs or an interest that may terminate upon the occurrence (or nonoccurrence) of an event in the future.[3] The death of an individual without children or before a specific date are examples of such an event.

As a general rule, when a person retains an interest in a transferred property, but that interest is contingent on the person remaining alive, Section 2033 does not pull such an interest into gross estate.

A vested remainder is pulled into a remainder person's estate by Section 2033 when he/she dies before obtaining such property interest.[4] However, a remainder interest is limited to the remainder person's life since his/her interest in the property interest terminates at his/her death.[5]

EXAMPLE 1. Don transfers assets to a trust with income to Ann for life, remainder to Bob (if living), and any remainder to Carl (or Carl's estate). If Bob dies but is survived by Ann, nothing will be included in Bob's estate since the interest evaporates at his death. If Carl dies, survived by Ann but not Bob, Carl's interest is included in his estate. Carl's interest became vested upon Bob's death. Obviously, for tax-planning purposes it is advantageous to give a person a remainder that is dependent upon his/her survival (that is, "if living") rather than an absolute interest (that is, "or to his/her estate").

Dower or Curtesy Interest

The gross estate of a decedent includes the value of all property passing to the surviving spouse as dower or curtesy or by virtue of a statute creating an estate in lieu of dower and curtesy as determined by the laws of the specific state. A dower (to the wife) or curtesy (to the husband) is a statutory provision in a common-law state which directs a certain portion of the estate to the surviving spouse (often one third of the estate). However, state law does not determine the tax status of that interest under the federal statute.[6]

EXAMPLE 2. Wife is killed in a car accident without a will (that is, intestate), leaving an estate of $900,000. Under the state law, husband is entitled to one third of the wife's estate. The $300,000 that the husband receives is included in wife's gross estate under Section 2034.

Retained Life Interest

A transfer with a retained life interest is included in the gross estate. Included under this provision is the value of all property or property interest transferred by a decedent, by trust or otherwise, if the decedent retained it for life or for any period not ascertainable without reference to death or for a period of time that in fact does not end before the decedent's death. Specifically, under the federal statute, such interest is identified by

1. The possession, right to income, or other enjoyment of the property [Section 2036 (a)(1)].

2. The right, either alone or in conjunction with any other person, to designate who shall possess or enjoy the property or the income therefrom [Section 2036(a)(2)].[7]

According to Reg. 20.2036-1, the use, possession, right to the income, or other enjoyment of the property is considered as having been retained by the decedent if it is to be applied to the discharge of any of his/her legal obligations, including the obligation during lifetime to support a dependent. The phrase "right...to designate the person or persons who shall possess or enjoy the transferred property or the income therefrom" does not apply to a power held solely by a person other than the decedent. But if the decedent reserved the unrestricted power to remove a trustee at any time and appoint himself/herself as trustee, the decedent is considered as having the powers of the trustee.

EXAMPLE 3. Husband created a trust naming an independent party the trustee. Any income from this trust was to go to his three minor children to be used to help satisfy his obligation to support them. After the children reached age 18, the income interests were to continue for each of their lives. At the death of each child, one third of the trust was to pass to each child's children. Husband died when his children were 12, 15, and 23 years of age. Since two thirds of the trust income was being used to satisfy the legal obligation of support, two thirds of the trust assets would be included in husband's gross estate under Section 2036.

EXAMPLE 4. Husband deeds house to his wife, but continues to live in the home. More than three years later husband dies. As long as there is not an implicit agreement that the husband may live in the house, Section 2036 would not pull the house into the decedent's estate. (See *A. D. Gutchess,* 46 T.C. 554 (1966), acq. 1967-1 C.B.2.)

Retaining the right to vote, either directly or indirectly, shares of stock of a controlled corporation is considered to be a retention of the enjoyment of the stock for purposes of Section 2036(a). Control refers to the ownership of or the right to vote stock possessing at least 20 percent of the total combined voting power of all classes of stock. The transfer of nonvoting shares would not seem to fall within Section 2036(b), even where the decedent retained shares with voting rights.

A relinquishment or cessation of voting rights is treated as a gift in contemplation of death under Section 2035. However, this is a problem only if the corporation was a controlled one at some time after the transfer and within three years of death.

Property Transfers

Transfers taking effect at death must be included in the gross estate under Section 2037. The decedent's gross estate must include the value of any interest in property transferred by the decedent in any way, except for an adequate and full consideration in money or money's worth, if all the following conditions are met:

1. Possession or enjoyment of the property could, through ownership of the interest, have been obtained only by surviving the decedent.
2. The decedent has retained a reversionary interest in the transferred property by the expressed terms of the instrument of transfer.
3. The value of the reversionary interest immediately before the death of the decedent exceeds 5 percent of the value of the transferred property.

For purposes of this section, the term *reversionary interest* includes the possibility that property transferred by the decedent may return to the decedent or his/her estate or may be subject to a power of disposition by the decedent. This term does not include rights to income only. The value of such reversionary interest is determined by the usual methods of valuation, including the use of mortality tables and actuarial principles.[8] In essence, whereas a transfer with a retained life estate (Section 2036) pulls in the entire amount of the property, a transfer taking effect at death (Section 2037) pulls in some of the property.

EXAMPLE 5. An individual (decedent) transfers property to a trust with the income payable to his wife for life and with the remainder payable to the decedent or, if he is not living at his wife's death, to his daughter or her estate. The daughter could not obtain possession or enjoyment of the property without surviving the decedent. Assume the decedent's reversionary interest immediately before his death exceeded 5 percent of the value of the property; the value of the property, less the value of the wife's outstanding life estate, is includable in the decedent's gross estate under Section 2037.

Revocable Transfers

Revocable transfers are drawn back into the gross estate under Section 2038. Property transferred during the decedent's lifetime is includable in the decedent's gross estate if at the time of his/her death the enjoyment of the property is subject to change through the exercise of a power to alter, amend, revoke, or terminate by the decedent, either alone or in conjunction with another person.[9] However, according to Reg. 20.2038-1 this provision does not apply (1) to the extent that the transfer was for adequate and full consideration in money or money's worth, (2) if the decedent's power could be exercised only with the consent of all parties having an interest in the transferred property, or (3) to a power held solely by a person other than the decedent.

EXAMPLE 6. Husband creates a trust with income to wife or wife's estate for husband's life and remainder to his son or son's estate. Husband, as the trustee, retains a power to give the remainder to his daughter. If husband dies, everything is pulled into his gross estate under Section 2038.

EXAMPLE 7. Grantor transfers some securities to his minor daughter (age two years) under the Model Gifts of Securities to Minors Act. Grantor is the custodian of the stock. Although this is a valid technique for income tax purposes, if the grantor dies before the daughter reaches majority, the securities are included in the grantor's gross estate under Section 2038. Of course, to avoid this unfavorable tax result, someone else should be appointed the custodian (for example, the grantor's spouse).

The regulations provide actuarial tables that must be used for determining life estates, annuities, terms for years, remainders, and reversions. Only if the individual is known to have been afflicted at the time of the transfer with an incurable physical condition that is in such an advanced stage that death is clearly imminent may conditions other than the tables be considered.[10]

Annuities

The gross estate includes the value of an annuity or other payment receivable by a beneficiary by reason of surviving the decedent under any form of contract or agreement, including employment plans and agreements (except life insurance contracts) when the value of the annuity or other payment is attributable to contributions made by the decedent or his/her employer. This inclusion is true if (1) the payment or annuity was payable to the decedent or (2) the decedent possessed the right to receive such annuity or payment, either alone or in conjunction with another, for his/her life or for any period not ascertainable without reference to death or for any period that does not in fact end before his/her death.[11]

The amount included in the gross estate under such a contract is limited to the part of the value of the annuity receivable that is proportionate to the part of the purchase price contributed by the decedent's employer. For this purpose, any contribution made by the decedent's employer or former employer as a consequence of his employment is considered as being contributed by the decedent. There is excluded, however, the value of annuities or other benefits receivable by a beneficiary (other than the estate) under certain qualified employee benefit plans. This exclusion applies only to the benefits attributable to the employer's contributions.[12] Further, an annuity that terminates at the decedent's death (that is, single-life, nonrefund annuity) is not included in the decedent's gross estate.

EXAMPLE 8.   Husband enters into a contract with an insurance company under which he paid the company $100,000, and his wife paid $50,000 from her funds. The company agreed that in 1988 they would pay husband $200 per month for life, and after his death the company would make like payment to his wife for life. Husband dies in 1985, survived by his wife. Two thirds of the value of the annuity would be included in husband's estate under Section 2039(b).

Powers of Appointment

The value of all property over which the decedent possessed a general power of appointment at the time of death is includable in his/her gross estate. A general power of appointment is one under which holders have the right to dispose of the property in favor of (1) themselves, (2) their estate, (3) their creditors, or (4) the creditors of their estate. In essence, if one should exercise a general power of appointment during lifetime, there is a taxable gift. But if the general power is held at death, the property is included in the gross estate under Section 2041.

There are some exceptions to this definition of a general power of appointment:

1. When the holder's right to consume or invade the property is limited by an ascertainable standard relating to his/her needs for health, maintenance, support, or education, the power is not considered to be a general power of appointment.

2. If power created on or before October 21, 1942, is exercisable by the decedent only in conjunction with another person, it is not general.

3. If power created after October 21, 1942, is exercisable by the decedent only in conjunction with the creator of the power or with a person having substantial interest in the property subject to the power in the decedent's favor, it is excluded.

4. If the power may be exercised both in favor of the decedent and the persons whose consent the decedent must have, the power is general to the extent of the decedent's fractional interest in it.[13]

A general power is different from a special power of appointment. A special power of appointment may appoint anyone other than the four parties mentioned above. An individual may hold a special power of appointment at death and not include the property in the gross estate.

EXAMPLE 9. Decedent was granted a life estate in a trust with a power to invade corpus as desired in order to continue an accustomed standard of living. Since decedent possessed a power that was not limited by an ascertainable standard relating to health, education, support, or maintenance, decedent possessed a general power of appointment and the property would be included in her gross estate under Section 2041.

EXAMPLE 10. Decedent has a general power of appointment created in 1968 by grantor. However, decedent has the right to appoint all of the corpus of the trust to anyone, but only with the consent of Harvey. After decedent's death, Harvey alone will have the power to appoint corpus of the trust to anyone. Since Harvey can wait and get all of the trust (that is, an adverse interest), the trust corpus is not included in decedent's gross estate under Section 2041(b)(1)(c)(ii).

EXAMPLE 11. Property from a trust created by decedent's husband poured at her death into her revocable trust. Since this trust provided for distribution to her estate, creditor and creditors of her estate, then she had a general power of appointment under Section 2041.[14]

Life Insurance

Proceeds of insurance on the decedent's life, receivable by or for the benefit of the estate or by other beneficiaries, are included in the gross estate of the decedent under Section 2042. Life insurance, for estate tax purposes, includes not only the common forms of insurance taken out by people upon their lives but also the proceeds of certain other types of policies, including accident insurance, war risk insurance, and group insurance. Life insurance payable to named beneficiaries is subject to special rules. The proceeds of such a policy are included in the gross estate only if the decedent possessed at his/her death any incidents of ownership in the policy or certain reversionary interests.

The term *reversionary interest* includes the possibility that the policy or the proceeds of the policy may return to the decedent or the estate. For the proceeds of the policy to be included in the decedent's gross estate, the value of such reversionary interest must exceed 5 percent of the value of the policy immediately before the death of the decedent. The value of a reversionary interest is determined by the usual methods of valuation, including the use of mortality tables and actuarial principles.[15]

If a decedent/insured has a controlling interest in a corporation, there is a difference in treatment. Where the proceeds are payable to the corporate owner or for the corporate purposes, the proceeds become a factor in the valuation of the decedent's interest in the corporation.[16] Whereas if the proceeds are payable for noncorporate purposes, the corporate incidents of ownership are attributed to the decedent.[17] Similarly, insurance proceeds are includable in gross estate under Section 2042(2) where they are payable for other than partnership purposes.

Real Property Interests

There are various types of joint ownership of property. Tenancy by the entirety with rights of survivorship occurs between a husband and wife. Joint tenancy with rights of survivorship occurs between nonspouses. Before 1977, under both arrangements, each party was viewed as owning all under Section 2040. A tenancy in common (without rights of survivorship) is an undivided interest that can be transferred during life or at death. At death, the applicable portion of the undivided interest is included in gross estate under Section 2033. Community property occurs in seven states where each spouse is viewed as having one half vested property rights. At death, one half of the community property is included in the gross estate under Section 2033.

Joint Spousal Transfers after 1981

The rules for property held jointly by spouses with survivorship rights are fairly simple for tax years after 1981. Each spouse is to be treated as one-half owner of joint tenancy assets, regardless of which spouse furnished the funds to acquire the property and regardless of how the joint tenancy was created. Thus, the first spouse to die includes one half of the joint tenancy in gross estate, and only one half of any separate property will receive a step-up in basis. Step-up in basis is the difference between the price the decedent originally paid for an asset and its fair market value when an heir receives it. If an asset's value has increased, the resulting gain to the heir is not taxable to the heir, either when he/she receives the asset or when he/she eventually disposes of it. This is an extremely important concept in tax planning.

EXAMPLE 12. A married couple owns a $190,000 house (that cost them $40,000 many years ago) in a separate-property state. Husband dies in 1985 and one half of the value of the house is included in his gross estate, but it is not taxed because of the unlimited marital deduction. Wife receives the home under the will with a basis of $115,000 ($40,000 + $75,000).

EXAMPLE 13. Assume that in the prior example the husband owns the house outright and dies first. Husband could leave the house to wife and obtain a marital deduction for the will transfer, paying no estate taxes. Here the wife would receive a full step-up in basis to $190,000.

If the wife in Example 12 sells the home, she would have a $75,000 potential taxable gain, but the wife in Example 13 would have none. As these two examples demonstrate, joint ownership of property by married couples may no longer be appropriate because of the limited marital deduction. However, with the current high divorce rate, who is to own the property: husband or wife?

Jointly held property in a community-property state will include a full step-up in basis, including the surviving spouse's one-half interest in the community property.[18] Thus, joint ownership in a community-property state in order to avoid probate is still satisfactory.

EXAMPLE 14. Bill Raby owns his home in Texas (a community-property state) jointly with rights of survivorship with his wife, Mary. Bill paid $70,000 for their home. At the death of Bill in 1985, the house is valued at $230,000. Mary later sells the house for $240,000 and remarries. Mary would receive a full step-up in basis to $230,000, which is not taxable. However, the $10,000 difference between market value at Bill's death and the price she eventually receives for the house would be considered potential taxable gain.

Gifts

For estates of decedents dying after December 31, 1981, the gross estate must also include the amount of certain taxable gifts made after December 31, 1981, and within three years of the decedent's death. The amount to be added is the gross amount of the gift (without a reduction for the $10,000 annual exclusion) plus gift tax paid on the transfer (so-called gross-up of the gift tax.)[19] Basically, only a gift for which the decedent was not required to file a gift tax return is exempt from being pulled into the gross estate under Section 2035(a). However, this exemption does not apply to any transfers of life insurance policies.

EXAMPLE 15. T, within three years of death, made three gifts of $10,000 each to three donees. Also T made a $21,000 gift to another donee (paying a gift tax of $3,000). A total of $24,000 would be pulled into T's gross estate by Section 2035.

The purpose of the automatic three-year rule is to eliminate the problems involving gifts in contemplation of death that were experienced under the law before 1977. If the donor died within three years of making the gift, there was a rebuttable presumption that the gift was made in contemplation of death. Also, before 1977, there was no gross-up of the gift tax liability.

In general, the three-year rule about gifts in contemplation of death does not apply to certain decedents dying after December 31, 1981. Instead, the basis of appreciated property acquired by gift within one year of death is not adjusted to its fair market value at date of death if it returns to the donor or donor's spouse. However, the three-year rule will continue to apply to gifts of property covered by Sections 2036 (retained life estate), 2037 (tranfers taking effect at death), 2038 (revocable transfers), 2041 (powers of appointment), and 2042 (life insurance). Furthermore, all gifts made within three years of death are included for purposes of qualifying for current-use valuation under Section 2032A, for deferred payment of estate taxes under Section 6166, for qualified redemptions to pay estate taxes under Section 303, and for estate tax liens under Subchapter C of Chapter 64. As a result of these changes, deathbed gifts of cash and unappreciated property should become popular.

EXAMPLE 16. Leonard Molstad makes a gift of a rental house worth $72,000 to his father on September 1, 1982 (cost basis is $27,000). His father is seriously ill and dies on March 3, 1983, and the rental house returns to Mr. Molstad under his father's will. Mr. Molstad has a carryover basis of $27,000 in the rental house. The house would be included in the father's gross estate and taxed at a rate that might be higher than the 20 percent capital-gain tax that would have been paid if the rental house had been sold by Leonard Molstad.

In essence, under the law, both the gift and the gift tax liability attributable to the transfer must be included in the estate. This gross-up mechanism does not apply to gifts made more than three years before death or to any gift tax paid by a decedent within three years of death and which is treated as being paid one half by each spouse under the gift-splitting provision of Section 2513.

Even when it appears that a gift may be made in contemplation of death, such a gift may be worthwhile. The donor might live three years or more, and then there would be no transfer tax on any appreciation that occurred between the time of the gift and the donor's death. A donor who dies within three years may be in a high-income tax bracket, and then the transfer would place the income-producing property in the hands of a lower-tax-bracket donee.

EXAMPLE 17. Decedent obtains a life insurance policy, which had a face value of $125,000. She paid premiums on it for eight years. In the ninth year she transferred it to her sister. The sister paid two years of premiums, and the decedent retained no incidents of ownership. Decedent died two years after this transfer in 1985. Since the transfer was a gift in contemplation of death, eight tenths of the $125,000 face value of the policy is included in the decedent's estate.

Miscellaneous Assets

Section 2033 of the Internal Revenue Code requires the inclusion in the decedent's estate of a wide variety of property interests owned on the date of death. Reg. 20.2033-1 and many court cases have applied this section to many specific items of property interest. According to this regulation, property subject to homestead or other exemptions under local law must be included in the gross estate. Notes or other claims held by the decedent should be included even though they are concealed by the decedent's will. Accrued interest and rents are includable even though they are not collected until after death, and under certain circumstances dividends payable to the decedent are included. Bonds, notes, bills, and certificates of indebtedness of the federal government or its agencies, which are exempt from other taxes, are subject to the estate tax and are included in the decedent's gross estate. The tax treatments of many other particular property interests are covered, and some of these are discussed below.

As a general rule, accrued income, dividends, interest, compensation, and other items accrued at the time of the decedent's death should be included in the gross estate. However, this rule does not apply if any of these types of payments are made only as a matter of grace.[20] The following accruals have been held includable in the decedent's estate:

1. Executor's fees accrued at the date of the decedent's death.[21]
2. Accrued interest on the decedent's capital investment in a partnership.[22]
3. Accrued interest on Series G bonds even though they were held under six months.[23]
4. Salary and bonus paid under contract to the decedent's surviving spouse by employer.[24]
5. Commission.[25]
6. Dividends.[26]
7. Bonus.[27]
8. Partnership profits.[28]

For estate tax purposes, dividends accrue to the shareholder on the date of the record date. Thus, dividends that are payable to the decedent or the estate constitute a part of the gross estate if, on or before the date of death, the decedent was the shareholder of record. If the record date is after the date of death, the dividends are not included in the gross estate. This rule applies no matter how the gross estate is valued. However, if the record date is after the valuation date and the stock is selling ex-dividend on the valuation date, the dividend is added to the quotation to obtain the includable value of the stock.[29]

Any bonus paid to the decedent's estate or to a named beneficiary may be subject to tax as an accrual. However, the bonus is not included if the employer is under no duty to make the payment.[30]

Like any other accrual, partnership profits to date of death of the decedent are included in the gross estate.[31] In some instances, profits accruing after the deceased partner's death are included in the gross estate.[32] If a partnership agreement stipulates that the deceased partner's estate is to share in the profits for a definite period of time after death, then such profits accruing to the estate are included in the gross estate.[33]

Any property owned as a tenancy in common is included in the decedent's gross estate to the extent of his/her fractional interest in such property.[34] Even cemetery lots are included in the decedent's gross estate under certain circumstances. If any part of a cemetery lot not designed for the interment of the decedent and the members of the family has a salable value, then that salable value is included in the gross estate.[35]

All valid and enforceable claims or choses in action owned by the decedent are included in the gross estate. The following types of claims and choses in action are includable: right to executor's commissions,[36] contingent-fee legal services,[37] debts due the decedent,[38] trustee's commission,[39] claims against a partner,[40] computed value of claim for advance,[41] and others. Any notes held by the decedent are included in the gross estate unless the obligations end on death.[42]

Depending on the nature of the payment, death benefits provided for in pension or profit-sharing plans may or may not be included in the decedent's gross estate. Even though the decedent had the right to appoint his/her share of the fund to beneficiaries, the proceeds paid from such a trust fund are not included in the gross estate if the decedent did not have a vested interest in the fund.[43] If the decedent did have an enforceable vested interest in such a fund to his beneficiaries, this is included in the gross estate.[44]

Cases, revenue rulings, and income tax regulations apply Section 2033 of the Internal Revenue Code to many more miscellaneous items of property and property interest. These situations are too numerous to discuss in detail, but most of the important ones have been briefly covered.

NOTES

1. *Internal Revenue Code of 1954*, Section 2031. (The remaining footnotes from the Internal Revenue Code of 1954 will be cited as Sections 2031, 2033, etc.)
2. Rev. Rul. 55-438, 1955-2 C.B. 601.
3. *Estate of Ull*, 38 T.C. 512 (1962).
4. *Frazer*, 6 T.C. 1255 (1946).
5. *Field*, 22 BTA 915 (1931).
6. Section 2034.
7. Reg. 20.2036-1(b)(3) seems to override the Code by striking the phrase "or the income" from Section 2036(a)(2). This regulation was held valid in *Farrell* v. *U.S.*, 533 F.2d 637 (Ct. Cl. 1977).
8. Section 2037.
9. Section 2038.
10. Rev. Rul. 80-80, 1980-1, C.B. 194.
11. Section 2039(a).
12. Section 2039(b), and (c).
13. Section 2041.
14. *Smith* v. *U.S.*, 557 F. Supp. 723 (D. Conn. 1982).

15. Section 2042.
16. Reg. 20.2031-2(f).
17. Reg. 20.2042-1(c)(b).
18. Section 1014(b)(6).
19. Sections 2035(a) and (b).
20. *Maas Exec. (Sakas) et al.* v. *Higgins,* 312 U.S. 443 (1941), 61 S. Ct. 631, 85 LL. Ed. 940, 25 AFTR 1177.
21. *Est. of Percy McGlue,* 41 BTA 1199 (1940).
22. *Est. of John F. Degener,* 26 BTA 185 (1932).
23. *Est. of Willis L. King, Jr. (Mellon Nat. Bank & Trust Co.),* 18 TC 414 (1949).
24. *Est. of Paul G. Leoni,* 48, 213 P-H Memo TC (1948).
25. *Est. of Harry Eliot Robinson,* 42, 018 P-H Memo BTA.
26. Revenue Ruling 54-399, 1954-2 C.B. 279; *Estate of George McNought Lockie,* 21 TC 64 (1952).
27. *Est. of Leonard B. McKitterick,* 42 BTA 130, dismissed (2 Cir.; 1941).
28. *Bull, Exec* v. *U.S.,* 295 U.S. 247 (1935), 55 S. Ct. 695, 15 AFTR 1069, rev'g 6 F. Supp. 141, 13 AFTR 262 (1934).
29. Revenue Ruling 54-399, 1954-2 C.B. 279; *Estate of George McNought Lockie,* 21 TC 64 (1952).
30. *Est. of Leonard B. McKitterick,* 42 BTA 130, dismissed (2 Cir.; 1941).
31. See note 8 above.
32. *Est. of George Wood,* 26 BTA 533 (1932); *Est. of John F. Degener,* 26 BTA 185 (1932).
33. Revenue Ruling 66-20, 1966-1 C.B. 214.
34. *Harvey, Exr.* v. *U.S.,* 185 F. 2d 463 (7 Cir.; 1950).
35. Regulation 20.2033-1(b).
36. *Est. of G. Perry McGlue,* 41 BTA 1199 (1940).
37. Rev. Rul. 55-123, 1955-1 C.B. 443.
38. *Est. of Heran F. Hammor,* 10 BTA 43 (1928).
39. *Est. of Harry Eliot Robinson,* 42, 018 P-H Memo BTA.
40. *Isaac W. Baldwin Est.,* 59, 203 P-H Memo TC (1959).
41. *Est. of Theodore O. Hamlin (Lincoln Rochester Tr. Co.),* 9 TC 676 (1947).
42. *Comm.* v. *Austin,* 73 F. 2d 483, 43 AFTR 748 (1934).
43. *Hammer* v. *Glenn,* 212 F. 2d 483 (6 Cir.; 1954).
44. *Est. of Charles B. Wolf,* 29 TC 441 (1957), 3 AFTR 2d 1797.

3

Valuing the Gross Estate

The thing generally raised on land is taxes.

—*Will Rogers*

Once a determination has been made of what property should be included in the gross estate, a value must be assigned to each of these items of property. There are three major options available for valuing items of property: fair market value, alternate valuation, and special-use valuation. Each of these options is discussed below in relation to the tax basis to beneficiaries. Generally, all assets must be valued at their fair market value at the date of death or on the alternate valuation date. Fair market value is normally defined as the price at which the property would change hands between a willing buyer and a willing seller, neither being under any compulsion to buy or sell and both having reasonable knowledge of all relevant facts.

For estate and gift tax returns filed after 1984, there is a special penalty rule for undervaluations. For both estate and gift tax purposes, where a tax underpayment is at least $1,000 as a result of a valuation understatement, Section 6660 provides a penalty ranging from 10 to 30 percent (depending on the percentage of understatement). This penalty is imposed if the claimed value of an asset is less than two thirds of its determined correct value. The IRS may waive this penalty for good faith undervaluations having a reasonable basis.

FAIR MARKET VALUE

The fair market value is never determined by a forced sale price or by the sale of the item in a market other than that in which the item is most commonly sold. Therefore, if a particular item of property is normally retailed, the fair market value of the item to be included in the decedent's gross estate is the price at which the item or a comparable item would be sold at retail.

For example, an automobile is generally retailed; thus, its fair market value would be the price at which a similar automobile could be purchased by a member of the general public, and is not the price for which the particular automobile of the decedent would be purchased by a dealer in used cars. The selling price of tangible personal property sold at a public auction or through newspaper classified advertising will be deemed the retail price for estate tax purposes. To qualify, the sale must be made within a reasonable period following the applicable valuation date, when there is no substantial change in market conditions or other circumstances affecting the value of similar items between the time of sale and the applicable valuation date. Further, for estate tax purposes, property shall not be valued at the basis at which it is assessed for local tax purposes unless that assessed value represents the fair market value on the applicable valuation date.[1]

In determining the fair market value of any item of property, all the relevant facts and elements of value on the valuation date must be considered. The following paragraphs discuss the normal means of valuing particular types of property.

Stocks and Bonds

Stocks and bonds are included in the decedent's gross estate at their fair market value per share or per bond on the valuation date. This fair market value is the mean value between the highest and lowest selling prices on the date of valuation. When there are sales on dates within a reasonable period of time both before and after the valuation date but no sale on the valuation date, the fair market value is the weighted average of the means between the highest and lowest sales on the nearest dates both before and after the valuation date. This average should be weighted inversely by the respective numbers of trading days between the valuation date and the nearest selling date. If there are no actual sales within a reasonable period of time of the valuation date, then the fair market value is considered to be the mean between the bona fide bid-and-asked prices on the date of valuation.

If it can be established that the value of such stocks and bonds determined on the basis of selling prices or on bid-and-asked prices does not reflect the fair market value, then other relevant facts and elements must be considered in determining the fair market value. For example, if the block of stock were so large in relation to actual sales on the existing market that it could not be liquidated in a reasonable time without depressing the market, or if the block represents a controlling interest, then the price at which other lots change hands may have little relation to the true market value.[2]

An argument can be made for a marketability discount. That is, to the extent a prospective buyer will have difficulty reselling shares of stock in a corporation, such purchaser will pay less than he would if given a convenient method of disposing of the shares. The discount for lack of marketability ranges from 10 to 30 percent.

A minority-interest discount reflects the inability of a minority shareholder to have any influence on the decision-making process of a corporation. Thus, in theory the minority interest is worth less than the proportionate share of the underlying assets in the corporation. The IRS will often fight both the minority-interest discount and the marketability discount.

If no actual sales prices or bona fide bid-and-asked prices exist, then other factors must be considered in determining the fair market value. In the case of bonds, the soundness of the security, the interest yield, the date of maturity, and other relevant factors must be considered. The factors to consider in the case of shares of stock are the company's net worth, prospective earnings, dividend-paying capacity, and other relevant factors. Some of the other relevant factors are goodwill of the business, the economic outlook of the industry, the company's position within the industry, and, of course, its management capability.[3]

There is no theoretical standard or general formula for valuing stock of closely held corporations or any other unlisted stock.

A hypothetical marketplace must be established, but the IRS admits that valuation is not an exact science. IRS instructions to appeals officers indicate that they should not expect an appraiser to arrive at the same valuation conclusion as the appeals officer.

The factors to be considered in determining the value of such stock vary with the particular facts involved. The weight to be given to any factor depends on the specific circumstances of that case. The following fundamental factors should receive careful analysis in every case:

1. The nature of the business and the history of the enterprise from its inception.
2. The economic outlook in general, and the condition and outlook of the specific industry in particular.
3. The book value of the stock and the financial condition of the business.
4. The earning capacity of the company.
5. The dividend-paying capacity.
6. Whether or not the enterprise has goodwill or other intangible value.
7. Sales of the stock and the size of the block to be valued.
8. The market price of stocks of corporations engaged in the same or a similar line of business and having their stocks actively traded in a free and open market, either as an exchange or over the counter.[4]

Business Interests

The fair market value of a decedent's interest in any business is the net amount a willing buyer would pay a willing seller for such interest, neither being under any compulsion to buy or to sell, and both having reasonable knowledge of all the facts. A fair appraisal should be made of the earning capacity of the business and of all its assets, including goodwill. These elements should be considered in determining its net value.[5] However, the value of a business interest may be fixed by a mutual buy-and-sell agreement. For such an agreement to be effective for estate tax purposes, it must bind the estate to sell, either by giving the survivors an option or by binding all parties, and the price must not be so grossly inadequate as to make the agreement a "mere gratuitous promise."[6]

Cash Accounts

All cash belonging to the decedent, including that in the possession of others and that deposited in banks, is included in the gross estate. The bank account may be reduced by valid and bona fide checks that are outstanding on the date of death, but that are subsequently honored by the bank.[7] The fair market value of any secured or unsecured note held by the decedent is presumed to be the principal face amount of the note plus interest accrued to the date of death. Under certain circumstances, the executor may establish that the value of the note is something less or even worthless.[8]

Personal Property

Generally, the fair market value of the decedent's household and personal effects is considered to be the price that a willing buyer would pay to a willing seller. There should be a room-by-room itemization of these articles. A separate value should be listed for each item; however, all articles in a room worth $100 or less may be grouped together. Instead of making such an itemized list, the executor may, under the penalties of perjury, submit a written statement containing the aggregate value of the property as appraised by a competent appraiser. But if there are included among these household and personal effects any articles having an artistic or intrinsic value of more than $3,000, the appraisal of an expert must be filed with the estate tax return. Before the executor may sell or distribute any of the household or personal effects in advance of an investigation by an officer of the IRS, he must give the district director notice of such action. This notice must be accompanied by an appraisal of such property.[9]

Real Property

Real property is to be valued under Reg. 20.2031-1 at its "highest and best use." This phrase means the most profitable use to which the property might logically and probably be put. The one exception is the special-use valuation method under Section 2032A (discussed later).

The three generally recognized methods used to value real property are

1. Comparable-sales approach.
2. Income-capitalization method.
3. Replacement-cost approach.

The comparable-sales method involves comparing the property being valued with similar properties that have been sold recently in arms-length transactions. Rev. Proc. 79-24, 1979-1 C.B. 565 gives guidelines for the comparable-sales approach in appraising unimproved real property. The comparable-sales approach is used often for valuation of unimproved real estate.

The capitalization-of-income method is based on a projection of the real property's net income over its reasonable economic life which is capitalized to convert the income stream into a market value. The capitalization-of-income approach is used often for valuation of industrial and commercial property.

The approach subject to the greatest risk of error is the replacement-cost method. This valuation method is based on the construction costs of replacing property similar to the property being valued.

Annuities, Insurance, and Other Term Contracts

The fair market value of annuities, life estates, terms for years, remainders, and reversions is their present value. The regulations provide tables to be used in calculating the present value of these assets.[10] The value of a contract for the payment of an annuity or an insurance policy on the life of another person is the price for which such a contract could be acquired on the date of the decedent's death from a company regularly engaged in selling contracts of that character. If further premiums are to be paid on a life insurance policy on the life of another person, the value of such a policy may be approximated by adding to the interpolated terminal reserve at the date of the decedent's death the proportionate part of the gross premium that was last paid before the decedent's death and that covers the period extending beyond that date.[11]

ALTERNATE VALUATION

Although all property belonging to the decedent on the date of death is included in the gross estate and is generally appraised at its fair market value, the executor may elect to value the estate either at the date of the decedent's death or as of the date six months after the decedent's date of death. This latter date is referred to as the alternate valuation date (AVD).

If the alternate valuation date is to be used, the executor must make such an election on the estate tax return. In no case may such an election be made or a previous election be changed after the date of the tax return. When the AVD is elected, it applies to all property of the gross estate and is valued according to the following rules:

1. Any property distributed, sold, exchanged, or otherwise disposed of within six months after the decedent's death must be valued as of the date on which it is disposed of.

2. Any property not distributed, sold, exchanged, or otherwise disposed of within six months after the decedent's death must be valued as of the date six months after the decedent's death.

3. Any property, interest, or estate that is affected by a mere lapse of time must be valued as of the date of the decedent's death. However, it must be adjusted for any change in value not due to a mere lapse of time within six months after the decedent's death or as of the date of its disposition, whichever occurs first.[12]

Of course the purpose of the alternate valuation date is to permit a reduction in estate taxes whenever there is a shrinkage in the aggregate value of the estate property. However, there are some interrelated income tax consequences that should be evaluated before selecting the most advantageous valuation date, especially since the alternate valuation date may not be elected unless the valuation amount decreases both the value of the gross estate and the estate tax liability of the estate.

EXAMPLE 1. Decedent's gross estate at the date of death is $380,000 in 1985, but its value six months later is $420,000. There would be no estate tax whether or not the alternate valuation date election were made because the threshold filing requirement for the year is $400,000 ($500,000 in 1986 and thereafter). Thus, for purposes of a possible stepped-up basis (see the next section), the executor could not elect AVD per Section 2032(c).

Income earned subsequent to death but prior to the alternate valuation date is not included in the gross estate. Such property includes post-death interest accrued on interest-bearing obligations, rental payments accrued after the date of death and before the subsequent valuation date, and ordinary dividends out of earnings and profits declared to shareholders of record after the date of the decedent's death.[13] One district court indicates that proceeds from the sale of oil and gas during the alternate valuation period is not includable in the gross estate.[14]

Even when a decedent's will directs the executor to sell assets to a specified individual for less than an adequate and full consideration, the assets are includable in the decedent's gross estate at their fair market value on the applicable valuation date.

SPECIAL-USE VALUATION

For estates of U.S. decedents dying after December 31, 1976, a special-use valuation is available in the case of property being used for farming purposes or closely held businesses.[15] Any property so qualified may be valued at the fair market value of its actual use rather than any speculative value (that is, "highest and best" use) that it might have. This special valuation process may be used to reduce the value of an estate by as much as $600,000 in 1981, $700,000 in 1982, and $750,000 thereafter.[16] For example, if a decedent's estate contains special-use property that is valued at $2.3 million at its highest-and-best use, but only at $1.2 million at its current use, the estate would be valued at $1.55 million in 1985 ($2.3 million less $750,000).

In order to qualify for this special-use valuation, several tests must be met:

1. The value of the closely held business or farm must be at least 50 percent of the adjusted value of the gross estate (determined on the basis of its highest-and-best use).
2. The value of the real property must be 25 percent of the adjusted value of the gross estate.
3. The property must be located in the United States.

4. The property must pass to a qualified heir (e.g., family).

5. The real property must have been used by the decedent or a member of his/her family as a farm or other closely held business, and the decedent or a member of his/her family must have participated materially in its operation during five out of the eight years preceding his/her death. This special method probably cannot be used for real property that the decedent has rented.[17]

The formula for computing this current special-use value for farmland may be shown as follows:

$$SUV = \frac{R - T}{I}$$

where

SUV = Current special-use value
 R = Average annual gross cash rent per acre for comparable farming land in the same locality
 T = Average annual state and local real estate taxes per acre for comparable land
 I = Average annual effective interest rate for all new federal bank loans

There is no special-use valuation for purposes of valuing property for the lifetime-gift provision.

EXAMPLE 2. A farmer died in 1985, meeting all the requirements necessary to qualify for the special-use valuation. The highest-and-best-use value of his 1,000-acre farm is $2.5 million. The average annual gross cash rental per acre is $140, and the average annual state and local real estate taxes per acre are $60. The average annual effective interest rate for all new Federal Land Bank loans is 8 percent. Thus, under the special-use valuation, the farmer's land is worth $1,000 per acre [($140 − $60) ÷ 8% = $1,000]. Therefore, the value of the farm as determined under the special-use valuation is $1 million, but under no circumstances may this special method reduce the decedent's estate by more than $750,000. Therefore, the farm would be valued at $1.65 million ($2.5 million − $0.75 million).

For closely held business property or farm property where comparable land cannot be found, Section 2032 A (e)(8) provides several methods of valuation based primarily on the capitalization of income.

A dual election of the AVD and the special use valuation (SUV) is allowable.[18] Further, community property is treated in the same manner as separate property. Therefore, if property is held by a decedent and spouse as community property, the entire value of the property is taken into consideration.[19]

Tax benefits of SUV are recaptured if, within 10 years after the decedent's death but before the death of the qualified heir, such heir either disposes of any interest in the property to a nonfamily member or ceases to use the property for the qualified use. A cessation of qualified use also triggers recapture. In general, the recapture amount is the excess of the estate tax liability that would have been paid had the SUV not been elected over the estate tax paid based on SUV.

Be careful, because the IRS insists that the procedural aspects of an SUV election be followed closely. The Deficit Reduction Act of 1984 (DRA) directed the IRS to develop a procedure to allow estates to correct certain defects in timely filed SUV elections.

Gift of a Remainder Interest

A gift of a remainder interest with a reserved term can be a valuable estate-freezing technique. A reserved interest trust occurs when a grantor makes a present-interest gift to a remainder person of a future interest in property while retaining for a specified time the right to the income or its use. The grantor has a gift on the fraction of the present value of the property placed into the trust.

Valuation tables in Reg. 25.2512-5(f) are used to determine the value of both the present interest and the remainder interest. Under the new 10 percent interest rates, the income tax value of the income stream from the property is larger, but the remainder interest placed in the trust is smaller. Assuming the remainder interest appreciates in value, this amount is no longer in the estate. A reserved-interest trust can freeze a grantor's estate at a low gift tax cost.

EXAMPLE 3. P. Grantor places property having a fair market value of $100,000 into a trust, reserving the right to any income from the property for 15 years. Referring to Table B in Reg. 25.2512-5(f), the factors .760608 are found in column 3 and .239392 in column 4. Therefore, P. Grantor has made a gift of a future interest of $23,939 ($100,000 × .239392), subject to a unified credit. The value of the retained interest is $76,061.

Sale of a Remainder Interest

Another technique to limit the value of the assets in an estate is to sell a remainder interest in the assets before death. The result is to place in the estate currently the value of the remainder interest (in the form of proceeds from sale) and to leave the estate with a life interest in the asset(s) itself. The future value of the remainder interest (a highly appreciating asset) is passed on to a purchaser, a family member. Since the life estate expires at death, only the unused accumulation from the amount received from the sale of the remainder interest is included in the estate.

An extension of this technique is to sell the remainder interest in an asset to a family member (i.e., heir) for a disappearing note. The potential heir pays the note over a period of time that is slightly less than the life expectancy of the taxpayer. The older taxpayer continues to own the asset until death, and the heir does not receive the asset until the death of the taxpayer.

This disappearing note is called a self-canceling installment note (SCIN). In other words, the sale instrument contains a clause that causes any unpaid balance of the sale price to be extinguished when the taxpayer dies before all the payments are made.

Estate Freeze

The value of an estate that includes a large block of stock can be limited by an "estate freeze." Most estate freezes involve the use of a tax-free recapitalization whereby fixed-income preferred stock can be given to the older generation (i.e., parent). The preferred stock would be protected from future appreciation (i.e., estate freeze). Appreciation and control could be shifted to the younger generation (i.e., child) through issuance of common stock.

EXAMPLE 4. Closer, Inc. is worth approximately $1 million, owned by Fred Planner. It is estimated that the corporation will be worth $2 million in 10 years. Fred gives one half of his common stock (the only class outstanding) to his son. In a recapitalization under Section 368(a)(1)(E), Fred exchanges his other half of common stock for newly issued preferred stock (worth about $500,000). If Closer, Inc. is valued at $2 million at Fred's death, in theory the value included in his estate would be the frozen $500,000 recapitalization value. Approximately $1 million would escape the estate tax at Fred's death.

The IRS has attacked the recapitalization as an estate planning technique from several points of view. Avoidance of the preferred stock being classified as Section 306 stock is a major hurdle. If stock is considered to be Section 306 stock, any gain on sale or redemption of such stock is treated as ordinary income (and not capital gain).

If only preferred stock is received in a tax-free recapitalization in exchange for all of a shareholder's common stock, then no Section 306 taint occurs.[20] However, generally where both common and preferred stock are received, the preferred stock is tainted Section 306 stock.[21] In order for the IRS to rule that nonconvertible preferred stock is not Section 306 stock, it must not be pursuant to a plan to avoid federal income taxes. Further, it must be widely held, and it must not be redeemable by its terms for five years.[22]

A gift tax liability may also arise from a recapitalization. The IRS may assert that there has been a substantial gift from the parent (who receives the preferred stock) to the child (who receives the common stock). There may be a constructive dividend to the parent to the extent of the excess redemption premium attributable to the preferred stock.[23] Furthermore, the IRS may challenge the right of an estate to receive a discount for the lapse at death of voting rights on the preferred stock received as a part of the estate freeze.[24]

Buy-Sell Agreements

An alternative technique to the questionable estate freeze is the use of a buy-sell agreement. The two most common arrangements for the transfer of stock at death are the cross-purchase agreement and the stock-redemption agreement.

These agreements offer various estate planning advantages. For example, an agreement can provide for an orderly settlement with the heirs of the decedents. The estate is eliminated from the picture, and control is retained by the remaining shareholders. Further the process may create a basis for placing a value on the stock owned by the decedent.[25] However, the buy-sell agreement cannot provide the discount some believe to be available with a recapitalization.

In order for an agreement to limit the estate value, four requirements must be met:[26]

1. The purchase price must be fixed or determinable according to a formula.
2. An estate must be obligated to sell at such price at the death of the decedent.[27]
3. Any obligation to sell must be binding on the decedent during his/her lifetime as well as on the estate after death.[28]
4. Any agreement must be a bona fide business arrangement and not a device to pass the decedent's stock to the natural heirs for less than adequate and full consideration in money or money's worth.[29]

In a cross-purchase plan, the stock of the decedent is purchased by the surviving shareholders, whereas under a stock-redemption agreement, the ownership interest of the deceased is purchased by the corporation. Each type of agreement has advantages and disadvantages, and no one plan is clearly superior to the other in all situations.

TAX BASIS TO BENEFICIARIES

For estates and heirs of decedents, the basis of inherited property is stepped up to the property's value at the time of the decedent's death (or six months later if the alternate valuation date is elected).[30] Thus, if an heir sells the property shortly after inheriting it, there may be little or no income tax due, even though the property might have appreciated in value substantially while owned by the decedent.

If the executor or administrator of the estate elects to value the estate's property for estate tax purposes at a date six months after the decedent's death, the asset's basis is the value at such alternate valuation date. (As explained earlier, if property is disposed of before six months after the decedent's death, the value is determined on the date of disposition.) Where the special-use valuation is elected for property used for farming purposes or closely held businesses, such lower value is the basis of the inherited assets.[31]

EXAMPLE 5. Decedent died on January 12, 1985, and his will directs his executor to transfer a certain asset to a beneficiary. This asset had a fair market value of $500,000 at the decedent's date of death and $440,000 six months later. On April 13, 1985, the property was distributed to this beneficiary, at which time the property had a fair market value of $450,000. Assuming that no election is made by the executor, this asset is includable in gross estate at $500,000, and the beneficiary receives a $500,000 stepped-up basis. If the executor elects the alternate valuation method under Section 2032, the includable value of the asset is $450,000 with a stepped-up basis of $450,000 to the beneficiary.[32]

A carryover basis was available to certain taxpayers dying between January 1, 1977, and November 7, 1978. Also, as mentioned in Chapter 2, the basis of appreciated property acquired by gift within one year of death is not adjusted to its fair market value at date of death if it returns to the donor or the donor's spouse.[33]

Because substantial income tax savings may result, any assets that have increased in value (especially if the taxpayer is elderly) should be retained until death so that the heirs will receive the step-up in basis.

A high valuation of the assets that pass to a surviving spouse (which qualifies for the unlimited marital deduction) will result in a high income tax basis without a federal estate tax burden. Further, where an estate has a value below the unified exemption equivalent ($600,000 in 1987), an executor should increase the value of the assets up to the exemption amount (without federal estate tax consequences) in order to provide a higher income tax base for purposes of depreciation and later sale.

The death of an individual eliminates any potential depreciation recapture. Regs. 1.1245-2(c)(1)(iv) and 1.1250-3(b)(2) indicate that the depreciation adjustment acquired from a decedent is zero, assuming the basis is determined under Section 1014(a).

Investment credit property is treated more favorably. Under Reg. 1.47-3(b)(1) there is no investment credit recapture when the estate or beneficiary disposes of the assets that would have given the decedent an investment credit recapture.

NOTES

1. Reg. 20.2031-1(b).
2. Reg. 20.2031-2(a)-(e).
3. Reg. 20.2031(f).
4. Rev. Ruling 59-60, 1959-1 C.B. 237.
5. Reg. 20.2031-3.
6. Rev. Ruling 59-60, 1959-1 C.B. 237.
7. Reg. 20.2031-5.
8. Reg. 20.2031-4.
9. Reg. 20.2031-6. For example, see D. L. Crumbley and J. Curtis, *Donate less to the IRS* (Vestal, N.Y.: Vestal Press, 1982). ($9.00, Information Services, P.O. Box 9027, College Station, TX 77840.)
10. Reg. 20.2031-7.
11. Reg. 20.2031-8.
12. Section 2032.
13. Reg. 20.2032-1(d).
14. *Estate of Johnston,* 586 F. Supp. 500 (DC Tex, 1984); but see Rev. Rul. 70-317, 1971-2 C.B. 328 and Ltt. Rul. 8432012.
15. Section 2032A(a).
16. Section 2032A(a)(2). The full amount of this limitation is allowed for community property interest held by a decedent. Rev. Rul. 83-96, 1983-2 C.B. 156.
17. Section 2032(A)(b). *Estate of Trueman,* 84-2 USTC ¶13,590, 1984 P-H 148,788 (Cls. Ct. 1984).
18. Rev. Rul. 83-31, 1983-1 C.B. 225.
19. Section 2032A(e)(10).
20. Rev. Rul. 59-84, 1959-1 C.B. 71.
21. Rev. Rul. 79-274, 1979-2 C.B. 131.
22. Rev. Proc. 77-37, 1977-2 C.B. 568.

23. Rev. Rul. 83-119, 1983-2 C.B. 57.
24. Doc. 8401006.
25. Reg. 1.691(a)-2(b), ex. 4.
26. D. Dickey, "Buy-Sell Agreements Can Conclusively Limit Value Without Recapitalization Problems," *Estate Planning,* September 1984, p. 269.
27. See *Worcester County Trust Co.,* 134 F.2d 578 (1st Cir. 1943).
28. See *Estate of Salt,* 17 T.C. 92 (1951), Acq.
29. *Estate of Bischoff,* 69 T.C. 32 (1977).
30. Section 1014(a)(1).
31. Section 1014(a)(3).
32. Rev. Rul. 77-180, 1977-1 C.B. 270.
33. Section 1014(e).

4

Reductions in Gross Estate

A taxpayer is someone who doesn't have to take a civil service examination to work for the government.

—Anonymous

A number of reductions—deductions and credits—are allowed in arriving at the estate tax liability of a decedent. An intermediate step in the calculation of the tax liability is taxable estate.

ALLOWABLE DEDUCTIONS

The taxable estate is the gross estate reduced by all allowable deductions. Some are discussed below.

Administration and Funeral Expenses

A deduction is granted to the extent allowable under local law for funeral expenses. Funeral expenses include a reasonable expenditure for a tombstone, monument, burial lot, and the cost of transportation of the person taking the body to the place of burial.[1]

All reasonable and necessary expenses incurred in the administration of the decedent's estate are deductible from the gross estate. The administration of the estate includes the collection of the assets, the payment of debts, and the distribution of property to the proper beneficiaries. The three types of administrative expenses are executor's commissions, attorney's fees, and miscellaneous expenses.

An executor normally is named by a decedent in his/her will. If there is no will, the state court will appoint an administrator. The executor manages the estate's personal property and real estate; collects assets; pays debts, administrative expenses, and funeral expenses; and distributes the remainder according to the will. Selection of a well-qualified executor is enormously important.

A deduction for executor's commissions is allowed to the extent that such an amount has actually been paid or for an amount which at the time of the filing of the estate tax return may reasonably be expected to be paid, but no deduction is allowed if the commission is not collected. When the executor is also a major beneficiary, he may wish not to receive a commission because it is taxable as ordinary income. Instead, the executor may wish to receive a larger share of inheritance, which is not taxable to the executor. Place a mechanism in the will for the executor to disclaim any commission, if so desired.

Legal Cost Deductions

In selecting a lawyer, remember that estate planning is a small part of the practice of most lawyers. Be very careful in selecting an attorney. A listing of lawyers can be found in *The Bar Register* and *The Martindale-Hubbell Law Directory,* which may be found in a local library. *The Bar Register* lists only those "lawyers who enjoy fine professional reputations."

Attorney fees actually paid or reasonably expected to be paid are deductible. These attorney fees do not include charges incurred by beneficiaries incident to litigation as to their respective interests.

Miscellaneous administrative expenses include court costs, surrogate's fees, clerk hire, and similar charges. All expenses necessarily incurred in preserving and distributing the estate are deductible, including the cost of storing or maintaining property of the estate when immediate distribution to the beneficiaries is impossible.[2]

Expenditures that are not essential for the proper settlement of the estate, but that are incurred for the individual benefit of heirs, legatees, or devisees, are not deductible (e.g., broker's commission on sale of house by surviving spouse because house is too large). Reg. 20.2053-3(d)(2) indicates that expenses for selling property of the estate are deductible if the sale is necessary in order to pay the decedent's debts, expenses of administration, or taxes; to preserve the estate; or to effect distribution.

Under Section 642(g), expenditures may not be used to offset the sales price of assets for income tax purposes unless a waiver of the right to deduct such an item on the federal estate tax return is filed.

Claims Against the Estate

A deduction is allowed for all bona fide and legally enforceable claims against the estate for debts incurred by the decedent, to the extent paid from property included in the gross estate. Thus, any income or gift taxes owed at the date of death would be deductible under this provision. Also, a deduction is allowed from the decedent's gross estate for the full unpaid amount of a mortgage or other indebtedness with respect to any property included in the gross estate at its full fair market value. This deduction includes an amount for interest accrued to the date of the decedent's death.

Two lines of decisions now coexist with respect to whether post-death events are or are not to be considered in ascertaining the value of deductions permitted against a decedent's estate. Under the *Ithaca Trust Co.* principle, post-death events are not to be considered.[3] In *Ithaca* the Supreme Court held that a widow's life estate should be valued as of the decedent's date of death on the basis of mortality tables without considering the widow's premature death.[4]

The IRS and some lower courts have taken the position that post-death events should be considered especially for disputed or contingent claims against the estate.[5] For example, courts have held that claims valid at death but later waived, barred, or not enforced are not permitted as deductions to the estate.[6] The Tax Court subscribes to this anti-*Ithaca* approach. To be deductible a claim must be a bona fide obligation at the time of the decedent's death, and the estate must actually satisfy the claim.[7] The IRS follows this line of reasoning,[8] which is supported by the Eighth Circuit.[9]

Especially for a claim by a relative, there should be a written agreement entered into between the claiming relative and the decedent during the lifetime of the decedent. Courts will normally disallow oral agreements. The claim must be allowable and enforceable against the estate under local law and must be a matured claim and not contingent or barred by the statutes of limitations (or any other defenses).

Postmortem Planning

Portmortem planning is possible with administrative expenses. An executor may elect to claim certain administrative expenses and medical expenses, either as a deduction on the federal estate tax return (Form 706) or as a deduction in computing the estate income tax (Form 1041), but not on both. If the executor elects to claim the deduction on Form 1041, he must file a waiver of the deduction for federal estate tax purposes (Form 706).[10]

Where the marginal estate tax bracket is less than the marginal-income rates of the beneficiaries, the deductions become more valuable to the individuals. As to mechanics, Reg. 1.642 (g)-1 requires the fiduciary to file a statement, in duplicate, stating that the items claimed as income tax deductions have not been allowed as a deduction from gross estate. This statement also must provide that all rights to have such expenses allowed as estate tax deductions under Sections 2053 and 2054 are waived.

The value of the gross estate is reduced by any losses incurred during the settlement of the estate arising from fire, storms, thefts, or other casualty. The amount of this deduction is limited to the losses not compensated for by insurance or otherwise under Section 2054.

Any bequest, legacy, or devise made to certain religious, charitable, scientific, or educational organizations, or to the United States, any state, or any political subdivision is deductible. Unlike the charitable deduction for income tax purposes, there are no percentage limitations, and the payment does not have to be made to domestic organizations.[11] The use of a specific bequest/disclaimer in favor of a charity in a will can maximize the benefit of a charitable bequest (see Chapter 10).

MARITAL DEDUCTIONS

The marital deduction originated with the Revenue Act of 1948, which also allowed the income-splitting advantages of filing joint returns. The purpose of the marital deduction is to eliminate the tax advantages held by those persons domiciled in community-property states.* These statutes provide all taxpayers the same tax treatment that was once theoretically and actually possible only in community-property states. Thus, for tax purposes, Congress made the community-property system applicable to all the states.

For estate tax purposes, a marital deduction is allowed for the value of all property passing outright to the surviving spouse. Before 1982, this deduction was limited to 50 percent of the value of the adjusted gross estate unless this amount was less than $250,000 (in which case several adjustments had to be considered). The adjusted gross estate was found by subtracting from the entire value of the gross estate the community property and the adjusted amount of the deductions allowed for funeral expenses, administrative expenses, debts of the decedents, and casualty and theft losses (i.e., Sections 2053 and 2054 expenses).[12]

For a decedent dying on or after January 1, 1982, an unlimited marital deduction is available on estate tax for property passing to a surviving spouse, including community property. Keep in mind that if all the assets are left to the surviving spouse, the survivor may be pushed into a very high estate tax bracket. Of course, as long as the surviving spouse marries someone young and then dies first, a new generation-skipping technique may develop. Theoretically, as long as each surviving spouse marries someone young and dies first and as long as there are no simultaneous deaths, assets may escape the estate tax indefinitely.

EXAMPLE 1. If Alex Grant dies in 1987, leaving his entire $1.2 million estate to his wife, Charlotte, he would pay no estate tax. Assuming that Charlotte does not remarry and dies, her estate would have a tax of approximately $330,000

---

*Arizona, California, Idaho, Louisiana, Nevada, New Mexico, Texas, and Washington.

(considering only the marital deduction). Assume, however, that Alex leaves $600,000 to Charlotte and $600,000 in a trust for the children, giving Charlotte a lifetime-income interest in the trust. Here, there will be no estate tax on Alex or Charlotte. Because of the $600,000 unified credit, Charlotte can leave her estate to the children upon her death. Thus, by using the optimum marital deduction and all of the two unified credits, a couple can transfer a $1.2 million estate to their children without incurring any estate tax.

A will with a formula marital deduction clause should be examined and possibly revised after January 1, 1982. However, a taxpayer may wish to limit the amount of the estate passing to the surviving spouse. There are still reasons for having a formula-type will. The surviving spouse may be a spendthrift, or a decedent may wish to protect the children in case the surviving spouse remarries. By using enough of the unlimited marital deduction, a well-planned will can reduce the taxable estate in any given year to the amount passing free of tax to the heirs because of the unified credit (that is, $192,800 in 1987).

There is a transitional rule which provides that the unlimited marital deduction does not apply to transfers resulting from an executed will (or trust) created before September 12, 1981. This transitional rule applies if the decedent dies after December 31, 1981, the will contains a maximum marital deduction formula, the formula was not amended to refer to the unlimited deduction, and there are no state laws construing existing formula clauses to refer to the new unlimited marital deduction.

After December 31, 1981, there is an unlimited gift tax marital deduction. This unlimited deduction means that less tax planning is necessary, since the taxpayer now can make unlimited gifts to a spouse at death using the unlimited estate tax marital deduction. Heirs receive a step-up in basis.

Shared Property Interests

Transfers that qualify for the marital deduction include property interests taken by the surviving spouse under the will, under the laws of intestacy, by rights of survivorship by the entirety or as joint tenants, as a beneficiary of life insurance, and other interests. Normally, in order to qualify for the marital deduction, the property must pass outright.

Terminable Interest

If the surviving spouse receives a terminable interest in the property, it does not qualify for the marital deduction. A terminable interest is an interest that will terminate or fail after a certain period of time or upon the occurrence of some contingency or upon the failure of some event to occur.[13] For example, a "naked life estate" to a spouse is a terminable interest: the decedent leaves income from assets to the surviving spouse but leaves the assets themselves in trust to the children. Section 2056(d)(3) lists a number of items that qualify as passing to the surviving spouse:

1. The interest bequeathed or devised to the spouse.
2. The interest inherited by the spouse.
3. The dower or curtesy interest (or statutory interest in lieu thereof) of such person as surviving spouse of the decedent.
4. Interest transferred to the spouse by the decedent at any time (that is, a gift in contemplation of death).
5. Property held in joint ownership with right of survivorship.
6. Power to appoint such interest, if such interest has been appointed.
7. Proceeds of life insurance received by the surviving spouse.

EXAMPLE 2. Husband dies, leaving his entire estate to a trust, with income to be paid to his wife for life and the remainder to his children. The transfer to the trust does not qualify for a marital deduction because it is a terminable interest under Section 2056(b).

EXAMPLE 3. Husband sold property to one son, subject to his continuous use of the property for 15 years, for $30,000 (the fair market value of the remainder interest transferred to the son). When husband died, he still had the right to use the property for eight more years; he left this right to his wife. Since Section 2056(b)(1)(A) is not met, this transfer qualifies for the marital deduction. Assume that, instead of selling the property to the son, husband had given the property to him. Section 2056(b)(1)(A) would be met and the transfer would not qualify for the marital deduction.

Three exceptions to the terminable interest rule apply to property passing to the surviving spouse that would otherwise be considered a terminable interest and would be nondeductible. The three exceptions that may still qualify for the marital deduction are:

1. Property passing to the surviving spouse with the only condition being that he/she survive by a period not to exceed six months, and in fact, he/she does survive the decedent by such a period.[14]

2. Property passing from the decedent either in trust or as a legal life estate where the surviving spouse has a general power of appointment and is entitled to all income from such property. This income must be paid to the survivor at least annually.[15]

3. Life insurance or annuity payments held by the insurer with a general power of appointment held by the surviving spouse. If the proceeds are payable in installments, the installments or interest must be paid to the surviving spouse at least annually.[16]

EXAMPLE 4. A decedent's will provides for the creation of a marital trust, with income to be distributed at least quarterly to the surviving spouse. At the death of surviving spouse, trust income is to be accumulated and added to principal for a period of two years, after which the trust terminates and all assets are to be paid to such individuals as the spouse has designated by will. This testamentary general power of appointment could be exercised in favor of the surviving spouse's estate.

The corpus of the trust would be included in the surviving spouse's estate because there was a general power of appointment. But in Rev. Rul. 76-502, 1976-2 C.B. 273, the IRS indicated that this testamentary power did not conform to Reg.

20.2056(b)-5(g)(2), and a marital deduction was not allowed. Thus, the continuation of a trust beyond the death of a powerholder that was not completely attributable to a default of exercise of temporary administrative difficulties will result in a denial of the marital deduction.

EXAMPLE 5. A decedent bequeathed to her husband an income interest in her property for life, payable annually, and a lifetime power of invasion exercisable on the surviving spouse's behalf in all events. A fee-simple absolute interest in the property is not necessary for a marital deduction. Thus, this interest in property qualifies for the marital deduction under Section 2056(d)(5).

Qualified Terminable-Interest Trust (QTIP) Property

Certain types of qualified terminable-interest property (QTIP) qualify after 1981 for both the estate and gift tax marital deductions. Where a spouse receives certain life estates, at the election of the executor (or donor), such property is deemed to pass to the spouse without a tax. However, the spouse (or spouse's estate) will be subject later to a tax at the earlier of (1) the time of disposal or (2) the time of death. In essence, the property passing to the QTIP trust qualifies for the marital deduction and is not taxed to the decedent. The income goes to the surviving spouse for life, and the decedent determines where the property eventually goes, such as to specific children. However, the property is eventually taxed in the surviving spouse's estate at death.

The following dispositions can qualify for QTIP treatment:

1. A gift to a spouse of a legal life estate.
2. A gift to a spouse of a lifetime-income interest along with a special testamentary power of appointment over the principal.
3. A gift to a spouse of a lifetime-income interest with a discretionary power in the trustee to invade the principal on behalf of the spouse.
4. A gift to a spouse of a lifetime-income interest with a power to withdraw annually the greater of $5,000 or 5 percent of principal.[17]

A failure to elect QTIP treatment on the estate tax return results in an irrevocable nonelection, and no subsequent election can be made. Since a QTIP election is irrevocable and changes cannot be made later to reflect IRS audit results, a person should use a formula election if the person wishes the audit changes to be considered. That is, add language such as the following in the will: "taking into account final estate tax values."

The QTIP technique may be beneficial if there is a multiple marriage and one spouse desires to control the passing of property to children of the first marriage. Or a person may believe that his/her spouse needs the protection of a restraining trust. However, since property given to a qualified terminable interest trust is eventually taxed, the surviving spouse may be pushed into a higher estate tax bracket. There may be a need for life insurance on the life of the surviving spouse so that there will be sufficient cash to pay this added tax burden.

EXAMPLE 6. Husband includes the following provision in his will, giving his wife a lifetime-in-all income: My trustee shall pay to my wife for her life all the net income of the trust in quarterly or more frequent installments. Upon the death of my wife, any income received or accrued by the trust prior to the time of her death and not paid to her shall be paid to her personal representative as part of her general probate estate.[18] This is a typical example of a QTIP election.

A decedent may wish to give the QTIP trustee a discretionary power to make principal distributions to the surviving spouse. The surviving spouse can later reduce the value of the QTIP trust payable to the surviving spouse's estate by a program of gift giving. In other words, the principal distribution from the trust can be given as gifts to a younger generation. Of course, the surviving spouse is provided with some influence over who shall receive the decedent's assets.

Formula Bequests

In order to secure the maximum marital deduction, many wills drawn before 1982 contain a formula bequest expressed in terms of 50 percent of the adjusted gross estate or the maximum allowable marital deduction. Such a clause may now lead to unfavorable tax results.

COMPUTATION OF TAX

To determine the tax base, the taxable estate must be increased by the adjusted taxable gifts made after December 31, 1976. The adjusted taxable gifts are simply the sum of all taxable gifts made after December 31, 1976, and before three years prior to the decedent's death. One point of caution is necessary here: the gross amount of gifts is less all deductions such as the annual exclusions and the marital deduction.

Gross Estate Tax

The gross estate tax is computed by using the unified rate schedule found in Section 2001. These rates, which apply to citizens and residents of the United States, range from 18 percent on the first $10,000 to 50 percent on the entire taxable estate in excess of $2.5 million in 1985.[19] The tax computed at these rates, however, is subject to reduction by various credits allowed on account of other taxes. Some of the credits allowed as deductions from the gross estate tax payable, when calculating the net estate tax payable, are state death tax credit, a credit for tax on prior transfers, credit for foreign death taxes, and the unified estate and gift tax credit. These credits are discussed below. (The unified rate schedule can be found in Appendix B at the end of this book.)

Credits Allowable

A credit is allowed against the federal estate tax for the amount of any estate, inheritance, legacy, or succession taxes actually paid to any state, territory, or the District of Columbia with respect to any property included in the decedent's gross estate. If the decedent's taxable estate does not exceed $40,000, there is no credit allowed for state death taxes. If the taxable estate exceeds $40,000, the credit is limited by an amount determined by the table in Section 2011(b).

EXAMPLE 7. Decedent's taxable estate is $300,000 and his executrix paid $3,800 state estate taxes. The taxable estate is reduced by $60,000 before the maximum credit for state death taxes is looked up in the table in Section 2011(b). The maximum allowable credit is $3,600.

The credit for state death taxes is limited to those taxes that were actually paid. Basically, the credit must be claimed within four years after the filing of the estate tax return for the decedent's estate.

Since a credit is allowed only up to the amount of state taxes paid, care should be taken to supply the required information in full. This is particularly important when a deposit is made with the state as security for the payment of the state tax. It is also important when discounts or refunds may be allowed by the state. The information to be furnished to the district director should disclose the total amount of tax imposed by the state, the amount of any discount allowed, the total amount actually paid in cash, and the identity of the property for which the state tax has been paid or is to be paid.[20]

Postmortem Planning

Postmortem estate planning is possible with state death taxes. Instead of claiming state death taxes (imposed on a transfer for public, charitable, or religious uses) as credit, an executor may elect to deduct these expenditures. The conditions for making this election are outlined in Reg. 20.2053-9(b).

Prior Transfers Credit

For all or a part of the estate tax paid with respect to the transfer of property to the decedent by someone who died within 10 years before or within 2 years after the decedent's death, a credit is allowed against the estate tax. The credit for tax on prior transfers is allowed only for prior estate taxes, not gift taxes. Also, within limits, it is allowed for more than two successive decedents. If the transferor died within two years before or after the present decedent's death, the credit allowed for the tax is 100 percent of the maximum amount allowable. If the transferor predeceased the decedent by more than two years, the credit allowable is reduced by 20 percent for each full two years by which the death of the transferor preceded that of the present decedent.[21]

The credit for tax on prior transfers is limited to the smaller of the following amounts:

1. An amount that bears the same ratio to the transferor's adjusted federal estate tax as the value of the transferred property bears to the transferor's adjusted taxable estate.

2. The amount by which the estate tax of the present decedent as determined without regard to a credit on prior transfers exceeds the estate tax for his/her estate as determined by excluding from the gross estate the net value of the transfer.[22]

Since many other countries levy death taxes on the transfer by nonresident aliens of property situated within their boundaries, the estates of many United States citizens are subjected to double taxes. Thus, our federal government has entered into estate tax conventions with a number of foreign countries to provide relief from such double taxation.

State Tax Credits

To protect against double taxation, the estate is allowed a credit against the federal estate tax for any inheritance, estate, legacy, or succession tax paid to a foreign country and its political subdivisions on any property that is included in the decedent's gross estate. The credit for foreign death taxes is limited to the smaller of the following amounts: the amount of the foreign death tax attributable to such property situated in the country imposing the tax and included in the decedent's gross estate, or the amount of the federal estate taxes attributable to such property.[23]

For the credit to be allowed, taxpayers must establish to the satisfaction of the secretary of state the amount of taxes actually paid to the foreign country, the amount and date of each payment, and the description and value of the property with respect to which taxes were imposed. Taxpayers may also have to submit other information necessary for the verification and computation of the credit.

Gift Tax Paid

To be allowed, this credit must be claimed within four years after the filing of the estate tax return.[24] Since under the law taxable gifts made after December 31, 1976, become part of the tax base and thus subject to the tax rate, any gift tax rate paid on gifts made after December 31, 1976, may be subtracted from the gross estate tax. Thus, in essence, the tax paid on such gifts becomes a credit against the estate tax.

An executor may elect to deduct certain foreign death taxes (imposed on a transfer for public, charitable, or religious uses) rather than claim such taxes as a tax credit. The conditions to be met in order to make this election are outlined in Reg. 20.2053-10(b).

Unified Estate and Gift Tax Credit

As was mentioned in Chapter 2, the unified credit for both the estate tax and the gift tax will be increased gradually from $47,000 in 1981 to $192,000 in 1987 by the Economic Recovery Tax Act of 1981.[25] (Refer back to Table 1 in Chapter 2 for the figures for each year.) The equivalent exemption is the amount of the taxable estate that passes free of the unified estate tax at death.

This credit (like the other credits) is deducted directly from the gross estate tax to determine the net estate tax payable. The net estate tax payable is the amount that becomes due to the Internal Revenue Service within nine months after the death unless an extension of time is granted.[26]

The mechanical calculation of the estate tax can best be summarized by observing the simplified format developed by Barry R. Schimel, as shown in Box 1.

ESTATE PLANNING TIPS

The federal estate tax laws are quite complicated and involved. Therefore, an estate planner must have a firm understanding of these laws and be aware of their interrelationships with the income tax laws. Estate owners must consider the impact of the estate tax when planning their estates. They should try to maximize the use of their assets in the way they think best. However, some helpful hints to enable estate owners to minimize taxes may be outlined as follows:

1. The estate owner should keep accurate inventories of assets and investments. He/she should make certain that an-

BOX 1   Simplified Format to Estimate the Estate Tax

Total assets of estate	$ _____	
Gifts during last three years (1)	+ _____	
Gross estate		$ _____
Less: liabilities of estate	− _____	
expenses (2)	− _____	
Adjusted gross estate		$ _____
Less: marital deduction (3)	− _____	
Less: charitable deduction	− _____	
Taxable estate		$ _____
Gifts made after 1976 (4)		+ _____
Tentative taxable base		$ _____
Estate tax from unified rate schedule		$ _____
Less: gift taxes previously paid (5)	− _____	
Less: unified tax credit (6)	− _____	
Net estate tax payable		$ _____

Notes:

(1) If certain post-1976 gifts are made within three years of death, the full amount of the gift, including the amount of gift taxes paid, less the $10,000 annual exclusions, is includible in the gross estate.

(2) Funeral and medical expenses estimate $4,500–$5,000. Administrative expenses estimate 3 percent of the gross estate or 5 percent of the probate estate.

(3) The actual amount passing to the surviving spouse not to exceed $250,000 or 50 percent of the adjusted gross estate, whichever is greater (if before 1982).

(4) Taxable gifts made after 1976, with the exception of certain gifts within three years of death (see item 1 above). The taxable gift is the amount of the gift minus the marital deduction and the $10,000 annual exclusion.

(5) Gift taxes actually paid on gifts after 1976, including gifts in items 1 and 5 above.

(6) Varies depending on year of death:

$$1982 = \$ \; 62,800$$
$$1983 = \$ \; 79,300$$
$$1984 = \$ \; 96,300$$
$$1985 = \$121,500$$
$$1986 = \$155,800$$
$$1987 \text{ and after} = \$192,800$$

Gifts made from September 9, 1976, to December 31, 1976, will reduce the unified credit by 20 percent of the portion of the previous lifetime exclusion used.

SOURCE: B. R. Schimel, "Estimating the Estate Under the 1976 Reform Act," *Journal of Accountancy,* July 1977, p. 42. Reprinted with permission. © 1977 by the American Institute of Certified Public Accountants, Inc.

other person knows the location of his/her will and inventory of assets.

2. A taxable estate should not be closed in less than six months after the date of the decedent's death. Only then can an administrator determine whether the alternate valuation date should be elected.

3. An excellent way to reduce an individual's estate tax liability is to reduce the gross estate by a systematic program of lifetime giving. Succeeding subsections discuss ways in which a portion of an estate can be transferred without incurring a gift tax.

4. Generally, the advantage of a step-up in basis to the estate and heirs of a decedent indicates that an individual should try to retain until death any noncash property that has substantially appreciated in value. Although such a procedure maximizes the estate tax, it eliminates any income tax that would have resulted if the property had been sold before death.

5. In order to get the marital deduction, there must be a surviving spouse. If there is a common disaster, the law presumes that each survived the other. Therefore, neither will inherit from the other and there will be no marital deduction. If one of the estates is much larger than the other, a provision should be placed in the will stating that the beneficiary survived the spouse with the larger estate. However, with the larger marital deduction, it may be better to include some of the assets in the smaller estate in order to qualify for the estate tax marital deduction. Some simple language in the will should accomplish this objective.

6. To a limited extent a decedent can bypass or skip a generation. For example, a father can pass to his son (or daughter) only the right to receive income from certain assets, with the remainder to go to his grandchildren. There is no tax on generation-skipping transfers to grandchildren up to $250,000 per child on the date of the termination of the grantor-children life income interest. Thus, to a limited extent, the assets are not included in the child's estate and the estate tax is avoided. For example, if a grantor has three children (who

also have children), up to $750,000 can be transferred to the grandchildren tax-free.

7. A husband should consider giving up all "incidents of ownership" in insurance policies (i.e., change the beneficiary, surrender or cancel the policy, pledge the policy for a loan, revoke an assignment, or borrow against). The right to convert a policy from group term to individual whole life is not an incident of ownership. If his wife owns all the insurance policies covering his life, none of the policies will be included in his gross estate. The husband should also own the policies on his wife's life. Remember, only the value of the policy on the date of the gift is included in "taxable gifts." Of course, this assignment is not for everyone (i.e., the marriage may be unstable). Also, if the spouse has very little experience in managing money, some type of trust arrangement may be appropriate.

For example, a life insurance trust may be established with all incidents of ownership of the insurance policy. The trust would collect the insurance proceeds, and the trustee would have certain discretionary powers, such as lending money to the estate. Or the trustee could be empowered to use the trust income for the surviving spouse and/or children.

8. Where there is a chance that a donor will die before the donee reaches 21 years of age, the donor should not be the custodian of a transfer under the Uniform Gifts to Minors Act. If the donor is the custodian and dies, the value of the custodian property will be included in the estate.

9. Flower bonds are certain treasury bonds that bear a low interest rate and may be bought at a discount but are redeemable at par in payment of a decedent's federal estate tax. However, the bonds must be included in the estate at face value. The excess of the face value of the bonds above their purchase price escapes the income tax because the tax basis of the bonds is stepped up to their face value on date of death. This excess is not taxable when the executor uses the bonds to pay the federal estate tax.

10. When satisfying charitable bequests, the executor may wish to distribute property with the lowest carryover ba-

sis to charitable organizations. Such a procedure allows the executor to distribute the higher-basis property to the family of the decedent.

11. Before revising a will that was in existence on April 30, 1976, estate owners must consider the fact that any revision may cause the will or trust to fall within the generation-skipping tax area.

NOTES

1. Section 2053; Reg. 20.2053-2.
2. Section 2053; Reg. 20.2053-3.
3. 279 U.S. 151 (S. Ct., 1929).
4. See also *Estate of Van Horne,* 720 F.2d 1114 (9th Cir. 1983).
5. See for example, *Propstra,* 680 F.2d 1248 (9th Cir. 1982).
6. *Du Val's Estate,* 152 F.2d 103 (9th Cir. 1945).
7. *Estate of Hagmann,* 60 T.C. 465 (1973).
8. *Jacobs,* 34 F.2d 233 (8th Cir. 1929).
9. Section 2053; Reg. 20.2053-6 and 7.
10. Reg. 20.2053-1(d); Reg. 1.642(g)(1).
11. Section 2055.
12. Section 2056.
13. Section 2056(b).
14. Section 2056(b)-3.
15. Section 2056(b)-5.
16. Section 2056(b)-6.
17. See S. Sherman, "How to Draft QTIP Trust Provisions for Maximum Flexibility," *Estate Planning,* May 1984, pp. 158–63.
18. Ibid., 159.
19. Section 2001.
20. Reg. 20.2011-1(b)(2).
21. Section 2013.
22. Reg. 20-2013-2 and 20-2013-3.
23. Section 2014.
24. Section 2014(d)(e).
25. The unified credit and equivalent exemptions for 1977–1980 were as follows:

Year	Credit	Equivalent Exemption
1977	$30,000	$120,667
1978	34,000	134,000
1979	38,000	147,333
1980	42,500	161,563

26. Sections 6075 and 6151.

5

Deferral and Financing of the Estate Tax Liability

The mere fact that a taxpayer chooses one road in preference to another, in order to avoid the hot sun of taxation, is no reason to deny he actually traveled the first road.

—*Hugh C. Bickford*

An estate tax return (Form 706) is due within nine months of a decedent's death. The district director's office is authorized to extend the time for filing up to six months upon written request and showing of a reasonable cause. Some situations that may be recognized as reasonable cause are pending litigation, illness of the executor or attorney, or circumstances that make it impossible to determine the nature or extent of an asset. Except in the case of a taxpayer who is abroad, the extension cannot be for more than six months. Receiving an extension does prevent a delinquency penalty from being assessed, but interest accrues under Section 6621(a) during the extension at the statutory rate of 13 percent per year during the first six months in 1985 (11 percent in 1984). If no extension is obtained, 13 percent interest during the first half of 1985 is charged on the amount of tax not paid by the due date; likewise, there is a nondeductible .5 percent penalty tax due per month up to a maximum of 25 percent.[1] This statutory rate is established by the secretary of the treasury.

PAYMENT OF TAX LIABILITY

The tax liability must be sent to the district director's office with the return, unless the estate qualifies for special treatment under one of the provisions that allows an extension of time for payment. The extensions apply to reasonable cause, reversionary or remainder interests, and large interests in closely held corporations. If payment cannot be made with the return, due to reasonable cause such as being forced to liquidate assets in a depressed market, the district director's office may extend the time for submitting the payment. The extension can be granted for a period ranging from one year to a maximum of 10 years. As is true with all extensions, interest accrues from the due date of the return. Prior to December 31, 1976, exceptional circumstances had to be shown in order to receive this extension. The Tax Reform Act of 1976 substitutes the phrase "reasonable cause" for "undue hardship" in this provision. If a farm or closely held business constitutes at least 35 percent of the adjusted gross estate, then reasonable cause is presumed to exist.

If an estate includes a reversionary or remainder interest, an extension of time for payment may be elected by the executor under Section 6163. The tax attributable to the value of the interest may be postponed up to six months after the termination of the decedent's interest in the property for reasonable cause. The district office may postpone the payment date for a reasonable period, up to a maximum of three years. Since the extension applies only to the tax on the reversionary or remainder interest, the portion of the tax attributable to the other assets must be submitted with the estate tax return.

The two extensions discussed above must be requested in writing on or before the due date of the tax return. The reasonable-cause extension is discretionary with the district office, but the postponement for reversionary or business interests may be elected by the estate if the requirements are met. Extensions of time for payment are usually applied for simultaneously with the filing of the return. Both extensions are available to postpone the payment of any deficiency that may arise from a subsequent audit of the return, provided the requirements are met at that time.

DEFERMENT AND EXTENSION

Fourteen-Year Installment Provision: Section 6166

Effective after December 31, 1981, there is a 14-year installment provision for qualifying interest in a closely held business. An executor may defer all payments of tax for four years and pay only interest for such period. For years 5 through 14 after the decedent's death, the tax is payable in equal installments. A low 4 percent interest rate applies to the first $345,800 of estate tax (less the available unified credit).

In order to qualify, the interest in the closely held business (proprietor, partner, and stockholder) must exceed 35 percent (65 percent before 1982) of the decedent's adjusted gross estate (AGE). AGE refers to gross estate less expenses, debts, claims, and losses (Sections 2053 and 2054), but before marital and charitable deductions. In order to qualify, it may be worthwhile to give securities or other property to heir(s) before death in order to make sure that the required proportion of the estate consists of farm or business property. Further, a taxpayer may wish to delay giving children a share of the family business before he/she dies.

An interest in a closely held business refers to

1. An interest as a proprietor in a trade or business.

2. An interest as a partner in a partnership where 20 percent or more of the total capital interest in such partnership is included in determining the gross estate of the decedent or the partnership has 15 or fewer partners.

3. Stock in a corporation where 20 percent or more is included in the gross estate or the corporation has 15 or fewer shareholders.

4. Indirect ownership of a closely held business interest through a holding company (after July 18, 1984). However, such holding company stock must have no market value on a stock exchange or on an over-the-counter market at the time of the decedent's death. (Here, however, the 5-year deferral and 4 percent interest rate are not available; only the 10-year installment payments are available).

In order to determine the value of any interest in a closely held business, the value of its passive assets is not includable. A passive asset is any asset other than an asset used in carrying on a trade or business. For example, suppose a corporation owns real estate not used in the business. The value of the decedent's stock attributable to this passive asset must be eliminated in order to determine if the decedent's stock meets the 35 percent test in Section 6166(a)(1).

Under this 5-year deferral and 10-year installment payment plan in Section 6166, any interest payable by the estate on deferred payments is deductible as an administrative expense under Section 2053 for purposes of determining taxable estate and estate taxes. Thus, this deduction can have a significant impact on reducing the estate tax. The stock interest in two or more businesses may be aggregated for testing purposes (that is, the 35 percent test) where the decedent owned 20 percent or more of the outstanding stock of each corporation.

The payment of the estate tax is accelerated if one third or more of a decedent's qualifying interest is disposed of or if there is a withdrawal of money (or other property) in an amount equal to one third of the value of the decedent's interest (a Section 303 redemption is excepted).

A disposition of holding company stock (which is treated as business company stock) or the withdrawal of money or other property from the holding company is treated as a fatal disposition or withdrawal (i.e., acceleration of the estate tax).

Where an election is made to pay taxes in installments under Section 6166, a special lien procedure may be elected so that an executor will not be personally liable for the taxes. The executor and all beneficiaries with an interest in the qualifying property must file a written agreement, consenting to the creation of a lien, and must designate a responsible person to deal with the IRS as an agent for the appropriate parties.

Redemption under Section 303

Owners of corporations should not overlook a Section 303 redemption that provides an opportunity to take assets out of a family corporation at a favorable sale or exchange treatment (that is, capital-gain treatment). Under this provision an estate or the heirs of the stockholder of a corporation may withdraw cash or property from the enterprise without paying a dividend tax, provided the amount is equal to the sum of federal and estate death taxes and funeral and administrative expenses. Further, the gain may be reduced on such a redemption, since the stock may have received a step-up in basis under Section 1014. The purpose of this special redemption is to help the financing of the estate taxes in situations where the estate consists mainly of shares of stock in a closely held corporation.

An option can be created to give the administrator for the decedent's estate the right to require the corporation to redeem from the estate an amount of stock that will provide the necessary liquid assets to pay death taxes and funeral and administrative expenses under Section 303. Such an option can be placed in a written agreement between the stockholder and the corporation, and should be so designed as to meet the requirements of Section 303.

REQUIREMENTS AND LIMITATIONS

A number of requirements and limitations must be satisfied in order to obtain capital-gain treatment under Section 303:

1. There must be a distribution of property to a stockholder by a corporation in redemption of all or part of the stock of such corporation.

2. Such stock must be included in determining the gross estate of a decedent for purposes of the federal estate tax.

3. The value of the stock included in the decedent's estate must be more than 35 percent of the adjusted gross estate (50 percent before 1982).[2]

4. The amount treated as a capital gain can be no greater than the sum of the death taxes and the funeral and administrative expenses allowable under Sections 2053 or 2106.

5. Qualifying redemptions are limited to those post-1976 stockholders whose interest in the estate is reduced directly (or through a binding obligation to contribute) by any payment of death taxes or funeral and administrative expenses.

6. Any distribution made more than four years after the decedent's death is subject to additional limitations.[3]

Inclusion in an Estate

The redeemed stock must be included in the gross estate of a decedent for federal estate tax purposes.[4] The IRS takes the position that the stock must be taxable to the decedent's estate (and not stock that is includable in the estate under Section 2035 for purposes of making the 35 percent computation). Thus, a gift of stock within three years of death may eliminate the availability of a Section 303 redemption. If an estate has liquidity problems, try to avoid disposing of the closely held stock.

Such included stock must have a federal estate tax value more than 35 percent of the value of the adjusted gross estate. Adjusted gross estate (AGE) is defined as gross estate less the sum of the deductions allowable under Sections 2053 or 2054.[5] These allowable deductions include the following:

1. Funeral expenses.
2. Administrative expenses.
3. Claims against the estate.
4. Unpaid mortgages and other indebtedness.
5. Losses incurred by the estate.[6]

Note that the term *allowable* (rather than *allowed*) will permit an executor to claim administrative expenses as income tax deductions without adversely affecting qualification under the 35 percent test.[7] Prop. Reg. 1.303-1(a)(5) takes the harsh position that only qualifying deductions incurred within nine months of death (plus extensions) may be used to offset the value of the gross estate. Thus, it may be beneficial to obtain as many extensions of the estate tax return due date as possible.

A special rule applies to an estate that includes stock of two or more corporations. If neither block of stock satisfies the 35 percent requirement, this special rule permits treatment of the combined holdings as stock in a single corporation. To qualify, however, the estate tax value of the stock held in each corporation must be more than 20 percent in value of the outstanding stock of such corporation. For purposes of this 20 percent test, the surviving spouse's community property interest in such stock is treated as if it were included in the decedent's gross estate.[8]

EXAMPLE 1. The gross estate of a decedent, Pete Rose, has a fair market value of $1 million, and the Sections 2053 and 2054 expenses are $125,000. Included in the gross estate are stocks in three corporations:

	Adjusted Basis	Fair Market Value
Bay	$110,000	$200,000
Melk	125,000	300,000
Whip	75,000	200,000

The stock of Bay and Melk included in the estate is all the outstanding stock of the two corporations. Neither of the stockholdings satisfies the 35 percent of adjusted gross estate test. However, since Bay, Whip, and Melk meet the 20 percent test, the stock of each corporation can be treated as stock of a single corporation valued at $700,000. Clearly, $700,000 is greater than 35 percent of AGE [35% × ($1 million − $125,000) = $306,250].

The 35 percent test is critical to the use of a Section 303 redemption. If the stockholdings do not satisfy this test, certain steps may be taken to ensure qualification. The value of a stockholder's interest in a corporation may be increased, the stockholder's adjusted gross estate may be decreased, or a combination of both can be employed in order to qualify for Section 303 treatment. For example, a stockholder could purchase more shares in the corporation. Further, assets other than closely held stock may be given away more than three years before death in order to help satisfy the 35 percent test.[9]

There is one exception to the requirement that the stock must be included in the gross estate. Section 303(c) provides exchange treatment to a redemption of stock possessing a substituted basis acquired from stock that was included in the gross estate. For example, stock may have been included in the decedent's gross estate and later exchanged for other stock in a nontaxable reorganization. The latter stock can qualify under Section 303.

Limitation of Amount

Even if an estate has sufficient liquid assets in order to pay its taxes and expenses without a redemption, qualified stockholders can still obtain the benefits of Section 303. In fact, Section 303 is applicable even though the proceeds are not used to pay federal estate taxes or even when there is no federal estate tax due.[10] However, the amount of the redemption is limited to the total of the death taxes and the funeral and administrative expenses of the estate.[11]

When there is more than one redemption distribution during the prescribed time period, the distribution is applied against the total amount that qualifies for exchange treatment, in the order in which the distributions were made. All distributions are considered, including distributions that fall under a different code provision.[12]

EXAMPLE 2. Decedent's gross estate is $800,000, and the sum of death taxes and funeral and administrative expenses is $225,000. Included in determining gross estate is stock of a corporation that is valued at $450,000 for estate tax purposes. In the first year of administration, one third of the stock is distributed to a legatee, and shortly thereafter the corporation redeems it for $150,000. In the second year, another one third of the stock includable in the estate is redeemed for $150,000. The first distribution is applied against the $225,000 that qualifies for Section 303 treatment as payment in exchange for stock under Section 302(a). On the second distribution, only $75,000 is treated as in-full payment in exchange for stock under Section 303.

Time Limitations

This special time-limitation treatment applies only to distributions made in redemption of such stock in either of two situations:

1. The period between the decedent's death and the 90th day after the expiration of the limitation period in Section 6501(a) (that is, three years). Since the federal estate tax return is due nine months after the decedent's death under Section 6075(a), the qualified limitation is approximately four years.

2. In the case of Tax Court litigation, the permissible time period is extended for 60 days after the Tax Court's decision becomes final.[13]

If an election is made under Section 6166, relating to the extension of time to pay the estate tax attributable to a farm or closely held business, the Section 303 period is identical with the extension period.[14] However, any amounts distributed after the four-year period are still limited to the sum of the death taxes and funeral and administrative expenses.[15]

Qualifying Stockholders

For estates of decedents dying after 1976, a qualifying redemption is limited to those stockholders whose interest in the estate is reduced (directly or through a binding obligation to contribute) by the payment of the death taxes and funeral and administration expenses, and to the extent of such reduction.[16] Thus, items such as property qualifying for the marital deduction are not eligible for Section 303 treatment.

Special rules apply to generation-skipping transfers. Where stock in a corporation is subject to a generation-skipping tax, such stock will be included in the gross estate of the deemed transferor. Any tax imposed under Section 2601 will be treated as an estate tax, thereby increasing the amount available for Section 303 treatment. The period of distribution is measured from the date of the generation-skipping transfer, and the relationship of the stock to the decedent's estate is measured with reference solely to the amount of the generation-skipping transfer.[17]

Step-up in Basis

Section 303 redemptions are favorably affected by the step-up-in-basis rule under Section 1014. Most of the stock being redeemed will have appreciated in value, and the redemption will produce little capital gain subject to taxation. Of course subsequent redemption, in order to raise funds to pay such income taxes, is not protected by Section 303.

EXAMPLE 3. Decedent's gross estate is $1 million, and the Sections 2053 and 2054 expenses are $225,000. Included in determining gross estate is stock of a corporation that is valued at $450,000 for estate tax purposes (adjusted basis of $150,000). In the first year of administration, one third of the stock is distributed to a legatee, and shortly thereafter the corporation redeems it for $150,000. In the second year, another one third of the stock includable in the estate is redeemed for $160,000. During the first year, the entire distribution would qualify for exchange treatment. Thus, no capital gain would be recognized ($150,000 − $150,000) for the first year because of the step-up in basis. As for the second year, only $75,000 of the distribution may be protected by Section 303. Thus, there would be a $4,687.50 capital gain [$75,000 − ($75,000/160,000 × $150,000)]. The remaining $150,000 distribution must qualify under a "safe harbor" in Section 302; otherwise the $150,000 would be treated as a dividend.

Installment Sales of Real Estate

There is an exception to the 10 percent minimum rate of interest imputed on installment sales that do not provide for at least 9 percent interest. Real estate sales between related parties after June 30, 1981, qualify for this special rule. Up to $500,000 per year in installment sales of land to a spouse, children, ancestors, and lineal descendants is eligible for a lower 7 percent rate of interest. No party involved in the sale may be a nonresident alien.

This exception should work well with an installment gift technique. Assume that a parent sells real property—that is, land—to a child in return for 7 percent interest-bearing notes, payable $10,000 per year ($20,000 if married). The notes can be secured by deed of trust on the land. The value of the promissory notes should be equal to the value of the property transferred. As each payment becomes due, the parent forgives the note.

The advantages of this installment-sale technique are threefold. The gifts are spread over a number of years to take advantage of the annual $10,000 exclusion; the parent's annual forgiveness is a present-interest gift. Since the transferee is vested immediately with absolute ownership, the transferor's estate is relieved of any subsequent appreciation. Finally, the transferee gets a step-up in basis equal to the selling price. Of course, the transferor may have to recognize income taxes on any gain on the sale (excess of selling price over adjusted basis). Although the Tax Court agrees with this technique,[18] the IRS will hold that since the donor never intended to enforce the installment notes, the notes were not a valuable consideration for the transfer of the property. Thus, the IRS may assert that the gift was made in the year of transfer.[19]

Another technique has been approved by the IRS—installment gifts of the property. In Revenue Ruling 83-180 a taxpayer wished to make a gift of real estate.[20] Every year the taxpayer obtained an appraisal of the land, and based on such appraisal made a gift of a portion of the land equal to or less than the annual exclusion (i.e., $10,000 or $20,000), until all the land was transferred. The IRS ruled that each annual gift transferred to the donee was a present unrestricted right to the immediate use and enjoyment of an ascertainable interest in the land, and the taxpayer retained ownership and control of the remaining portion. Therefore, the taxpayer made a separate gift each year, and each gift qualified for the annual exclusion. Although annual appraisals can be expensive, apparently the IRS insists on an annual appraisal to make this technique qualify.

Using ESOPs/Worker-Owned Cooperatives

An employee stock ownership plan (ESOP)[21] or an eligible worker-owned cooperative[22] that purchases employer securities from a decedent may assume all or part of the estate tax liability (which would otherwise be paid by the decedent's estate). The employer must guarantee payment of the estate tax liability, along with any interest payable under Section 6601. A worker-owned cooperative includes farmers' cooperatives and corporations owned on a cooperative basis. The majority of the membership must be composed of employees who own a majority of the voting stock of the corporation.

Since the assumption of the liability is treated as a leveraged purchase of stock, the acquisition must take place at not less than fair market value. If the business qualifies for deferral and 4 percent interest rate (on the first $1 million) under Section 6166, an ESOP (or cooperative) should qualify for the same benefits.

Where employer securities move from the decedent or executor to an ESOP (or cooperative), an executor may elect Section 2210 and file agreements by the ESOP (and the employer) or the cooperative to guarantee payment of the estate tax. The executor of the estate is then relieved of any liability for the estate tax assumed by the ESOP or cooperative. The appropriate election must be made and the agreements filed by the executor before the due date (including extensions) for filing Form 706 (estate tax return).

The amount payable by the ESOP (or cooperative) is limited by the value of the employer securities acquired by the ESOP (or cooperative) from the decedent and includable in the decedent's gross estate. An ESOP probably cannot bind itself in advance to purchase employer securities. Therefore, a person should put directions in the will indicating that the transfer is contemplated. Authorize the executor to carry out such a transfer where beneficial.

Obviously, more than one Form 706 may be required when Section 2210 is elected—one by the executor and one by the ESOP (or cooperative). The benefits of Section 2210 are available for estates of decedents which are required to file estate tax returns on a date after July 18, 1984.

NOTES

1. Section 6651.
2. Section 303. Before 1977, the stock so included must have had a federal estate tax value of either (*a*) more than 35 percent of the gross estate, or (*b*) 50 percent of the taxable estate.
3. See Section 303(b).
4. Section 303(a).
5. Section 303(b)(2)(A).
6. Sections 2053 and 2054.
7. Rev. Rul. 56-449, 1956-2 C.B. 180.
8. Section 303(b)(2)(B).
9. See also L. Chan, "Planning a Sec. 303 Redemption," *The Tax Adviser,* January 1976, p. 7.
10. Section 3039(a).
11. Rev. Rul. 56-60, 1956-1 C.B. 443.
12. Reg. 1.303-2(g)(1).
13. Section 303(b)(1)(A) and (B).
14. Section 303(b)(1)(C).
15. Section 303(b)(4).
16. Section 303(b)(3).
17. Section 303(d).
18. *Estate of Kelley,* 63 T.C. 321 (1974), nonacq. *Story,* III, 38 T.C. 936 (1962).
19. Rev. Rul. 77-299, 1977-2 C.B. 343.
20. 1983-2 C.B. 169.
21. Section 4975(e)(7).
22. Section 1042(c)(2).

6

Lifetime Gifts

Estate planning is the process of passing from this world into
the next without passing through the Internal Revenue
Service.

—*Robert Brosterman*

The federal gift tax is a tax levied upon transfer of gifts from
one person (donor) to another person (donee). The difference
between a gift and inheritance is that a gift is the trans-
mission of property from one living person to another. To further qualify as a gift, property must be given without any
consideration.

The federal gift tax originated in the Revenue Act of 1932.
Its primary purpose was to act as a backstop to the federal
estate tax; it was not intended to raise revenues. The establishment of the gift tax prevented people from avoiding the
progressive federal estate tax by distributing assets during
their lifetime. An interesting note is that, although the yield
of this tax and the dollar value of gifts are relatively small,
lifetime giving is almost universal in the higher wealth
categories.

Before 1977, the gift tax rates were 25 percent less than
federal estate tax rates, and a systematic pattern of lifetime
giving could significantly reduce people's federal estate tax
liability as well as their income tax payments. This old two-

tax-rate system was eliminated after December 31, 1976, and a single, progressive transfer tax is now imposed on the cumulative total of both lifetime gifts and property owned at death. The unified tax rates are presented in Appendix B at the end of this book.

REQUIREMENTS OF A GIFT

The statutes fail to give an exact definition of a gift. As set forth by Section 2511(a), the gift tax applies "whether the transfer is in trust or otherwise, whether the gift is direct or indirect, and whether the property is real or personal, tangible or intangible." Further, Regulation 25.1512-8 states that

> Transfers reached by the gift tax are not confined to those only which, being without a valuable consideration, accord with the common-law concept of gifts, but embrace as well sales, exchanges, and other dispositions of property for a consideration to the extent that the value of the property transferred by the donor exceeds the value in money or money's worth of the consideration given therefor. However, a sale, exchange, or other transfer of property made in the ordinary course of business (a transaction which is bona fide, at arm's length, and free from any donative intent) will be considered as made for an adequate and full consideration in money or money's worth, as love and affection, promise of marriage, etc., is to be wholly disregarded, and the entire value of the property transferred constitutes the amount of the gift. Similarly, a relinquishment or promised relinquishment of dower or curtesy, or of a statutory estate created in lieu of dower or curtesy, or of other marital rights in the spouse's property or estate, shall not be considered to any extent a consideration "in money or money's worth."

The Tax Court has stipulated that the six following items are essential elements of a bona fide gift.[1]

1. A donor competent to make a gift.
2. A donee capable of taking the gift.
3. A clear and unmistakable intention on the part of the donor to absolutely and irrevocably divest himself of the title, dominion, and control of the subject matter of the gift in presents.
4. There is an actual irrevocable transfer of the present legal title and of the dominion and control of the entire

gift to the donee, so that the donor can exercise no further active dominion or control over it.

5. A delivery to the donee of the subject of the gift or of the most effective means of commanding the dominion of it.

6. Acceptance of the gift by the donee.

In viewing items 2 and 6, Regulation 25.2511-2(a) indicates that, regardless of the fact that the identity of the donee may not then be known, a gift is considered valid.[2] Also, donative intent on behalf of the donor need not be present in order to incur a gift tax.[3]

PARTIES SUBJECT TO THE TAX AND TIMING OF THE TAX

Under Reg. 25.2511-2(b) the date of the gift is the date the donor's dominion and control over the property ceases. For example, a gift made by check is not completed until the check is paid, certified, accepted by the drawee bank, or negotiated for value by a third person.

Beginning in 1982, gift tax returns are filed and taxes paid on a calendar-year basis on April 15 following the year of transfers. However, for a deceased donor, the gift tax return shall be filed no later than the date for filing the federal estate tax return (which is generally nine months after the date of death).

EXAMPLE 1. Dean Winner makes a taxable gift on March 13, 1985, but he dies from a strange illness on May 1, 1985. The due date of the gift tax return is nine months later on February 1, 1986 (not April 15, 1986).

An important factor is the status of the donor at the time of the gift and not the location of the gift property. Thus, a transfer of gift property, wherever situated, is taxable (to the extent that value exceeds deductions and exclusions) if the donor is a citizen or resident of the United States. This tax is payable by the donor as stipulated in Section 2502(c). For nonresident aliens, the gift tax is applicable only to the transfer of real and tangible personal property that is located in the United States. Gifts of intangible property made by nonresident aliens for the calendar year 1967 and years thereafter are not subject to gift tax except in the case of certain expatriate U.S. citizens.

ANNUAL EXCLUSION AND UNIFIED CREDIT

Beginning in 1982, the annual exclusion per donee per year was increased from $3,000 to $10,000 ($20,000 for consenting-spouse gifts). A married couple electing to split gifts can exclude $20,000 of present-interest gifts per year for each donee. Further, there is an unlimited exclusion for amounts paid for the benefit of a donee for certain medical-care expenses and school tuition. The donee does not have to be related to the donor. Medical or tuition "gifts" must be made to the service provider (rather than the donee).

Tuition refers to amounts paid to an educational organization which normally maintains a regular faculty and curriculum and normally has a regularly enrolled body of pupils or students in attendance at the place where its educational activities are regularly carried on.[4]

EXAMPLE 2. Beginning in 1985, Rich and Cathy Daf decide to establish a program of giving to their four children over the next 10 years. The couple would be able to give $800,000 tax-free to their children over a 10-year period. Remember that income-producing property may be shifted to the children, thereby decreasing the overall income tax payable.

There is no $10,000 annual exclusion for gifts considered to be future interests (discussed later).[5] In order to have a present interest in property, an individual must currently have the right to use, possess, or enjoy the property. There must be a substantial present economic benefit for the person to have a present interest and qualify for the annual exclusion.[6]

To see the unified credit figures for the gift tax between 1981 and 1987, refer back to Table 1 in Chapter 2.

Gift Splitting

By gift splitting a husband and wife could combine their pre-1977 lifetime exemptions for a total of $60,000 and also their annual exclusions, which would total $6,000. For years after

1976, a husband and wife can combine their unified credits and their annual exclusions. The consent of the spouses to treat a gift as a split gift must be made on a calendar-year basis. The husband signifies his consent to split gifts on the wife's return, and the wife signifies her consent on the husband's return in the place provided on Form 709.

EXAMPLE 3. In July, Mr. Giving and his wife made a gift that exceeds $25,000. The decision to treat it as a split gift must be made no later than the date on which the gift tax return is filed (that is, April 15). When this option is chosen, the gift to a third party is considered to be shared halfway by each spouse. Where one spouse has little or no estate, gift splitting is appropriate, since a unified estate tax credit would be wasted.

In most cases it will benefit the taxpayer to take the unified credit as soon as possible. The federal gift tax is progressive and cumulative, and there is no valid reason for saving portions of the credit for future years. If portions of the unified credit are saved for future periods, gift tax rates might very well be less and therefore would reflect an illusory tax savings. But if one considers the loss of earning power of gift taxes paid immediately as the result of any "saved" credit, then this saving will be deceptive, and the net result will probably be an economic loss. The concept of the time value of money seems appropriate here in that money (or gifts) received today will be worth more than the same amount received at some future date.

A husband and wife are allowed to give away tax free an astounding amount of property in a 10-year period. If a family has four children and the spouses agree to split their gifts, a total of $2 million can be transferred without paying any gift tax (using the 1987 unified credit). Each spouse has a $192,800 unified credit (1987) and an annual exclusion of $10,000, which is accumulated as shown below:

$20,000 (annual exclusion) × 4 children	= $	80,000	per year
		× 10	years
	$	800,000	
$600,000 (1987 exemption equivalent) × 2 spouses	=	$1,200,000	
		$2,000,000	

What may be difficult to appreciate is the concept of using the unified credit as soon as possible. Other things being equal, a taxpayer should give away enough assets to use up the unified credit. Think of it as borrowing the unpaid tax from the federal government. Keep in mind that if income-producing property is given away, income can be shifted to a donee in a lower tax bracket.

A couple should not automatically elect to gift-split, especially where there is a chance that the gift will be a gift in contemplation of death. In such a situation the full amount of the gift (including the $10,000 exclusion) is included in the decedent's gross estate along with any gift taxes in fact paid by the decedent.

This gross-up does not include any gift tax paid by the other spouse, since the spouse's payment of such a gift tax does not reduce the decedent's estate at death. When the other spouse dies, one half of the gift is added to the second spouse's taxable estate as an "adjusted taxable gift." Although the statutes are not clear, the second spouse should receive a credit for the gift tax paid by the second spouse.

EXAMPLE 4. Husband makes a gift to his son of $200,000, and his wife agrees to gift-split. Husband includes $90,000 in his taxable gifts and his wife includes $90,000 in her taxable gifts. If husband dies within three years of this gift, a total of $200,000 is includable in his gross estate under Section 2037. When wife dies, she also adds $100,000 to her adjusted taxable gift. Notice that this same gift is includable one and a half times (that is, completely in the husband's estate and one half in the wife's estate).

Marital Deduction

Since April 2, 1948, a donor has been allowed an exemption on separate property that at the time of the gift belonged to the donor's spouse. In order to establish equity between separate and community property, a donor was permitted until 1977 to deduct one half of any gifts to his/her spouse. From 1977 through 1981, there was an unlimited marital deduction for the first $100,000, and a 50 percent deduction for gifts above

$200,000. Thus, a much larger amount could be given to a spouse between 1976 and 1981 without paying a tax. Apparently, this $100,000 limitation was a per-donor limitation (that is, no extra amount for a second marriage).

EXAMPLE 5. Husband transfers $250,000 to his spouse in 1977, his first gift to her. He would be allowed a total marital deduction of $125,000.

After December 31, 1981, there is an unlimited gift tax marital deduction. This change simplifies tax planning since the taxpayer now can make unlimited gifts to a spouse at death, using the unlimited gift tax marital deduction. In effect, a spouse can give everything to the other spouse without incurring a gift tax.

Community property is not applicable to this marital deduction. In the transfer of property, the status of the donor is the critical factor (not the status of the donee). For example, a nonresident alien donor is not allowed a marital deduction, whereas a resident donor is not denied a deduction merely because the donee is a nonresident alien.

Although a "permanent interest" or present interest qualifies as a marital deduction, a "terminable interest" is not allowed, except for qualified terminable-interest property (QTIP). Generally speaking, a permanent interest does not cease with the death of the donee and is eventually included in the donee's gross estate unless the gift is disposed of before the donee's death. To state this another way, the donee spouse must have full power to dispose of the gift property before a marital deduction is allowed.

Aside from the QTIP exception discussed in Chapter 4, two other major exceptions to the terminable-interest rule exist. The first exception occurs when the donee has enough control over the gift property to make the donee the owner of the property. Before this exception is applicable, the following conditions must be met:

1. The donee spouse must be entitled for life to all income from the entire interest.
2. Such income must be payable annually or at more frequent intervals.

3. The donee spouse must have the power (exercisable in favor of the donee or donee's estate) to appoint the entire interest.

4. Such a power must be exercisable by the donee spouse alone and (whether exercisable by will or during life) must be exercisable by the donee in all events.

5. No part of the entire interest must be subject to a power in any other person to appoint any part thereof to any person other than the donee spouse.

When this "life estate with power of appointment in donee spouse" occurs, the transferred property qualifies for the marital deduction.

A gift of joint interest is the other exception to the terminable-interest rule. If the property is transferred to a donee spouse as a sole joint tenant with the donor or as tenant by the entirety, the interest of the donor in the gift property—which exists solely because of the possibility that the donor may survive the donee spouse, or that there may occur a severance of tenancy—can still qualify for the marital deduction. For this exception to apply, such a transfer must be between husband and wife, and the spouses must be the only joint tenants.

Deduction for Charitable Gifts

A deduction is allowable on the federal gift tax return for certain gifts to qualified charities. If the gift to the charity is $10,000 or less and is a present-interest gift, such a transfer does not have to appear on a gift tax return. If the gift exceeds $10,000 or is a future-interest gift, the transfer must eventually be reported on a gift tax return. However, even if the charitable gift is reported, the taxpayer is allowed a deduction for the gift (that is, a "wash" effect). There is no percentage limitation as to the amount deductible on the gift tax return.

A *qualified charitable transfer* is defined as a transfer where a deduction is allowable under Section 2522 for the full amount of the gift. For example, if a person gives outright securities to a qualified charitable organization, he/she is entitled to a charitable deduction and would not have to file a special return for such gift.

But suppose a person transfers property in trust to a son for life, with the remainder to a charitable organization after the son's death. This gift would not be a qualified charitable transfer, since a gift tax charitable deduction is now allowable in an amount equal to the full amount transferred. Thus, the donor must file a return reporting the entire gift to the split-interest trust by April 15. The donor may have to pay a gift tax for the interest transferred to the son.

Gifts made to religious, charitable, scientific, literary, and educational organizations (including the encouragement of arts and the prevention of cruelty to children or animals) are normally deductible. But a gift made to a public institution is deductible only if made to the United States, any state, territory, any political subdivision thereof, or the District of Columbia.

A citizen or resident is allowed a gift tax deduction for transfers to a charitable organization, regardless of whether the organization is a United States institution or foreign institution. On the other hand, a nonresident alien may obtain a deduction only for gifts to a domestic corporation; and a nonresident alien may not deduct gifts to a foreign trust, community chest, fund, or foundation unless the gift is used within the United States for charitable purposes.

Certain deductions are disallowed for gifts to or for the use of organizations or trusts described in Section 5508(d) or Section 4948(c)(4).

A charitable deduction is allowed for certain future interests in property given to a charity. The future interest (except for a future interest in a personal residence or farm) must be in the form of a charitable remainder annuity trust, a charitable remainder unitrust, or a pooled-income fund.[7]

Charitable remainder annuity trust. This is a trust that is to pay its income beneficiary (or beneficiaries) a specific sum which is not less than 5 percent of the initial fair market value of all property placed in the trust. At the death of the income beneficiary, or at the end of a term of years (not greater than 20 years), the remainder interest must be paid to a qualified organization described above.[8]

Charitable remainder unitrust. This is a trust that is to pay the income beneficiary (or beneficiaries) a fixed percentage which is not less than 5 percent of the net fair market value of its assets (as valued annually).[9] There are two exceptions. The trust instrument may provide (1) that for any year, the trustee is to pay the income beneficiary the amount of trust income where this amount is less than the portion required to be distributed by the particular unitrust, and (2) that the trustee is to pay the beneficiary an amount of trust income in excess of that required to be distributed, to the extent he/she paid less than that portion in prior years because of the requirement to pay only the amount of the trust income.[10]

Pooled-income fund. This is similar to a charitable remainder trust except that the donor's irrevocable gifts are commingled with similar contributions in a fund maintained by the organization to which the remainder interest is contributed. This fund must meet six strict rules.[11]

Table 2, compiled by the CPA firm Deloitte Haskins & Sells, compares the characteristics of these three types of trusts.

An individual may establish a charitable income trust (often called a charitable lead trust), give away some of the income from the property, and still keep the property. A charitable income trust must be either an annuity trust or unitrust.

A charitable remainder trust is the opposite. The donor retains the income from some property and gives away the entire principal. A remainder trust must be in the form of an annuity trust, a unitrust, or a pooled-income trust. For both a charitable income trust and charitable remainder trust, a donor receives a current income tax deduction which is equal to the present value of the interest in the asset given to the charity (using 10 percent present worth annuity tables).

The value of the charitable deduction is computed by using the actuarial tables in Publication 723, *Valuation of Last Survivor Charitable Remainder,* available from the U.S. Government Printing Office.[12] The new 10 percent actuarial tables increase the gift and estate tax value given to the income interest and reduce the value given to the remainder.

One other exception to this denial of a charitable deduction (where the donor retains a life interest in the property) applies to gifts of personal residences and farms. A donor may still obtain a charitable deduction for a gift to a publicly supported charity (but not to a trust) even though he/she retains a right to live in the residence or use the farm.[13] However, the law does severely restrict the contribution of future interest in personal property (for example, paintings, jewelry, antiques) where the donor wishes to retain the enjoyment of the property during his/her lifetime. Further, some contributions of

TABLE 2 Features of Three Kinds of Trusts

	Type of Trust		
Trust Features	Annuity Trust	Unitrust	Pooled Income Fund
Required distribution to income beneficiary.	Fixed sum, but not less than 5 percent of the value of assets at transfer date.	Fixed percentage, which is not less than 5 percent, of the value of the annually revalued assets.*	Varies with earnings of the trust.
Term of trust.	Up to 20 years or life of beneficiary.	Up to 20 years or life of beneficiary.	Life of beneficiary.
Protection of trust principal.	Depending on the type of investments, principal normally remains intact.	Depending on the investments and trust earnings, principal may not remain intact.	Principal is not normally distributed.
Hedge against inflation.	Least protection.	Best protection.	Varies with actual earnings of trust.
Additional trust contributions after creation.	None allowed.	Allowed.	Allowed.

*If trust so provides, distribution may be limited in a year to actual trust income if it is a lesser amount.
SOURCE: Deloitte Haskins & Sells, *The Week in Review,* December 11, 1981. Used with permission.

tangible personal property to public charities result in a 50 percent reduction in the appreciation portion of the property (see Chapter 10).[14]

PRESENT VERSUS FUTURE INTEREST

Earlier, the criticality of determining whether a gift is a present or future interest was mentioned. This topic deserves a more thorough discussion. The definition of a present interest is an "unrestricted right to the immediate use, possession, or enjoyment of property or the income from property (such as a life estate or term certain)."

The entire amount of any gift of future interest in property must be included in taxable gifts, with the exception of certain gifts to minors (discussed later in more detail). "Reversions, remainders, and other interests or estates, whether vested or contingent, and whether or not supported by a particular interest or estate, which are limited to commence in use, possession, or enjoyment at some future date or time" are all included in the term *future interest.* From a decree by the Supreme Court we find that "the critical test is whether there has been a postponement of the rights of the donees to use, possess, and enjoy the property."[15] The law has stipulated that any remainder interest, even though marketable, is a future interest.

It is advisable, then, to make sure that the gifts made are of a present interest if it is expected that any exclusions from the amounts of these gifts will be taken. Gifts of present interest are the only forms of gifts to which an exclusion can be applied. The classification of gifts as either present or future interest should be made prior to the gift by the donor so as to take the optimum advantage of the tax consequences.

EXAMPLE 6. An unmarried person transfers assets to a trust for Sam for life, with the remainder to Deater. Sam's life estate value is $2,700 and Deater's remainder interest is worth $9,300. The taxable gift is $9,300 because there is no exclusion on the future-interest gift.

Gifts to Minors

A transfer of property by gifts to minors can be an effective planning tool. One very important exception to the future-interest rule is a transfer under the Uniform Gift to Minors Act. In a typical situation, a taxpayer irrevocably transfers securities, cash, or life insurance to a minor by registering the property in the name of the custodian or guardian designated by the donor. The donor should not be the custodian so as to ensure that the given property will not be included in the donor's gross estate if he/she dies before the minor reaches the age of majority. This selection can be a very important event, since Rev. Rul. 59-357 indicates that if the donor is the custodian and dies before the donee has reached the age of 21 years, it is quite likely that the gift will be included in the gross estate of the donor.[16] This exception to the future-interest rule will be the case if all three of the following conditions are met:

1. Both the property and its income may be expended by or for the benefit of the donee before he/she attains the age of 21.
2. Any portion of the property and its income not disposed of under condition 1 will pass to the donee when he/she attains the age of 21 years.
3. Any portion of the property and income not disposed of under condition 1 will be payable either to the estate of the donee or to whomever the donee may appoint under a general power of appointment if he/she dies before attaining the age of 21 years.[17]

In essence, the first condition means that the trust instrument must not impose any substantial restrictions on the trustee's ability to determine the amount of income or property distributed and the purposes for which the expenditures are made. A trustee, however, may be required to consider the donee-beneficiary's other available resources before distributing any principal or income to the donee. A gift will qualify for the annual exclusion where the restrictions in the trust instrument are no greater than the restrictions imposed on a guardian by the state law. The trustee also can be instructed to invest solely in life insurance policies.

The second condition requires any corpus and accumulated income to pass to the donee at age 21. Suppose the donor does not wish to distribute the principal to the beneficiary at age 21. This can be accomplished by gifting the assets to a 10-year reversionary trust, with the income earned in the trust to be distributed to a Section 2503(c) trust for the donee. The accumulated income qualifies as a present interest until the donee reaches 21, and the donor can obtain the corpus property after 10 years.

If a donee dies before age 21, the trust corpus and income must be payable to the donee's estate or to someone the donee may appoint under a general power of appointment. By giving a donee a power to demand the trust property for a reasonable period of time after reaching age 21, the trust may continue beyond the donee's 21st birthday. However, the donee must have a general power of appointment over the trust income/corpus or the property must pass automatically to the donee's estate.

There are also income tax benefits of making a gift to minors. In 1985, a minor could receive up to $1,100 of dividend income tax free (composed of the $1,000 personal exemption and the $100 dividend exclusion). Thus, a sizable income tax savings can result from a shift of income-producing property to a child, since the minor will be in a lower tax bracket. Furthermore, such gifts can insulate assets from the grips of creditors. Where the donor has the responsibility to support the donee, this income tax savings can be diluted. Regardless of the relationship of the donor or of the custodian to the donee, income from the gift property used to discharge the donor's support obligation is taxable to the donor. Private school costs and other nonessential items are outside the support obligation. Whether college expenditures are considered to be support depends on state law. Even if college expenses are outside the support obligation, a parent should not become contractually obligated to pay the minor's education costs. Such an obligation would cause payments by the trust for college costs of the minor to be taxed to the parent.

EXAMPLE 7. A father transfers securities worth $90,000 to a trust for the benefit of his son, Harvey. The property and income may be expended by or for the benefit of the minor prior to his attaining 21 years of age and, if not so expended, will pass to the donee upon his attaining majority, or in the event of his prior death, will be payable to his estate or to whomever he may appoint under a general power of appointment. Assuming gift-splitting, the minimum taxable gift (ignoring the unified credit) is $70,000 ($90,000 − $20,000).

In a closely held corporation situation, gifts of stock may be a useful tool for family income splitting. But the donor should not retain any interest in the transferred stock and all gifts should be "for real." The commissioner may use the general principles of the *Gregory* or *Knetsch* cases, in which the transfer of the property did not have an economic reality.[18] For example, in one court decision a father gave 25 percent of a Subchapter S corporation to each of his two minor sons. Although he filed a gift tax return, he paid no gift tax and waited one year before he typed his wife's name in as the custodian. The donor prepared and signed tax returns and paid the tax liabilities from his own funds. Custodian bank accounts were not established for the donees until several years later. The Tax

Court ruled that the stock transfers had "no economic reality" and were thereby not bona fide.[19] As one would expect, gifts other than shares of stock must also be of economic reality.

Valuation of Gift Transfers

In order to determine "taxable gifts," a proper valuation of the gift property must be made. Gifts of money cause no valuation problems, but this is not true of gifts of property.

In general, a gift is valued at its fair market value on the date of the gift. There is no alternate valuation date as there is for estate tax purposes. Where property is transferred for less than adequate and full consideration, then the amount by which the fair market value of property exceeds the value of the consideration is deemed to be a gift. A gift occurs even if later facts indicate that the donor never enjoyed anything possessory and did not really transfer anything. One must look to see if there was any value on the date of the gift.[20]

In general, the same rules for valuation of property for estate tax purposes apply in a gift tax situation. Reg. 25.1512-1 defines value of the property as the price at which the gift property would change hands between a willing buyer and a willing seller (that is, when neither is under the compulsion to buy or sell), and that value is not a forced sale price. Nor is the value of the gift property the sales price in a market other than that in which such an item is normally sold to the public. This means that most gifts would be valued at the price at which the item would be sold at retail. For gift tax purposes, for example, a fur coat would be valued at the price for which a coat of like description would be purchased by the general public.

Since the donor is primarily liable for the tax, the amount of the gift is the fair market value of the property passing from the donor and is not the value of the property received by the donee. The value is generally determined at the time of the gift of each unit of property. The assessed value for state and local purposes is generally not the basis for gift tax purposes.

Sometimes the donee agrees to pay the gift tax. Here the value of the gift is reduced by the amount of the gift tax due. This calculation requires an interrelated computation which can be found in Rev. Rul. 75-72.[21] The reduction, however, in the value of a gift is limited to the amount of the gift tax actually assumed by the donee, and not for any amount of the gift tax absorbed by the donor's unified credit.[22]

With one exception, the donor also must include in income the amount by which the gift tax exceeds the donor's basis in the property. The payment of gift tax by a donee does not result in income to the donor for a net gift made before March 4, 1981.[23]

COMPUTING THE GIFT TAX

Although the gift tax is imposed separately in each calendar year on the total taxable gifts made during a given year, the applicable tax payable is determined by the total of all gifts made by the donor during that year and in all prior years. That is, the gift tax rates are cumulative and progressive. From the standpoint of gift tax rate alone, there is no benefit gained by spreading gifts over a number of years; however, it may be beneficial to spread gifts over a number of years in order to take advantage of the $10,000 annual exclusion and other deductions. There are six major steps in computing the gift tax.

Step 1: Determine the amount (fair market value, FMV) of the taxable gifts for the calendar year for which the gift tax return is being prepared. This step is broken down into a formula which follows.

Step 2: Ascertain the total FMV of all taxable gifts made by the donor for all prior calendar years.

Step 3: Sum the amounts in steps 1 and 2. Compute the tax on this total by using the unified estate and gift tax rates.

Step 4: Compute the theoretical unified gift tax on the amount in step 2.

Step 5: Subtract the tax computed in step 4 from the tax computed in step 3 in order to determine the tentative gift tax payable.

Step 6: Subtract the applicable unified credit from the amount in step 5 to arrive at the gift tax payable.

Step 1 above can be expanded into this formula:

Gross gifts (FMV)	XX
Less:	
Annual exclusions, if any, of $10,000 per	
donee per year of present-interest gifts	<u>X</u>
	XX
Less other deductions:	
FMV of charitable gifts X	
Marital deduction on gifts to spouse <u>X</u>	<u>X</u>
Taxable gifts	XX

Notice that pre-1977 gifts are used in computing gifts for preceding calendar years. However, the unified rates are used in figuring the tax on these pre-1977 gifts, even though such tax is greater than the amount produced under the old rates.

EXAMPLE 8. A husband made no gifts prior to 1977. In 1985, he made the following gifts: $70,000 to wife, $40,000 to daughter, $40,000 to grandson, and $20,000 to a cousin. The wife does not gift-split with husband. The husband would be allowed a total exclusion of $30,000 and a marital deduction of $70,000, resulting in a taxable gift of $70,000 ($170,000 − $70,000 − $30,000). A tentative gift tax liability of $15,600 is reduced by a unified credit of $15,600, resulting in no gift tax due.

Any U.S. citizen or resident who makes a gift to anyone other than his/her spouse which is not excluded under the $10,000 present interest exclusion must file Form 709. Simplified Form 709-A may be used by a married couple who elects gift-splitting for gifts which are nontaxable because they are covered by the annual exclusion. This short form is available only for present-interest gifts to third parties which do not exceed $20,000.

If a donor fails to pay any gift tax due, Section 6324(b) provides that the donee is personally liable for the donor's gift tax. The donee is not liable for filing the return.

The use of the unified credit to offset a gift tax liability is not an assessment or payment of tax for purposes of Section 2504(c). Thus, if no tax is paid, the statute of limitations does not start to run, so any valuation issues remain open indefinitely.[24]

If a gift tax is reimbursed to a taxpayer because of erroneous advice of a consultant, such reimbursement is not taxable income.[25]

Incomplete Gifts

A major objective of a lifetime gift is to remove the property from the gross estate of the donor. There are four major areas where this objective is not accomplished, since the gift is included in the donor's taxable estate: gifts in contemplation of death, transfers with a retained life interest, transfers taking effect at death, and revocable transfers. Each area is discussed below, with emphasis on ways of avoiding these incomplete gifts. Many transfers that are not complete for estate tax purposes may be complete for gift tax purposes. They are "not always mutually exclusive."[26]

Although no gift tax is due until a gift is complete, when a donor makes a transfer that he/she believes to be an incomplete gift because of a retained power over the property, the transfer still must be disclosed on Form 709. Such disclosure must be made in the year of transfer along with all relevant facts, including a copy of the instrument of transfer.

Gifts in contemplation of death. Under Section 2035(a), a decedent's gross estate is increased by the fair market value of certain gifts in contemplation of death. Prior to 1977, gifts made within three years prior to the date of the decedent's death were presumed to be made in contemplation of death.[27] Even if the property is sold by the donee before the donor's death, the FMV of the same property at the date of death is included. Any increase in value resulting from actions of the donee is not taken into consideration when determining the value.[28] However, if the donee has dissipated the property so that there is little left on the date of the transferor's death, the amount includable is not what actually exists, but rather is the present value of the property originally transferred.[29]

In order to overcome the three-year presumption, the administrator had to show by a fair preponderance of evidence that the donor had life motives rather than death motives for making the gifts. If the donor lived three years after making a gift, it was assumed that the gift was not in contemplation of death, and it was not included in the gross estate.

For gifts made after December 31, 1976, but before 1982, the rebuttable "gift in contemplation of death presumption" was deleted. Instead, any gifts made by a decedent or his/her spouse in these years, and during the three-year period ending on the date of the decedent's death, were automatically included in the gross estate. In effect, only the appreciation from the date of the lifetime gift to the date of death (or six months thereafter) was included in the estate, since the original "gift" was taxed by the unified estate and gift tax system. In other words, the date-of-gift value is included in the estate for gifts made more than three years prior to death, whereas the date-of-death value of the gift is included in gross estate if it is a gift in contemplation of death.

According to Section 2035(b)(2), the three-year rule about gifts in contemplation of death applies only to certain property for decedent's dying after December 31, 1981. This property (sometimes referred to as Section 2035(b)(2) property) must be covered by:

Section 2036. Retained life estate.

Section 2037. Transfers taking effect at death.

Section 2038. Revocable transfers.

Section 2041. Powers of appointment.

Section 2042. Life insurance.

Also, gifts made within three years of death are included for purposes of qualifying for current-use valuation under Section 2032A, for deferred payment of estate taxes under Section 6166, for qualified redemptions to pay estate taxes under Section 303, and for estate tax liens under Subchapter C of Chapter 64.

After 1981, deathbed gifts of cash and certain property should be a popular means of estate planning. For example, a person may give an unlimited number of less-than-$10,000 gifts on the deathbed, and any such gifts are removed from the gross estate. The exemption applies to gifts within three years of death only if no gift tax return was required. For maximum tax benefit, however, be careful to avoid deathbed gifts of the five categories just listed, such as life insurance.

EXAMPLE 9. Jane Swindle in March 1984 transfers a life insurance policy to her daughter, retaining none of the incidents of ownership. In February 1985, Jane dies. The insurance proceeds would be included in Jane's gross estate as a gift in contemplation of death under Section 2035(b)(2).

EXAMPLE 10. In 1981, Jim makes a gift to his daughter of Section 2035(b)(2) assets worth $100,000. When Jim dies in 1985, the property is worth $170,000. Since this transfer is not a gift in contemplation of death, only $100,000 (less a $10,000 exclusion) is taxed by the unified estate tax rate. If, instead, Jim dies in 1983 (within three years after making the gift) when the assets are worth $160,000, then a total of $170,000 is included in Jim's estate.

EXAMPLE 11. Assume in Example 10 that the property is worth $60,000 when Jim dies in 1983. Only the depreciated amount of $60,000 is included in Jim's estate. Obviously, Section 2035 is helpful if the Section 2035(b)(2) property depreciates in value, but harmful if the property appreciates in value.

If a gift is included in the gross estate as a gift in contemplation of death, the gift must be grossed-up. That is, the gift tax in fact paid by the decedent of the estate must be added back to the gift when it is included in the gross estate. However, since Section 2035 does not draw the $10,000-per-donee exclusion into the gross estate, deathbed gifts up to $10,000 per donee are still valuable. For example, four deathbed gifts of $10,000 would remove $40,000 from the gross estate. In a 50 percent estate tax bracket, such gifts would result in a $20,000 tax saving. In case of gift-splitting, the extra $10,000 is drawn back into the estate in the case of a gift in contemplation of death. Thus, where it appears that the donor will not live at least three years, gift-splitting is not appropriate.

Even when it appears that a gift may be in contemplation of death, a gift may still be advisable. The donor may live three years; if not, he/she may be in a high income tax bracket and the transfer can place the income-producing property in the hands of a lower-tax-bracket donee. Moreover, any gift tax paid is normally allowed as a full credit against any future estate tax, even if a spouse elects under Section 2513 to split a gift in contemplation of death.[30] In other words, the gift tax paid with respect to both halves of the gift is allowed as a credit on the donor's (decedent's) estate tax return, but there is no restoration of the unified credit used against gift taxes paid by the surviving spouse.

Transfers with retained life interest. If a donor retains a life interest in transferred property, such a transfer is not a complete transfer and will be included in the donor's estate under Section 2036(a). An interest in the property is defined as (1) the possession or enjoyment of, or the right to the income of, the property or (2) the right, whether alone or in conjunction with any person, to designate the persons who shall possess or enjoy the property or the income therefrom.[31]

The gift tax provisions do not follow the estate tax provisions. Whereas the full value of a transferred interest (where the donor has retained a life interest) is included in the gross estate upon death, such a transfer is subject to the gift tax. Of course the donor is allowed to deduct from the fair market value of the transferred property the value of the life interest retained. The difference is subject to the gift tax, and any income received by the donor is, of course, taxable income.

EXAMPLE 12. Grantor transfers $320,000 of stock (adjusted basis of $140,000) to a trust, but retains power to change the beneficiaries. Although grantor may divest herself or any power to revoke the trust or to make herself a beneficiary, this is not a complete gift.

EXAMPLE 13. Grantor transfers property with a reservation of a life estate. When he dies, the entire property is included in his estate. The remainder interest is valued at $123,000, and the life interest is valued at $29,000. There would be a complete gift as to the $123,000 interest.

Transfers taking effect at death. If a donor transfers property but retains a reversionary interest, such property is included in the gross estate under Section 2037(a). The gift is incomplete for estate tax purposes if three elements are present:

1. Possession or enjoyment of the property could, through ownership of the interest, have been obtained only by surviving the decedent.

2. The donor retains a reversionary interest in the transferred property. (Different rules apply for transfers before October 8, 1949.)

3. The value of the reversionary interest immediately be-

fore the donor's death exceeds 5 percent of the value of the property. The reversionary percentage is computed from the applicable actuarial tables.[32]

Such a conditional gift causes all or some of the value of the property to be included in the gross estate of the donor.

If the donor transfers the property in trust for at least 10 years and one day, any income from the property escapes the income tax under Section 673(a). As for gift tax purposes, the donor must give up dominion and control over such property to escape this tax. But the estate and gift tax rules are not perfectly coordinated. As long as the donor cannot revest the interest in himself/herself alone (or change with someone who has a substantial nonadverse interest), or dispose of the property directly for himself/herself or others (or by an ascertainable standard by a trustee), a completed gift of all the property has occurred. Thus, if a donor retains a power exercisable only in conjunction with a person having a substantial adverse interest (even a family member), the gift is complete. Furthermore, even when a reversion is retained by the donor, such a reversion will not make the gift entirely incomplete, but it will reduce the amount of taxable gift (even if less than a 5 percent reversionary interest).[33] But where a trustee can invade corpus of a trust on behalf of the donor, the gift would be incomplete to the extent that the definite standard is enforceable.

Revocable transfers. A final incomplete gift may occur when the donee's enjoyment of the transferred property is subject (at the donor's death) to any change through the exercise of a power by the donor to alter, amend, revoke, or terminate the interest. If Section 2038 is applicable, any gift property would be includable in the donor's gross estate.[34] This section does not apply if

1. Transfer was for adequate and full consideration.
2. Donor's power could be exercised only with the consent of all parties having an interest in the transferred property.
3. Power was held solely by a person other than the donor.[35]

A revocable transfer is an incomplete gift. If the power to revoke is held by the donor in conjunction with a person who has a substantial adverse interest, the gift would be incomplete. In contrast to the estate law, a reserved power to merely change the time and manner of the enjoyment of the beneficiary by the donor would not make the gift incomplete.[36] Yet a "time and manner" reserved power would draw the property into the gross estate under Section 2038. As Reg. 25.2511-2(g) indicates, if a donor transfers property to himself/herself as trustee (or to himself/herself and some other person not possessing an adverse interest), and retains no beneficial interest in the trust property and no power over it except fiduciary powers, the exercise or nonexercise of which is limited by an ascertainable standard to change the beneficiary of such property, the donor has made a complete gift. Therefore, the gift tax consequences of a revocable gift coincide with the estate tax consequences.

EXAMPLE 14. Apple transfers property worth $122,000 in trust for Karl, but reserves the power to revoke the trust with the trustee (who is unrelated to Apple or Karl). Since the trustee is not an adverse interest, this is not a complete gift.

EXAMPLE 15. Eileen transfers property to a trust for Yual for life, with remainder to Xexe. But Eileen reserves the power to revoke the trust with the consent of Yual. If the life estate is worth $28,000 and the remainder interest is worth $93,000, only $28,000 is a complete gift.

Property Settlements

A transfer is not subject to a gift tax if it is made for adequate and full consideration. Section 2516 provides that certain transfers of property between spouses pursuant to a settlement agreement are considered to be for full and adequate consideration. The husband and wife must enter into a written agreement relative to their marital and property rights and divorce must occur within a three-year period beginning on the date one year before the agreement is consummated. If the divorce decree does not become final before the due date for Form 709 for the calendar year in which the agreement is made, the transfer is treated as nontaxable but must be disclosed on the tax return for that year.

Are Lifetime Gifts Worthwhile?

There are disadvantages and advantages in making lifetime gifts. Some disadvantages are as follows:

1. Making taxable gifts results in prepayment of the transfer tax (that is, an interest-free loan is made to the federal government).
2. Lifetime taxable gifts increase the unified transfer tax rate effective at death.
3. Some gifts made within three years of death are included within the gross estate with a gross-up for any gift taxes paid.
4. To the extent that any portion of the unified credit is used against lifetime transfers, there is a reduction in the amount of the unified credit available at death. However, you may wish to make enough gifts during life to use up your unified credit (without paying a gift tax). Thus, you will make gifts without paying a tax, which is somewhat like borrowing such a deferred gift tax payable from the federal government.

Some advantages of making lifetime gifts are as follows:

1. These gifts eliminate future appreciation from the donor's estate.
2. They allow a donor to transfer income-producing property to beneficiaries who may be in low-income tax brackets.
3. Lifetime gifts of up to $10,000 per donee per year ($20,000 for married couples) are still tax-exempt transfers.
4. Gifts not in contemplation of death are not grossed-up in the donor's estate.

As people become older and the value of their assets increases, a program of lifetime gifts may be beneficial. Let us assume that a wealthy married man in a high tax bracket plans to leave a portion of his estate to his children. If the father's estate surpasses the exemption-equivalent level, it may be advantageous for him to make gifts while he is still living. If the children who receive the gifts are in a low tax bracket, the taxpayer may both obtain savings in income tax and also use his unified credit early by giving a portion of the assets to them. Since the children will eventually receive the assets anyway, it makes sense for the father to distribute them in the most advantageous manner. Although it is usually beneficial to make gifts, many people do not use this valuable tax-planning tool. Findings indicate that ignorance of potential tax savings and other nontax factors are the major reasons.

NOTES

1. *Robert W. Hite, Sr.,* 49 T.C. 580 (1968); see similar tests in *Lorenzo W. Swope Estate,* 41 B.T.A. 213 (1910).
2. *Robinette* v. *Helvering* 318 U.S. 184 (1943).
3. Reg. 25.2511-1(g)(1).
4. IRC Section 170(b)(1)(A)(ii).
5. IRC Section 2503(b).
6. *Fondren* v. *Commissioner,* 324 U.S. 20 (1945).
7. IRC Sections 170(f)(2)(a), 2055(e), 2106(a)(2)(E), and 2522(c).
8. IRC Section 664(d)(1).
9. IRC Section 664(d)(2).
10. IRC Section 664(d)(3).
11. IRC Section 642(c)(5).
12. Prop. Reg. 25.2522(c)-3(c)(2)(v).
13. IRC Sections 170(f)(3) and (4).
14. IRC Sections 170(e)(A) and (B)(ii). See Chapter 10.
15. *Ryerson* v. *U.S.,* 312 U.S. 405 (1941).
16. 1959-2 C.B. 212.
17. Reg. 25.2503-4(a).
18. *Gregory* v. *Helvering,* 293 U.S. 465 (1935); *Knetsch* v. *U.S.,* 364 U.S. 361 (1960).
19. Duarte, 44 T.C. 193 (1965). See Crumbley and Davis, *Organizing, Operating, and Terminating Subchapter S Corporations* (Tucson, Ariz.: Lawyers & Judges Publishing Co., 1980).
20. *Goodwin* v. *McGowan,* 47 F. Supp. 798 (W.D. N.Y. 1942).
21. 1975-1 C.B. 310.
22. Rev. Rul. 81-223, 1981-2 C.B. 189.
23. DRA of 1984, §1026.
24. Rev. Rul. 84-11, 1981-1 C.B. 475.
25. Ltr. Rul. 847076.
26. *Estate of Stanford* v. *U.S.,* 308 U.S. 45 (1939).
27. Section 2035(b).
28. Reg. 20.2035-1(e).
29. *Humphrey Estate* v. *Commissioner,* 162 F.2d 1 (1947), cert. den. 332 U.S. 817.

30. Reg. 20.2012-1(e).
31. Sections 2036(a)(1) and (2).
32. Prop. Reg. 25.2512-5(f).
33. Reg. 25.2511-1(e).
34. Section 2038(a); *Burnet* v. *Guggenheim,* 288 U.S. 280 (1933).
35. Reg. 20.2038-1(a).
36. Reg. 25.2511-2(d).

7

Below-Interest-Rate Loans

He who hesitates is taxed.

—*Anonymous*

For many years interest-free loans and below-market loans have been used by taxpayers to avoid a number of tax consequences. For example, corporation-to-shareholder loans have been used to avoid taxation at both the corporate and shareholder levels. Until recently, interest-free loans have been an effective and easy-to-use estate planning tool. Family loans (with no interest) were used to shift income to lower-bracket taxpayers, thereby reducing both the income tax and the estate tax.

For over 20 years the courts have generally held that loans at below-market or interest-free rates resulted in little or no gift tax consequences and no income tax consequences. The IRS frequently disagreed with the courts' findings over the years and never gave up its persistent effort to eliminate this most popular shelter of income. In recent times the IRS has had considerable success in this undertaking, first with the Supreme Court decision in *Dickman* v. *Commissioner*[1] and then with the provisions of the Tax Reform Act of 1984.

BACKGROUND

Prior to the *Dickman* decision the nontaxable treatment of interest-free loans had been well established. In *J. Simpson Dean,*[2] the Tax Court held that an interest-free loan had no income tax consequences. The reasoning by the court was based on the assumption that any income which could be imputed to the borrower because of foregone interest payments could be offset by a corresponding interest deduction, had such payment been made, thus resulting in a wash. Although the decision was challenged a number of times in other court battles, the courts agreed that no income could be imputed when cash was lent interest free.[3] Therefore, taxpayers were in a fairly secure position concerning income tax consequences of interest-free or below-market loans.

The early history of the gift tax consequences of demand loans is similar to that of the income tax consequences. *Johnson* v. *U.S.*[4] was the first case involving the gift tax consequences of interest-free lending. In *Johnson,* the court noted that the purpose of the gift tax is to prevent the evasion of the estate tax through *inter vivos* gifts. Since the full amount of the principal of all demand loans would be included in the lender's estate, the estate would remain intact. The court further stated that the lender had no duty to enhance his estate by putting the loaned funds to their most productive use.

The IRS again attempted to attach gift tax consequences in *Lester Crown,*[5] but to no avail. In deciding *Crown,* both the Tax Court and the Seventh Circuit agreed with the reasoning in *Johnson.* In *Crown,* the court further stated that no property right had been transferred; therefore, there was no gift. In addition to the lack of a property transfer, the Seventh Circuit found flaws in the IRS's method of valuation. The gift tax statutes generally require the gift to be valued at fair market value as of the date of gift. For a demand loan, the court found that it was impossible to determine the value at the time the loan was made, since the length of the loan was unknown. Term loans, however, did not enjoy this exemption from gift tax, because a fair market value could be determined. In cases where interest rates and due dates were stated, but the interest rates were below the prevailing market rate, the courts had no problem in determining the transaction to be a taxable gift.

The *Crown* decision held consistently until the Eleventh Circuit, in *Dickman,* disagreed with the *Crown* decision. To resolve the conflict between the two circuits, the U.S. Supreme Court granted certiorari. On February 22, 1984, it announced its decision affirming the Eleventh Circuit's decision in the *Dickman* case, thereby subjecting interest-free lending to the gift tax statute. With the *Dickman* decision and the provisions of new Section 7872, estate tax planning using interest-free lending has been severely impaired.

DICKMAN V. COMMISSIONER

In the *Dickman* decision, the Supreme Court did not address the income tax consequences, but did find that interest-free demand loans resulted in taxable gifts. Earlier court decisions had already found interest-free or below-market-terms loans to have gift tax consequences.[6] In *Dickman* the court gave three primary reasons for their findings:

1. It applied a very broad interpretation to the language of Section 2511. The gift tax covers the transfer of property and property rights, whether the gift is direct or indirect.[7] The court held that the language of Section 2511(a) was sufficient to cover any indirect gift, including the use of valuable property—in this case money in the form of interest-free loans.

2. The Court found that interest-free demand loans do involve the transfer of property rights that are subject to legal protection. Interest-free loans constitute the use of valuable property. The amount of the taxable gift that results from an interest-free demand loan is the value of receiving and using the money with no corresponding obligation to pay interest.

3. The purpose of the gift tax would be circumvented by exempting interest-free demand loans. The court stated that one of the major purposes of the federal gift tax statutes was the protection of the federal estate tax and the federal income tax. The interest-free loans permitted income tax evasion by allowing the shifting of income from a high-bracket taxpayer to a taxpayer in a lower tax bracket. Also, the estate tax would be evaded (which conflicts with the *Johnson* ruling) by the lender because the earnings from the loan would never become a part of the lender's estate.

Dickman dealt another blow to estate and gift tax planners because the decision was not given "prospective only" effect. This would allow the IRS to ascribe gift tax consequences retroactively. The Supreme Court made no attempt to value the loan in *Dickman* but remanded this issue back to the Tax Court to determine appropriate valuation of the gift. To help resolve future valuation problems, Congress addressed this question in the committee reports to the Tax Reform Act of 1984.

In order to solve the retroactive valuation problem for demand loans, the IRS published News Release IR-84-60,[8] which provides guidance in valuing gifts made prior to January 1, 1984. According to the release, the value of the gift is calculated by multiplying the average outstanding loan balance for that period by the lesser of the statutory interest rate for refunds and deficiencies or the annual average for three-month Treasury bills. For years before 1960, the applicable rate will be the average rate for three-month Treasury bills.[9] This retroactive application can be applied as far back as 1932,[10] the beginning of the gift tax provisions.

For administrative convenience IR-84-60 contains several exemptions to gift tax reporting requirements for pre-1984 loans. No gift tax return is required if the average annual outstanding interest-free demand loan balance did not exceed $50,000 per year for each donee ($100,000 for married couples), or if the amount of the gift applicable to the interest-free loan in any one year was less than the gift tax annual exclusion available to the donor, even though the annual exclusion had previously been used. Also, the release exempts the filing of a gift tax return if the only reason for doing so is to elect gift-splitting between spouses with regard to the interest-free loan. Perhaps the most significant impact of the *de minimis* rules of IR-84-60 is their impact on future gift tax and estate tax marginal rates. By exempting these gifts from taxes that fall under these *de minimis* rules, many individuals will be spared the disagreeable task of amending their gift tax returns and adjusting marginal tax rates for future transfers.

Taxpayers falling outside the *de minimis* rule are not so fortunate. The situation must be fully evaluated as to the necessity of filing amended gift tax returns. If the taxpayer had not filed a gift tax return at all for the period in question, the statute of limitations would not have run, regardless of the time that had elapsed. If any gift tax return was filed for the year in question, the statute may have run or begun to run. Generally, the limitation period expires three years after filing,[11] except where the gift tax value of the interest-free loan exceeds 25 percent of the total amount of gifts reported on the return. In this case the statute of limitations is extended a total of six years from filing date.[12] IR-84-60 has no bearing on income tax matters, and is applicable only to loans of money. Additionally, IR-84-60 is not applicable to loans made or outstanding after December 31, 1983.

TAX REFORM BILL OF 1984

The *Dickman* decision in February 1984 created new problems and left many unresolved questions. The IRS had been unhappy with the income tax consequences of *Dean* (that is, interest-free loans did not result in income tax consequences), but up to this point attempts to set *Dean* aside had failed. The *Dickman* decision, however, gave new life to IRS efforts to establish income tax consequences for tax-free loans. This, along with the fact that Congress was seeking new sources of revenue, led to the codification of estate, gift, and income tax consequences of interest-free loans.

Section 7872 provides a comprehensive and complicated set of rules prescribing income, gift, and estate consequences for both interest-free and below-market loans. The law substantially changes the gift and income tax consequences of below-market or interest-free loans for transactions that are in the form of gifts, compensation, dividends, or other tax-avoidance schemes. Section 7872 reclassifies an interest-free or below-market loan as two arms-length transactions. First, the note to the borrower is characterized as requiring interest at a statutory rate. The lender is then deemed to make a transfer to the borrower for the foregone-interest element of the loan. Second, the borrower is deemed to have paid to the lender an amount equal to the annual interest on the loan.[13] In other words, the lender has interest income. The classification of the transfer from the lender to the borrower as a gift, dividend, compensation, or other depends on the relationship of the two parties.

For example, in a common situation where a parent makes an interest-free demand loan to a child, and where the foregone interest is a gift, the parent is deemed to make a taxable gift to the child for the amount of foregone interest at the end of each year for which the loan is outstanding. The child will be deemed to retransfer an equal amount back to the parent. The payment from the child will be considered taxable income to the parent and a deductible interest payment by the child. This effectively prevents the shifting of income on the loan from the parent to the child and adheres to the assignment of income doctrine.

If the transaction is between employer and employee or corporation and shareholder, the imputed payment from borrower to lender is classified not as a gift but as either compensation, dividend, or other type of payment depending on the facts of the transaction.

Below-market loans covered by Section 7872 are of two types: demand loans and term loans. A demand loan is considered to be a below-market loan if interest payable on the loan is at a rate less than the federal short-term rate in effect under Section 1274(d) for the interest period.[14] A term loan will be considered a below-market loan if the amount of the loan exceeds the present value of all payments due under the loan, discounted at the applicable federal rate.[15] A demand loan is any loan that is payable in full at any time upon the demand of the lender.[16] A term loan is any loan that is not a demand loan.[17] For determining income tax effects only, term loans among family members (gift loans) are deemed to be demand loans.[18]

There are five categories of below-market loans covered in Section 7872. They are (1) gift loans (loans where the foregone interest is in the nature of a gift),[19] (2) compensation-related loans (loans between employer and employee or between an independent contractor and his client),[20] (3) corporation-shareholder loans (all below-market loans, direct or indirect, between a corporation and shareholder of that corporation),[21] (4) tax-avoidance loans (any below-market loan in which one of the principal purposes is the avoidance of any federal tax),[22] and (5) other below-market loans (any below-market loans that do not fit into the other categories and the interest arrangements of such loans have a significant effect on any federal tax liability of the lender or the borrower).[23] The tax treatment depends on the type of below-market loan involved (i.e., demand or term, gift or compensation).

GIFT LOANS

For all below-market gift loans and other below-market demand loans the lender is treated as transferring, and the borrower receiving, the amount of foregone interest on an annual basis. In addition, the lender is treated as receiving from the borrower an equal amount as a payment of interest.[24] Foregone interest is the amount equal to the excess of (1) the amount of interest that would have been payable on the loan for the taxable period if interest accrued on the loan at the applicable federal rate (AFR) and was payable on the loan allocable to the taxable period.[25]

A gift loan will cause both gift tax and income tax consequences for the lender unless one of the exceptions granted by Section 7872(c)(1) or (2) is satisfied. For a gift loan, the lender is deemed as making a taxable gift equal to the amount of foregone interest. The amount of the gift is different for a gift-term loan and a gift-demand loan. For a gift-demand loan the taxable gift is equal to the foregone interest computed on a daily basis at the AFR, with the transfer treated as taking place on the last day of the calendar year.[26] The AFR for gift-demand and nongift-demand loans is the federal short-term rate in effect under Section 1274(d) for the period for which the foregone interest is being calculated.[27] For a gift-term loan, the foregone interest for gift tax purposes is computed on the day the loan is made and is the difference between the amount of the loan over the present value of all required loan payments discounted at the AFR compounded semiannually.[28] For gift tax purposes, the AFR for gift-term and nongift-term loans is the AFR in effect under Section 1274(d) compounded semiannually based on the loan term.[29]

Since gift-term loans are deemed as demand loans for income tax purposes, the income tax effects are the same for both types of gift loan. Because the borrower is treated as transferring the foregone interest back to the lender, the lender has interest income equal to that amount. The borrower has no taxable income because the transfer from the lender to the borrower is considered a gift. The borrower does, however, have an interest deduction. The borrower comes out ahead because he gets a deduction without having to make any cash outlay. The lender loses in the transfer because he not only is subject to the gift tax but also has to recognize income that he has not and will never receive.

EXAMPLE 1. Gift-Demand Loan. On January 1, 1985, married taxpayers (M and F), who are calendar-year taxpayers, make an interest-free demand loan of $165,000 to their child (D), who is also a calendar-year taxpayer. If an AFR of 12 percent is assumed, then the foregone interest for the year would be $19,800. If gift-splitting is elected, and assuming there are no other gifts to the donee, there would be no gift tax consequences since a $20,000 annual exclusion is allowed. Assuming M and F file a joint return for 1985, they would be required to report $19,800 of interest income. D would have no interest income, because the $19,800 was a gift, but would have an interest deduction of $19,800 in 1985. If D had no taxable income, the deduction would be lost.

EXAMPLE 2. Gift-Term Loan. On January 1, 1985, married taxpayers (M and F), who are calendar-year taxpayers, make an interest-free, three-year term loan of $165,000 to their child (S), who is also a calendar-year taxpayer. If an AFR of 12 percent is assumed, the foregone interest element for 1985 for gift tax purposes would be $48,592. Even if gift-splitting is elected, there would still be a taxable gift of $28,592 for 1985 (after the annual exclusion of $20,000). There would be no gift for the other two years because the transfer for the total amount of foregone interest is deemed as taking place on the date the loan is made. The income tax consequences for M and F and D for the three years would be as follows:

| | M and F | | D | |
	Interest Income	Interest Expense	Interest Income	Interest Expense
Year 1	$19,800			$19,800
Year 2	19,800			19,800
Year 3	19,800			19,800
Total	$59,400	–0–	–0–	$59,400

Because a gift-term loan is considered a gift-demand loan for income tax purposes, the foregone interest is computed at the end of each year using the gift-demand loan rules. M and F must report a total of $59,400 in interest income for the three years, which they did not receive; and D had a total expense deduction for the three years, which was never paid.

NONGIFT LOANS

Nongift loans, in some situations, produce more favorable tax consequences for the lender than do gift loans. Although the lender must report income equal to the foregone interest, if the nongift-demand loan can be classified as a compensation-related loan (the borrower is an employee of the lender or there is an independent-contractor relationship),[30] a deduction can be taken in that year equal to the interest received. The borrower will have taxable income in the amount of the foregone interest, but will also have a corresponding deduction for the imputed interest. Thus, the transaction for both borrower and lender can result in a "wash" for income tax purposes.

If the borrower is a shareholder, the transfer will be classified as a dividend, and no deduction will be allowed the corporation. Thus, the corporation would have taxable income with no offset. The shareholder could still have a wash transaction if the interest deduction were allowed as an itemized deduction or if it fell within the limits of the investment-interest deduction.

For a nongift-term loan the timing of the taxable investment income and interest deduction is different from that of the demand loan. However, the timing is the same for both gift and income tax purposes. For all nongift-term loans the lender is treated as transferring to the borrower, and the borrower is treated as receiving from the lender, cash equal to the excess of the amount of the loan over the present value of both principal and interest payments due under the loan.[31] The transfer is treated as occurring on the date the loan was made.[32] In addition, the excess of the amount of the loan over the present value of the payments due is treated as original issue discount.[33] Consequently, the borrower is treated as paying, and the lender is treated as receiving, interest at a constant rate over the life of the loan.

In the case of a compensation-related loan, the lender would have a business deduction on the date the loan was made for the excess (as determined above), but income would be reported over the life of the loan determined under the original issue discount rules. Similarly, the borrower would have compensation income equal to the excess when the loan is made and deduct the interest ratably over the life of the loan. Because the timing of the reportable income and deduction may not be matched, this may be a less desirable situation from the employee's perspective. Other term loans are handled similarly, depending on the lender-borrower relationship.

EXCEPTIONS

The Tax Reform Act of 1984 has essentially eliminated the use of below-market loans as an estate planning tool. There are, however, some escapes from the application of the new rule, provided by the *de minimis* exception and special rules for gift loans.

De Minimis Exceptions for Gift Loans

For income tax purposes, no amount is treated as transferred by the lender to the borrower, or retransferred by the borrower to the lender, for any day during which the aggregate amount of outstanding loans does not exceed $10,000.[34] This includes the aggregate amount of all loans between the lender and borrower, regardless of interest rates. For example, if the lender makes one loan for $10,000 to the borrower at a below-market rate of interest and another $10,000 loan at the appreciable federal rate, the exception would not apply. Also, the exception would not apply if the borrower uses the money to purchase or carry income-producing assets.[35]

De Minimis Exception for Nongift Loans

There is a similar $10,000 *de minimis* exception for compensation-related and corporation-shareholder loans; however, this exception does not apply if the principal purpose of the interest arrangement is the avoidance of any federal tax.[36]

Special Rules for Gift Loans

In the case of gift loans between two individuals where the aggregate amount of the outstanding loans does not exceed

$100,000, the amount of interest deemed to be retransferred to the lender will be the lesser of (1) the imputed interest on the loan or (2), the borrower's total net investment income.[37] In addition, if the borrower's total net investment income does not exceed $1,000 and the $100,000 test is met, then the retransferred amount is considered to be zero.[38] Net investment income is the excess of investment income, as defined in Section 163(d), over investment expense. However, this section does not apply if one of the principal purposes of the loan is tax avoidance. It should also be noted that gift tax consequences may still apply. In order to prevent abuse of the rules by deferral or distortion of investment income, deferred-payment obligations (market-discount bonds, short-term obligations, U.S. savings bonds, annuities, etc.) are treated as interest income in computing net investment interest.[39]

This $100,000 exception may prove useful where a taxpayer wishes to make a loan to persons who have little investment income and do not invest the proceeds of the loan.

EXAMPLE 3. On January 1, 1985, H and W make a $100,000 interest-free demand loan to their child (D). If D uses the money to purchase a home, and assuming D has net investment income of less than $1,000, there will be no income tax consequence to H and W or to D. Since D has net investment income of less than $1,000, H and W will not have any interest income from the loan, and D will not have an expense deduction. Assuming an AFR of 12 percent, if gift-splitting is elected the $20,000-per-donee exclusion will prevent any gift tax consequence. This exemption can be expanded by lending a like amount to D's spouse or child.

PLANNING ALTERNATIVES

While the tax benefits afforded in the past by the use of interest-free loans that combined estate freezing with income shifting may be diminished, some planning opportunities still exist. The Clifford trust will undoubtedly regain in popularity as an income-shifting device. Under Section 673, income from trust property will not be taxed to the grantor if neither the income or trust property revert to him/her within 10 years after the transfer of property to the trust. Income from trust assets will be distributed to the income beneficiary and taxed to the beneficiary at, presumably, lower tax rates. Since the corpus reverts to the grantor, only the income interest constitutes a taxable gift. Through careful planning, the grantor can use gift-splitting and the annual exclusion to avoid any gift tax consequence. The most undesirable feature of the Clifford trust is that the taxpayer must be willing to relinquish control of the assets for at least 10 years and one day.

Another available income-shifting device is the use of the short-term marital trust or the spousal remainder trust. The spousal remainder trust is similar to the Clifford trust, except that at the end of the trust term the assets pass to the grantor's spouse, rather than reverting back to the grantor. It is somewhat more flexible in that it does not have the 10-year time requirement. The income from the trust assets during the trust term, like that of the Clifford trust, can qualify for the annual gift tax exclusion. In addition, the remainder interest passes to the spouse and qualifies for the unlimited marital deduction.

Because the spousal remainder trust does not have a minimum time period, the grantor can transfer more assets than would be possible under the Clifford trust and still be within the annual gift tax exclusion. Since the assets do not revert to the grantor, the size of the grantor's estate is also effectively reduced.

For example, if gift-splitting is elected, assuming the statutory rate of 10 percent, a grantor can transfer up to $220,000 into a spousal remainder trust for a one-year period and still be within the annual gift tax exclusion, whereas the maximum contribution possible to a Clifford trust that avoids any gift tax on the income interest is $32,549.[40] Anyone interested in the specifics of such arrangements should consult their tax advisor.

The spousal remainder trust has its disadvantages. One is that it is irrevocable and the grantor can retain no reversionary interest. Thus, the grantor must be willing to transfer ownership of assets to his/her spouse. Of course, by the very nature of this trust, it is unavailable to unmarried persons.

Although the reciprocal-trust doctrine will prevent any benefits from a grantor and his/her spouse setting up separate trusts for the same beneficiary with remainder interest passing to each other, there is no reason why a spouse cannot, at the trust termination, establish a second trust with the original grantor as the remainder person. This will return the original assets back to the original grantor. Caution should be exercised here. There must not be any obligations to create the second remainder trust or any implication that it will be created. If such obligations exist, both trusts will be collapsed and all benefits will be lost.

Another potential planning opportunity is the gift-borrow-back technique. In this case, a high-bracket taxpayer should consider a gift to a child (or parent in a lower tax bracket) followed by a loan-back. Such an agreement would provide the donor-borrower with an interest deduction and the donee-lender with interest income. Care must be taken to show that a bona fide gift had been made and also that a bona fide indebtedness does not exist between the parties. If properly executed, such a transaction will be legitimate, but certainly will be subject to scrutiny by the IRS.

EXAMPLE 4. On January 1, 1985, H and W make a $20,000 gift to each of their children (D and S). After the bona fide gifts are made, H and W can borrow back the $40,000. H and W will have an interest deduction, and D and S will each have interest income for their loans. This allows H and W to remain in control of the $40,000, invest it, and through payment of the interest on the loan shift the interest income to the lower-bracket taxpayers, D and S.

Another option available using the gift borrow-back situation would be to have a high-bracket taxpayer make an interest-free gift loan to a trust, for the benefit of a child, then borrow the money back at an interest rate higher than the applicable federal rate at the time the loan was made.[41] The parent will have interest income but will also have a larger interest deduction. The child will report the net income from the trust, which will equal the difference between the income and deduction of the parent. Both of these situations will allow the use of the assets to remain with the higher-bracket taxpayer, while shifting income to the lower-bracket taxpayer. Again, caution must be used to insure a true debtor-creditor relationship.

A taxpayer may still create an interest-free gift loan of $100,000 or less to an individual who has less than $1,000 in net investment income and avoid income tax, but not gift tax, consequences. Also, the taxable gift would be only the imputed interest in excess of $10,000. If the loans are made to different individuals, for instance a loan to a son and another loan to the daughter-in-law, this would allow for the transfer of more funds, while still escaping taxation.

CONCLUSION

While some possibilities of income shifting and estate freezing still exist with the use of the interest-free loan, its availability is greatly diminished. Tax planners will likely look to more complex income and estate planning devices, such as the use of trusts or investments in tax-exempt securities in order to avoid income and gift tax consequences.

NOTES

1. *Ester C. Dickman,* 104 S. Ct. 1086 (1984).
2. *J. Simpson Dean,* 35 TC 1083 (1961).
3. See *Joseph Lupowitz Sons, Inc.* v. *Commissioner,* 497 F. 2d 862 (CA-3); *Fitzgerald Motor Co., Inc.* 508 F. 2d 1096 (CA-5); *Smith-Bridgman & Co.,* 16 TC 287 (1951).
4. *Johnson* v. *U.S.,* 254 F. Supp. 73 (N.D. Tex.).
5. *Lester Crown,* 67 TC 1960 (1977), aff'd, 585 F. 2d 334.
6. See *Estate of Berkman,* CCH Dec. 35, 866(M), 38 TCM 183 (1979).
7. Section 2511(a).
8. Internal Revenue Service News Release IR-84-60 (May 11, 1984).
9. Ibid.
10. In the *Dickman* decision the Supreme Court cited the Revenue Act of 1932 as the beginning of the present scheme of federal gift taxation.
11. Section 6501(a).
12. Section 6501(e)(2).
13. Conference Report on the Deficit Reduction Act of 1984, House Report 98-861 (to accompany H. R. 4170) June 23, 1984.
14. Section 7872(e)(1)(A).
15. Section 7872(e)(1)(B).
16. Section 7872(f)(5).
17. Section 7872(f)(6).
18. Section 7872(a).
19. Section 7872(f)(3).
20. Section 7872(c)(1)(B).
21. Section 7872(c)(1)(C).

22. Section 7872(c)(1)(D).
23. Section 7872(c)(1)(E).
24. Section 7872(a).
25. Section 7872(e)(2).
26. Section 7872(a)(2).
27. Section 7872(f)(B).
28. Section 7872(d)(2).
29. Section 7872(f)(A).
30. Section 7872(c)(1)(B).
31. Section 7872(b)(1).
32. Ibid.
33. Section 7872(b)(2).
34. Section 7872(c)(2)(A).
35. Section 7872(c)(2)(B).
36. Section 7872(c)(3).
37. Section 7872(d)(1).
38. Ibid.
39. Ibid.
40. See Reg. 25.2512-5 for valuation of interest in property for a term of years.
41. See H. McCue and P. Brosterhous, "Interest-Free and Below-Market Loans after *Dickman* and the Tax Reform Act of 1984," *Taxes—The Tax Magazine,* December 1984.

8

Trusts and Estates

The time will come when the poor man will not be able to wash
his shirt without paying a tax.

—*A Congressman in 1790*

One of the basic purposes of estate planning is to pass the
benefits of accumulated wealth from one family member to
another in a manner conducive to the best interests of the
estate owner and with a minimum reduction of that wealth
from taxes. Some of the most important advantages of trusts
are derived from the fact that trusts are based on the concepts
of property arrangement and property management. Therefore, trust departments are primarily interested in selling the
trust device as a means of preserving property and as a means
of efficiently administering the family assets for the benefit of
the beneficiaries.

The trust instrument is a valuable tool in estate planning,
primarily because it permits considerable flexibility in the
disposition and administration of property. The trust device
not only saves taxes but also provides the flexibility needed to
achieve many of the nontax objectives. Often other factors are
just as important as the savings of taxes, such as prudent
management of assets and the ability to give someone (the
trustee) the right to use discretion as to the amount and timing of income and principal distributions.

Since the trust provides so many opportunities and advantages in estate planning, no estate plan should be adopted until full consideration is given to the possibility of using a trust (or trusts) to carry out one or more of the desires of the estate owner. This chapter presents a brief introduction to trusts in general, to different classifications of trusts, and to some of the uses of trusts in estate planning.

INTRODUCTION TO TRUSTS

Before there can be any meaningful discussion of a trust, one must be familiar with the term, its definition, and its characteristics. One should also be familiar with the basic purposes for which trusts may be and are established. This section of the chapter contains a discussion of the definition, characteristics, and purposes of a trust.

Definitions and Characteristics of Trusts

The term *trust* is used by courts and lawyers in a variety of senses. Often it is used to include other fiduciary relationships such as bailments, executorships, guardianships, and agencies. However, in a narrower sense, the term is applied to a particular kind of fiduciary relationship that began in England when the courts of law and courts of equity in that country were separated. In this book, the term *trust* is applied only to trusts in this narrower sense.

Because of the way in which our laws are structured, a definition of any legal concept cannot properly be used as though it were a major premise so that rules governing conduct can be deduced from it. Since there is not one exact or perfect definition of the term *trust,* several definitions are given in an attempt to acquaint the reader with the legal concept. One author defines a trust as a fiduciary relationship in which one person holds property, subject to an equitable obligation to keep or use such property for the benefit of another person.[1] In its restatement of the law, the American Law Institute defined a trust as a fiduciary relationship with respect to property, subjecting the person holding title to the property to equitable duties in dealing with the property for the benefit of another person. This relationship arises as a result of a manifestation of an intention to create it.[2] Another writer defines a trust as a relationship between a trustee and a beneficiary with respect to rights in property, where legal ownership is divorced from equitable ownership, and legal title is held by the trustee exclusively for the benefit of the beneficiary because of the latter's equitable interest.[3] At least one court has defined a trust as a property right held by one party for the use of another.[4]

These definitions of the term *trust* (and many other definitions) seem concerned with the duty or obligation of the trustee, or with the rights of the beneficiary, rather than the nature of a trust. The trust in its modern sense is conceived to be the relationship in which the trustee holds the trust property subject to the trust agreement for the benefit of the beneficiaries.

Even though the preceding definitions are not exact or perfect, certain characteristics of a trust may be derived from them. These characteristics are (1) a trust is a relationship; (2) it is a relationship of a fiduciary character; (3) it is a relationship with respect to property; (4) it involves the existence of equitable duties imposed on the trustee for the benefit of the beneficiaries; and (5) it arises as a result of a clear intention to create the relationship. These characteristics give rise to our modern-day meaning of the term *trust.*

A trust is a relationship with respect to property held by the trustee. Such property is referred to as the trust property. The trust property may be defined as the interest in a thing—real or personal, tangible or intangible—which the trustee holds, subject to the rights of another.[5] Beside the trust property, the relationship usually involves three parties. The settlor (or grantor) of the trust is the person who creates or intentionally causes it to come into existence. Some other terms used to designate the settlor are *trustor, grantor,* and *donor.* The beneficiary is the person entitled to the benefits from the trust property. The third party to the trust is the trustee, who holds the legal title to the trust property for the benefit of the beneficiary.

In a fiduciary relationship, the law demands that one party of such a relationship must have an unusually high standard of ethical or moral conduct with respect to another party of the relationship. In a trust, the trustee is the one required to have such characteristics. Trustees must represent and act solely in the interest of the beneficiaries; they are not permitted to consider their own personal needs or desires. Due to the nature of a trust and the trustee's control over the trust property, he/she is expected to apply more than casual consideration and judgment in dealings with the beneficiary.

The settlor, in creating a trust, can state the necessary provisions with respect to the duties and powers of the trustee and the rights of the beneficiaries; unless these provisions are contrary to any local policy or law, they are valid and enforceable. Most of the legal principles and rules governing trusts are applicable only if the settlor does not provide otherwise. Thus, an estate planner must be familiar with trust law and know exactly what a particular trust can and cannot do before attempting to use it in an estate plan.

Purposes of Trusts

Trusts originated in England in the 15th century as an attempt to alleviate some of the rigid burdens of the common law. These trusts usually required the person who had legal right to the property to exercise the benefits of the property to whomever was equitably entitled to it. The usefulness of the trust concept became so apparent that it has been extended over the centuries and is still quite popular and useful today.

The trust concept has been utilized in many kinds of arrangements, such as a substitute for incorporation (the Massachusetts trust), real estate holdings, voting trusts, support of charities, and reserves set up for creditors. But the widest and most important use of trusts is in the field of family settlements. As the character of property ownership has changed, trusts have been established more and more to manage property other than land. As a result, most personal trusts at the present time consist of securities of one kind or another. But the basic purpose remains the same—the protection of the financial interests of the family.

INTRODUCTION TO ESTATES

Rather than eliminating taxation, death of an individual incurs several new tax responsibilities. For example, assume an individual dies on July 12. The executor must file tax returns for two separate entities. A regular Form 1040 return must be filed for the period before death, including the date of death (that is, July 12). Further, Form 1041 (estate income tax) must include any income or deductions that occur after death. Of course, if the estate is large enough, a federal estate tax is due on Form 706.

If the gross income of the estate is $600 or more, or if any beneficiary is a nonresident alien, the fiduciary must file Form 1041. The fiduciary may adopt a calendar year or a fiscal year. The calculation of estate income is similar to the calculation of trust income. Specific tax rates apply to an estate or trust. The remainder of this chapter discusses the tax aspects of an estate or trust.

TAXATION OF ESTATES AND TRUSTS

Any discussion of estate and trust taxation should begin with Sections 102(a) and 102(b). Section 102(a) provides the general rule that "gross income does not include the value of property acquired by gift, bequest, devise, or inheritance." Section 102(b) indicates that subsection (1) "does not exclude from gross income (1) the *income* from any property referred to in subsection (1); or (2) where the gifts, bequest, devise, or inheritance is of *income* from property, the amount of such income."

Generally, most people take for granted that any distributions from an estate or trust should be considered "income from property." But this same section indicates that "any amount included in the gross income of a beneficiary under Subchapter J shall be treated for purpose of paragraph (2) as a gift, bequest, devise, or inheritance of *income* from property." The key word is, of course, *income*. What the Code giveth it taketh away!

Subchapter J fills in this gap between Sections 102(a) and (b). In essence, the distribution rules of Sections 661 and 662 to a great extent neutralize the favorable treatment outlined in Section 102(a). The net result is that most distributions from an estate or trust are treated as taxable income, since they are considered an inheritance (or gift) of income under Section 102(b). There are two major safety valves:

1. Distributions that exceed distributable net income (DNI) are considered to be a tax-free transfer of income under Section 102(a).

2. A specific bequest of an amount of money or property under Section 663(a)(1) is not caught by the distribution rules in Subchapter J (that is, not taxable).

The taxation aspect of an estate or trust involves a number of unique concepts:

1. Fiduciary accounting income (FAI), Section 643(b).
2. Federal gross and net income of the trust, Section 61.
3. Tentative taxable income, Sections 643(a), 61, and 63.
4. Distributable net income (DNI), Section 643(a).
5. Distribution deduction (DD) or Section 651 deduction, Section 651(a) and (b).
6. Taxable income of the trust, Sections 641(b), 642, 61, and 63.
7. Adjusted gross income to the beneficiary, Section 652(a).

The term *fiduciary accounting income* (FAI) is not defined in the statutes. Instead, Section 643(b) indicates that FAI is to be determined on a state-by-state basis, since it is "determined under the terms of the governing instrument and applicable state statutes." Amounts realized from the sale or disposition of the corpus property are allocated generally to the trust (or principal), and day-by-day income items flowing into the trust (or estate) are allocated to fiduciary accounting income (that is, taxable interest, dividends, rent income, tax-exempt interest, and so on). Keep in mind that the trust instrument or will may alter the allocation of these income items. The amount designated as FAI is, of course, the amount required to be distributed to beneficiaries, in the case of a simple trust.

Federal interpretation of the gross income of an estate or trust is determined under Section 61, the same income-determination statute for other entities. Next, a figure called *tentative taxable income* is calculated under Sections 61, 63, and 643(a). As indicated in the prologue to Section 643(a), tentative taxable income is the starting point for calculating distributable net income.

EXAMPLE 1. Assume the following facts with respect to a calendar-year simple trust with two equal beneficiaries. No provision is made for a depreciation deduction. If the long-term capital gain (LTCG) is allocated to corpus, the appropriate calculations are shown in Table 3.

Under Section 643(a), tentative taxable income is modified in order to arrive at distributable net income (DNI). These modifications include the following:

1. No reduction of DNI is allowed for the distribution deduction.
2. No personal exemption is allowable.
3. Gains from the sale or exchange of capital assets are excluded to the extent that such gains are allocable to corpus.
4. Extraordinary dividends and taxable stock dividends are excluded when dealing with a simple trust.
5. Tax-exempt interest is included in DNI but is reduced by any deductions associated with the tax-exempt interest. Notice that the law mentions tax-exempt interest, but not other tax-free income. For example, a tax-free stock dividend is not included in DNI.[6]
6. Special rules apply to a foreign trust.
7. The $100 dividend exclusion is included in DNI.

This artificial concept of DNI is somewhat peculiar to fiduciary taxation. DNI acts as a limitation to the amount of income that can be taxed to a beneficiary when a distribution is made. The DNI amount also provides a limitation on the distribution deduction (DD) in order to stop tax avoidance through unlimited accumulation of income and use of gifts to charitable remainders. Think of DNI as a *quantitative* concept for measuring the amount of income taxable to an estate or trust.

The distribution deduction (DD) is, in most situations, a modified DNI. In order to avoid double taxation to an estate or trust, the statutes provide a deduction for purposes of computing the taxable income of the fiduciary, where imcome is distributed currently to the beneficiaries. This DD is the smaller of (1) the FAI required to be distributed currently under Section 651(a) or (2) modified DNI under Section 651(b). This "modified DNI" is DNI less any nontaxable income included in the DNI.

TABLE 3 Calculations for Example

Facts:

Taxable dividends	$ 4,000
Rental income	4,000
Taxable bond interest	1,000
Tax-exempt interest	1,000
Long-term capital gain	2,000
Trustee commissions	400 (to corpus)
Trustee commissions	500 (to income)
Rental expenses	1,500 (to income)
Tax-exempt expenditures	100 (to corpus)
Depreciation	1,000 (no provision)

Fiduciary accounting income:

Dividends	$ 4,000	
Rental income	4,000	
Taxable interest	1,000	
Tax-exempt interest	1,000	
	$10,000	
Less:		
Trustee commissions	$ 500	
Rental expenses	1,500	$ 2,000
FAI		$ 8,000

Gross income:

Dividends	$ 3,900*	
Rental income	4,000	
Taxable interest	1,000	
LTCG	2,000	
Gross income		$10,900

Tentative taxable income:

Gross income		$10,900
Less:		
Capital gain deduction	$ 1,200	
Rental expenses	1,500	
Personal exemption	300	
Trustee commissions	810†	$ 3,810
TTI		$ 7,090

*After the $100 dividend exclusion.

†The trustee commissions related to tax-exempt income are not deductible. The formula is: (tax-exempt income/gross FAI) × trustee commission = amount not deductible. Therefore: ($1,000/$10,000) × $900 = $90; $900 − $90 = $810.

EXAMPLE 2. Using the same facts as in Example 1, DNI may be calculated as follows, starting with tentative taxable income:

Tentative taxable income		$7,090
Personal exemption	$ 300	
Remainder of capital gain	(800)	
Tax-exempt interest	810*	
Dividend exclusion	100	+410
		$7,500

*$1,000 less $90 applicable to trustee commissions *less* the $100 tax-exempt expenditures.

Consider DD as a *qualitative* concept for determining the characterization of income items included in the beneficiary's adjusted gross income.

EXAMPLE 3. As in previous examples, DD is the smaller of (1) FAI required to be distributed, $8,000; or (2) modified DNI [$7,500 − $910 ($810 + $100) = $6,590]. Thus, the amount $6,590 is used as a deduction on the trust (or estate) tax return, and it is the largest amount that can be taxable to the beneficiaries.

Section 641(b) indicates that "taxable income of an estate or trust shall be computed in the same manner as in the case of an individual, except as otherwise provided in this part." Section 642 follows with special rules for credits and deductions involving an estate or trust. Thus, both Sections 61 (income) and 63 (deductions) are applicable to fiduciary taxation. Some of the special rules for estates and trusts (rules that do not apply to individual taxpayers) are:

1. A zero bracket amount (standard deduction) is unavailable.
2. Expenditures are not divided into deductions for adjusted gross income and deductions from adjusted gross income.
3. There is no percentage-of-income limitation on charitable contributions.
4. A simple trust is allowed a $300 personal exemption; in general, a complex trust is allowed a $100 personal exemption. If a complex trust is required to distribute

income currently, a complex trust can get a $300 exemption. A $600 personal exemption is available to an estate.

5. A trust or estate is allowed the special distribution deduction (DD) to the extent that distributions are made to the beneficiaries in order to avoid double taxation.

EXAMPLE 4. Using the facts given in the previous examples, taxable income of the trust may be calculated as follows, starting with the gross income figure from Example 1:

Gross income		$10,900
Less:		
Rental expenses	$1,500	
Capital gain exclusion	1,200	
Distribution deduction	6,590	
Trustee commissions	810	
Personal exemption	300	10,400
		$ 500

Keep in mind that this $500 amount is basically 40 percent of the long-term capital gain ($2,000), less the $300 personal exemption.

Section 652(a) indicates that the FAI required to be distributed currently by a simple trust* is to be "included in the gross income of the beneficiaries to whom the income is required to be distributed, whether distributed or not." If FAI exceeds DNI, the amount included in the gross income of each beneficiary is the figure that bears that same ratio of DNI as the amount of FAI required to be distributed to such beneficiary bears to the total amount of FAI required to be distributed to all beneficiaries. In arithmetic terms, this figure is:

$$\frac{\text{Amount of FAI to beneficiary}}{\text{Total FAI}} \times \text{DNI}$$

Section 652(b) indicates that the character of the income in the hands of the beneficiaries is the same as in the hands of the trust.

---

*A *simple trust* is defined as a trust in which all income is required to be distributed currently, does not distribute more than its current income, and has no charitable beneficiaries. All other trusts are complex trusts.

EXAMPLE 5. Assuming there are two equal beneficiaries in the previous distribution, the amount of $2,745 would be included in the adjusted gross income (AGI) of both beneficiaries. Notice in Table 4 that the entire rental expense (a direct expense) is allocated to the rental income.

Of the total $3,750 of potential gross income to a one-half beneficiary, $405 in nontaxable income. Thus, adjusted gross income of the beneficiary is calculated as follows:

Potential DNI	$3,750
Nontaxable	− 405
	$3,345
Dividend exclusion	− 100
	$3,245
Depreciation expense	− 500
	$2,745

TABLE 4

	Rent Income	Dividends	Interest	Tax Exempt Interest	Total
Gross income	$4,000	$4,000	$1,000	$1,000	$10,000
Rental expense	1,500	—	—	—	1,500
Trustee commissions	810	—	—	90	900
Tax-exempt expenses	—	—	—	100	100
Total expenses	$2,310	—	—	$ 190	$ 2,500
Total distribution	$1,690	$4,000	$1,000	$ 810	$ 7,500
Percentage	.50	.50	.50	.50	.50
Prorata distribution	$ 845	$2,000	$ 500	$ 405	$ 3,750

Depreciation expense provision. Whether or not an executor provides for a depreciation expense provision affects the calculation of the items listed above. If a depreciation reserve is not set up by the executor, FAI will be higher (to the extent of no depreciation deduction), which in turn affects the amount to be distributed. Since FAI must be distributed in a simple trust situation, the fact that no reserve is established reduces the principal (that is, the corpus of trust). In essence, the current beneficiaries receive a distributed part of the corpus. Where a trust is involved with a principal beneficiary and a remainder beneficiary, the "corpus" is being distributed to the primary beneficiary, and eventually there may be no corpus left for the secondary beneficiary. Obviously, a remainder beneficiary would prefer that a depreciation reserve be established in order to protect the corpus.

If the executor does not establish a depreciation reserve, the depreciation deduction "flows outside" FAI, DNI, and DD, and it is taken as a deduction by the beneficiaries. In Example 5, no reserve was established. Thus, the $500 depreciation expense deduction did not decrease FAI, DNI, and DD. Therefore, $500 more was distributed to the beneficiary. Of course, eventually the beneficiary was able to deduct the $500 depreciation expense.

If a depreciation reserve had been established by the executor, then FAI, DNI, and DD would have been $500 less than shown in Example 5. More importantly, there would be $500 less of FAI to be distributed to the beneficiary. Thus, the reserve protects corpus from being distributed to the beneficiaries.

In-Kind Property Distributions

As previously mentioned, a bequest of a specific sum of money or of specifically described property is not subject to the normal DNI distribution rules (i.e., treated as a distribution of property and not of income). The distribution must be paid all at once or in not more than three installments.

EXAMPLE 6. Decedent's will provides for a specific bequest of $36,000 to be paid to his daughter in not more than three installments within 12 months of his death, with the residuary estate to go to his wife. The financial, trust, and taxable net income of the trust for the 12-month period is $30,000. At four-month intervals $12,000 is paid to the daughter for a total of $36,000. Of this, $30,000 came from cash received as income and $6,000 from corpus. The fiduciary's book entry was a debit to corpus for the full $36,000. No part is deductible by the estate for income tax purposes, so that the wife as residuary legatee eventually bears the burden of the estate's income tax liability. Also, the daughter has no taxable income.

Specific bequests of appreciated property can be advantageous because the beneficiary receives a basis that is equal to the property's fair market value as of the date of the decedent's death.[7] Therefore, any unrealized appreciation avoids the income tax forever. Since a gift of appreciated property results in a carryover basis,[8] the unrealized appreciation will be taxed eventually.

In-kind distribution of nonspecific bequest property after June 1, 1984, is treated differently than a specific bequest or gift. At the election of the fiduciary, the beneficiary receives a carryover basis in the hands of the estate/trust *or* the gain or loss is recognized to the trust or estate. Once made, the election is irrevocable (unless consent is received from the IRS).[9]

Section 643(d)(3) allows the fiduciary to elect to recognize gain or loss on an in-kind distribution. If the fiduciary does not make the election on the tax return for the taxable year in which the distribution was made, no gain or loss is recognized, but the amount deductible by the fiduciary and taken into income by the beneficiary as a distribution of DNI (DD) is limited to the smaller of the basis or fair market value of the property. The beneficiary then takes a carryover basis.

The effect of the election is summarized in Table 5, using both appreciated and depreciated property.

TABLE 5

	Gain Property		Loss Property	
	No Election	Election	No Election	Election
Gain or loss to trust or estate	No	Yes	No	Yes: Estate No: Trust*
Distribution deduction	Adjusted basis	FMV	FMV	FMV
Income to beneficiary	Adjusted basis	FMV	FMV	FMV
Basis to beneficiary	Carryover	FMV	Carryover	FMV: Estate Carryover: Trust

*Section 267(b)(6) denies a loss between a trust and its beneficiary.

Complex trusts. The previous discussion has been limited to the taxation aspects of a simple trust. Although there are different sections in the statutes covering complex trusts, the basic rules applicable to a complex trust are similar to those for simple trusts and estates. Essentially a complex trust does not distribute all of the income to the beneficiaries, and, therefore, the trust itself is taxed on such income.

Multiple Trusts

After February 1984, two or more trusts are treated as one trust if they have substantially the same grantor(s) and substantially the same beneficiary(ies) and if *a* principal purpose for the existence of multiple trusts is the avoidance of federal income tax. A husband and wife are considered to be one person for the purpose of this provision. Tax avoidance must merely be *a* principal purpose rather than *the* principal purpose.

There were several advantages of multiple trusts before March 1984. Each trust was entitled to a $100 exemption, a $30,000 exemption from the alternative minimum tax, and a separate taxation on its own undistributed income. Now under Section 643(e) these trusts are consolidated and have only one exemption and only one run through the tax brackets.

Many multiple trusts created before March 1984, are irrevocable and will be an administrative burden. They will require a maintenance of separate books and records even though their income will be consolidated for tax purposes. Of course, no new sets of multiple trusts should be created under the present law.

NOTES

1. George C. Bogert and George T. Bogert, *The Law of Trusts and Trustees,* 2d ed. (St. Paul, Minn.: West Publishing, 1965), sec. 1.
2. American Law Institute, *Restatement of the Law, Second, Trusts,* 2d ed., vol. 1 (St. Paul, Minn.: American Law Institute Publishers, 1959), sec. 2.
3. Ralph A. Newman, *Newman on Trusts,* 2d ed. (Brooklyn, N.Y.: Foundation Press, 1953), pp. 3–4.
4. *Keplinger* v. *Keplinger,* 1916, 113 N.E. 292, 293, 185 Ind. 81.
5. Bogert et al., *Law of Trusts,* sec. 1.
6. See Section 305(a) and Rev. Rul. 67-117, 1967-1 C.B. 161.
7. Section 1014.
8. Section 1015.
9. Section 643(d)(3).

9

Using Trusts in Estate Planning

In levying taxes and in shearing sheep, it is well to stop when
you get down to the skin.

—*Austin O'Malley*

Trusts may be classified in many different ways: by purpose,
by manner of creation, or by revocable versus irrevocable.
There are also other ways to classify trusts. All the classifications just mentioned, as well as others, are discussed below.

CLASSIFICATION OF TRUSTS

Classified as to Purpose

There are many purposes for which trusts are formed. In fact,
a trust may be created to achieve any desired objective, as long
as the objective is not illegal or contrary to any public policy or
rule of law. Some of the more common types of trusts, classified
as to purpose, include insurance trusts, support trusts, charitable trusts, and marital deduction trusts.

Charitable trusts. Trusts that are originated in an effort to make one or more gifts to a charitable organization are
charitable trusts. The purpose of a charitable trust is to bring
social benefits to some portion of the public.[1] The American
Law Institute defines charitable purposes as (*a*) the relief of
poverty; (*b*) the advancement of education; (*c*) the advance-

ment of religion; (d) the promotion of health; (e) governmental or municipal purposes; and (f) other purposes, the accomplishment of which is beneficial to the community.[2]

A more thorough definition of a charitable trust appears in the *Restatement of the Law, Trusts,* by the American Law Institute:

> A charitable trust is a trust the performance of which will, in the opinion of the court of chancery, accomplish a substantial amount of social benefit to the public or some reasonably large class thereof.
>
> It is immaterial that the settlor had personal motives in creating the trust, if the trust has charitable effects, but the purpose must not include profit-making by the settlor, trustees, or others.
>
> A charitable trust is to be distinguished from an absolute gift to a charitable corporation.
>
> A trust for "benevolent" objects may be declared a valid charitable trust, if the word *benevolent* is used as a synonym of *charitable* but not if *benevolent* is construed as meaning any object which indicates merely goodwill toward mankind or merely liberality.[3]

The fundamental distinction between private trusts and charitable trusts is that private trusts have as their objectives the furnishing of financial benefits to individuals or corporations, whereas the charitable trust is used to benefit the general public or some large portion of the general public.

In practice, charitable trusts generally are of two types. In the first type, the charity is to receive the remainder interest of the trust after some noncharitable beneficiary has received the income from the trust for some period of time (a charitable remainder trust). In the second type of arrangement, the charity receives the income for a period of years, with the remainder returning to the grantor or some other designated beneficiary (a charitable lead trust or a charitable income trust) [see Chapter 6].

Also, consideration should be given to the tax effects of charitable trusts. If the trust is established during the settlor's lifetime, he/she receives an income tax deduction (see Chapter 10). On the other hand, if the trust is established by a will or as a testamentary transfer, the settlor could receive an estate tax deduction. Thus, careful consideration must be given to the types of transfers that should be made, if an estate planner wants to make a gift to a charitable organization.

Insurance trusts. The use of the trust for the disposition of life insurance proceeds is a comparatively new development. However, life insurance trusts today have become a significant part of estate planning. A person can transfer ownership of a life insurance policy on the transferor's life to a trust with a child as a beneficiary. The gift is taxable, but any gift tax incurred on the transfer is minimal. The advantage is that the proceeds of the assigned policy are not included in the transferor's estate (if all incidents of ownership are transferred).

A personal life insurance trust is primarily an arrangement whereby the proceeds of life insurance are to be held, invested, and managed by a trustee for the benefit of the beneficiary. Such a trust may be created by the estate owner's will (testamentary) or by a lifetime gift *(inter vivos)*.

Often assets other than the proceeds of life insurance are used as part of the corpus of such trusts. In fact, a trust of other property many constitute the vehicle for receiving and administering life insurance proceeds that mature upon the death of the insured. Thus, in a great many instances, a trust of life insurance proceeds is merged with a trust of other property. Such an arrangement constitutes the so-called pour-over method of implementing an estate plan.

Under the pour-over method, the will instructs the executor to collect all of the probate assets and pay all debts, expenses, and taxes. Next, the executor pours over all remaining assets into a trust—possibly an insurance trust. The trust, under the direction of a trustee, takes over the function of disposing of the assets in the estate.

Support trusts. In our society, it is generally deemed proper for people to want to help their families. Many times, however, it is not desirable to pass legal title to these beneficiaries. This restriction is especially true if the beneficiaries are minors, aged, surviving spouses, or incompetents who may not be capable of properly managing the property. If the taxpayer's objective is merely to support the beneficiary, a trust may offer certain advantages over an outright transfer of property or funds used to support the beneficiary. One of the main income tax advantages of using a trust is that all the income may pass through the trust to the beneficiary and the corpus returns to the grantor at the expiration of the trust.

A trust that is designed to provide support for the beneficiary is a support trust. This arrangement is designed to support beneficiaries who may be incapable of handling their own financial affairs. In other words, the trust funds are protected against the beneficiary's incapacity as well as against claims from creditors.

Another type of support trust is the short-term or Clifford trust (that is, one created for at least 10 years and one day). This type is especially advantageous when the grantor is in a high-income tax bracket but wants to reclaim the corpus after 10 years or more. The Clifford trust offers many tax advantages and should be given careful consideration by the estate planner, especially in situations that call for support trusts.

EXAMPLE 1. Father creates a Clifford trust in 1985 for his son's education with securities worth $10,000 that have a current yield of 10 percent. During the first year the trust earns $1,000 in dividends, which are distributed to the son. If the father is in the 50 percent tax bracket and the son has no other income, there would be a tax savings of $450. This savings occurs because the son has a $1,000 personal exemption, and $100 of dividends may be excluded from gross income. There may also be some state and city taxes saved.

	Father	Son
Dividend income	$1,000	$1,000
Taxes due	450	0
Net inflow	$ 550	$1,000

Although there is no gift tax on the transfer of the principal (the securities themselves), there may be a gift tax on the present value of the expected income over the life of the trust.

Assets may be shifted to a spousal remainder trust for a shorter period of time. However, the spouse of the grantor shall receive the remainder of the assets when the trust is closed. This type of trust can be used to shift income from the assets to a child to attend college.

Since the trust assets do not revert to the grantor, the spousal remainder trust is not burdened with the 10-year-plus Clifford requirement. By passing the remainder interest to the spouse of the grantor, such remainder interest qualifies for the unlimited spousal marital deduction. Further, the income paid from the trust to the beneficiary qualifies as a present interest (i.e., annual exclusion is available). A spousal remainder trust is irrevocable.

EXAMPLE 2. Mrs. Brown places $60,000 of stock into a spousal remainder trust. The trust earns 12 percent annually and pays a son, the sole beneficiary, $7,200 for four years. The son is in a much lower income tax bracket than is his father. After four years the trust is closed, and the stock goes to Mrs. Brown.

Do not allow the spouse of the grantor to set up another spousal remainder trust with the original grantor as the person to receive the second spousal remainder trust property. In such a situation the cross-trust doctrine shall apply (see subsequent discussion) to switch the grantors of the trust and stop the benefits of a spousal remainder trust. With proper care, spousal remainder trusts may become as common as was the Rubik's Cube a few years ago.

Grandfather and educational trusts. Still another type of trust is the grandfather trust. Here the grantor creates a trust providing for income to a son (daughter) for life, with the remainder to a grandson (granddaughter). An educational trust is a form of support trust. A parent in a high-income tax bracket is able to transfer income-producing assets to a trust for the educational benefit of children. As long as the income is not used for the "support of the children," the income is taxed at a much lower rate in the trust or in the hands of the children.

Another form of educational trust occurs when an employer makes contributions to a trust on behalf of an employee's children. These contributions and the accumulated income are used for the children's college education. A significant deferral of income taxes occurs, since the contributions are not taxed to the employee until payments are made toward the education of the children. Of course, the corporation is not allowed a deduction until a corresponding amount is included in the gross income of the participating employee.[4]

Marital deduction trusts. The two most widely used methods of securing the marital deduction are an outright bequest to the surviving spouse or the creation of a trust from which he/she is entitled to the lifetime income and has enough control over the corpus to make it includable in his/her gross estate at death. Taking advantage of the marital deduction has two primary advantages. First, management duties are shifted from the surviving spouse to the trustee, who is usually much more proficient at managing the trust property. Second, and perhaps most important, the trust may be set up in such a way that the surviving spouse would have to take positive action to prevent the remainder of the trust from passing to beneficiaries designated by the deceased spouse and creator of the trust.

For instance, the trust could be established so that the surviving spouse is to receive the income for life and have a general power of appointment with respect to the corpus; but if such power is not exercised, the remainder passes to the beneficiaries specified by the settlor. Because of the advantages discussed above and the fact that the marital deduction allows the estate owner to pass an unlimited amount to the surviving spouse tax free, it should be obvious that the marital deduction trust should be given careful consideration by the estate planner.

Frequently two trusts are established: a marital deduction trust and a nonmarital trust. The will instructs the executor to pay the exemption equivalent to a nonmarital trust (a bypass trust or an exemption-equivalent trust) to be held for the benefit of the surviving spouse. At the death of the surviving spouse, the assets in the nonmarital trust are not included in his/her estate. In effect, this exemption equivalent amount escapes taxation in both spouses' estates. The remaining assets pass either to a marital trust or directly to the surviving spouse, thereby qualifying for the marital deduction. These assets would be taxed, however, when the surviving spouse dies.

Various "sprinkling provisions" can be established to allow the trustee to invade the corpus for the surviving spouse or for the remainder person (often a child). For example, one beneficiary might get a larger amount one year because of a large medical bill. Of course, when the surviving spouse dies, the assets in the nonmarital trust pass tax free to the children.

Qualified terminable interest property trusts. A qualified terminable interest property (QTIP) trust may be created in order to obtain an elective marital deduction. A QTIP trust allows a person to provide income to a surviving spouse, but upon his/her death, the assets go to whomever the grantor (original spouse) chooses. The surviving spouse must have an income interest in the assets, and no person other than the surviving spouse may be given a life estate in the property.[5] The election to use a QTIP trust is made on the decedent's federal estate tax return, and once made it is irrevocable. This type of trust may be appropriate where there has been a second marriage. The decedent may wish to control the eventual disposition of the property (such as to the children of the first marriage) but still give an income interest to a surviving spouse and still obtain a marital deduction.

Once assets are transferred to a QTIP trust, these assets will be taxed at the surviving spouse's death or upon any earlier disposition of the income interest. The surviving spouse's estate is entitled to recover from the trust any tax attributable to the terminable interest assets.

A similar trust election is available to a donee-spouse when assets are transferred to the other spouse during the joint lives of the couple.

Classified as to Manner of Creation

Trusts are classified according to the manner of their creation as either made during the settlor's lifetime *(inter vivos)* or upon his/her death by a will (testamentary). An *inter vivos* or living trust is administered by the trustee, not only during the lifetime of the settlor but usually also after his/her death. On the other hand, a testamentary trust takes effect only upon death.

Living trusts. An *inter vivos* trust may be either revocable or irrevocable. The revocable *inter vivos* trust is one wherein the settlor reserves the power to terminate the trust at any time during his/her lifetime or to otherwise change its terms. Therefore, the settlor has the ability to completely cancel the trust or has the liberty to change the disposition of either the principal or income or both as circumstances change during his/her lifetime.

An irrevocable trust is just what the word *irrevocable* means. Once it is created, the trust agreement cannot be revoked and usually cannot be changed or modified. This means that no beneficiaries may be added.

There are a number of advantages of a living trust during the settlor's lifetime:

1. It is an easy way to have one's investments managed by a financial expert, to the extent desired.

2. It is a simple, expeditious, and inexpensive way of providing for the payment of bills for one's care if one becomes sick or incapacitated, thereby avoiding the need for a conservator or guardian of the estate.

3. It gives a settlor and his/her family the opportunity to get acquainted with the trustee. If they are dissatisfied with the way the trustee operates, they can replace him/her.

4. It serves as a good means of describing and segregating property according to its nature, the title to it, and the disposition to be made of it in accordance with sound estate planning practices.[6]

Some of the advantages of a living trust after the settlor's death include the following:

1. The trust assets do not become part of the decedent's probate estate and are not included in figuring the executor's commission or the attorney's fees.

2. Succeeding beneficiaries can receive trust income and principal immediately after the settlor's death unless tax considerations or the need to obtain releases cause delays.

3. A living trust has elements of privacy and confidentiality not afforded by a will, because the public does not have access to the trust document or trust assets as it does to the probate and court records.

4. The settlor, no matter where he/she lives, can ordinarily choose the state law that governs the trust (in most cases by choosing an attorney in that state). A will must be probated in the state and county of domicile.[7]

Testamentary trusts. The testamentary trust is usually created by the will of the settlor and therefore does not take effect until death. One of the advantages of this type of trust is that the settlor has complete control and authority over the trust property until death. Also, testamentary trusts are established for a variety of other reasons: doubt as to the ability of beneficiaries to manage the property, a desire to keep the property away from the present or future spouses of the settlor's children, or the need for keeping a business interest under continuous management. But probably the most compelling reason for establishing testamentary trusts, at least in recent years, is based on tax plans. The most common of the tax plans allows the property to pass free of tax on the death of the surviving spouse.

Revocable versus Irrevocable Trusts

People today are unduly tax conscious. Too often the only factor that they consider is whether or not there will be a tax savings and, if so, how much it will be. However, in estate planning of revocable and irrevocable trusts, the nontax considerations can be more important than the tax considerations. This characteristic (revocable versus irrevocable) is very important to the estate planner.

Characteristics of the two types. Generally, the irrevocable *inter vivos* trust is a vehicle for federal tax savings, while the revocable *inter vivos* trust is more suited for nontax objectives. The choice depends on the settlor's decision—either to transfer the property away forever (irrevocable) or to retain the right to get it back at a later date if circumstances should change (revocable).

The value of the revocable trust is appreciated only when one realizes that it is not permanently binding like an irrevocable *inter vivos* trust but is, in effect, a will. For the purposes of this chapter, *revocable inter vivos trust* is defined as a trust created during the settlor's lifetime in which "the settlor alone has the power to revoke and in which effect of his revocation is to force the return of the corpus to himself or to force the payment of the corpus as he may direct."[8]

The basic distinction between a revocable trust and a will, both created during the settlor's lifetime, is that the former effects a present transfer of property rights subject to "divestment" by exercise of the power of revocation. The will, until the taxpayer's death, creates only an expectancy. The fundamental advantage of wills seems to be that they enable people to determine who shall succeed to their property after their death without requiring them to part with it during their life.

The main disadvantage is that the testator's freedom of

disposition is often restricted. However, it is well settled that one has much greater freedom of alienation *inter vivos* than one has freedom of testamentary disposition.[9] Because the revocable *inter vivos* trust effects a present transfer of property rights, it should not be subject to the restrictions on testamentary dispositions. However, because the trust is revocable, the settlor does not run the risk of being unable to recall the property once transferred. There are also advantages to be considered after the death of the settlor.

Probate restrictions. A revocable *inter vivos* trust that continues after the settlor's death provides for an uninterrupted management arrangement. During the time of existence of the trust prior to death, the settlor has the opportunity to observe the management ability of the trustee and thus be assured that his/her directions will be followed.

Probate assets of a decedent are more or less in a suspended state until the executor can satisfy the claims of creditors and death tax obligations. The potential personal liability of the executor naturally defers the availability of the use of the estate assets by the beneficiaries until such liability is eliminated.

Also, probate property and its destination are revealed in a decedent's will, and the amount and nature are generally a matter of public record. Decedents may desire to keep their financial records and methods of caring for their families from becoming a part of such record, and to a considerable degree, this may be accomplished by an arrangement that avoids probate, which is usually a trust-property arrangement. However, the items in the gross estate (probate and nonprobate) will be disclosed in the federal estate tax return. Also, the instrument creating a revocable *inter vivos* trust will be filed with the return. However, the return and accompanying papers are not open to public scrutiny as are probate records.[10]

Various state laws may impose on the freedom of a property holder to decide who will be beneficiaries of his/her estate. To the extent that these restrictions apply only to probate property, they can be minimized by avoiding probate. To the extent that they are not limited to probate property, they may be avoided by placing the property under the jurisdiction of a more favorable state. Such a state may be selected by a property holder to establish a revocable *inter vivos* trust with the intention that its law control the trust, provided the trustee and the property are located there. (For a living trust, any state may be chosen.)

Tax advantages and disadvantages. Although the main advantages of the revocable trust are nontax considerations, a brief look at the tax situation is helpful. The Internal Revenue Code deals with taxation of trust income over which the settlor has a power of revocation. Section 676(a) provides as follows:

> The grantor shall be treated as the owner of any portion of a trust, whether or not he is treated as such owner under any other provision of the part, where at any time the power to revest in the grantor title to such portion is exercisable by the grantor or a nonadverse party or both.

Thus, under this section, income from the revocable trust property is taxed to the settlor just as if he had never made the transfer to the trustee. There is a possible method of avoiding this income tax. Section 676(b) provides:

> The income of a revocable trust shall not be taxed to the settlor if he cannot exercise the power of revocation affecting the beneficial enjoyment of the income until the expiration of a period of 10 years from the date of the transfer in trust. But the settlor may be treated as the owner of the income after such a period unless the power is relinquished.

Therefore, if the settlor suspends power of revocation for a period of more than 10 years from the date on which the trust was created (that is, a Clifford trust), the trust income for such a period will not be taxed to him/her. However, the income will become taxable to the settlor beginning with the date on which the power of revocation becomes exercisable, unless he/she relinquishes the power. This treatment is quite in contrast to the irrevocable trust examined below. *Warning:* Income from a trust may be taxable to the settlor to the extent such income is used to discharge a legal obligation of the settlor (that is, care of minor children).[11]

There is a major exception to the 10-year rule. The term of a Clifford trust can be limited to the life of the beneficiary, even when the life expectancy of the beneficiary is less than 10 years.[12]

EXAMPLE 3. Golden creates an irrevocable trust for the benefit of his aunt, who is 79. Upon her death, the trust is to end and the corpus revert to Golden. The income is not taxable to Golden, even though the aunt's life expectancy is less than 10 years. If the trust instrument is silent on capital gains and losses, then under local law net capital gains will be added to corpus. As a result, Golden will be currently taxable on them. Also, if there are net capital losses, Golden can currently deduct them.

Disadvantages of irrevocable *inter vivos* trusts. It has already been pointed out that the principal advantage of an irrevocable *inter vivos* trust is the saving of federal income and estate taxes. The major disadvantage of such a trust is that it results in the settlor's losing control of the property. Once made, the settlor of an irrevocable *inter vivos* trust can no longer change the terms of the trust to take into account any changed circumstances.

There may be instances when an individual would transfer property to an irrevocable *inter vivos* trust where the tax considerations are secondary. Suppose a man has accumulated an estate adequate enough to provide what he desires for his family, and he realizes that he is reaching an age at which he might not be able to trust himself to make good business decisions. If he makes the trust revocable, he might unwisely revoke the trust, but if it is irrevocable, he has protected himself against this possibility.[13]

Usually, however, when people decide to create an *inter vivos* trust other than a revocable one, they desire to accomplish the two following tax results:

1. The income from the trust will be removed from their taxable income.
2. The appreciation value that occurs after the transfer of the trust property will be removed from their gross estate.

The cost of accomplishing these results is mainly that the unified tax credit must be used, or, if the trust property is sufficiently large, the payment of a federal transfer tax must be made early. Considering other economic factors related to a reduction in one's wealth, a gift can still be a sound device for estate planning.

Property owners, by making outright gifts during their lifetime, shift the income tax liability from themselves to the people to whom they make the gift. Thus, if they make an irrevocable gift in trust, they may, according to the terms of the trust, shift the income tax liability to the trust or to the beneficiary. If the income is not distributed or is not distributable, it is taxable to the trust. If it is distributed or distributable, ordinarily it is taxable to the beneficiary. But, although the trust is irrevocable, the property owners may have reserved the right to leave themselves substantially the owners of the property, in which case the income would be taxable to them.

A trust under which the grantor retains the right to the income for life, with the remainder to someone else but which cannot be revoked, creates a situation that reduces the gross estate only by the amount of the gift tax paid (if any). The grantor is taxable on the income from such a trust because he/she has the right to receive it, and the value of the principal of such a trust is includable in gross estate for federal estate tax purposes. Thus, there is no major tax advantage to be gained by using such a trust.[14]

Sections 671–677 of the Internal Revenue Code spell out in detail the circumstances under which the settlor would be taxable on the trust income on the basis of dominion and control (sometimes called a grantor trust). The justification for including the trust income in the settlor's gross income must be found in these sections of Code. Examination of the Code provisions discloses the following factors to be considered in determining whether the settlor has eliminated the trust income from gross income.

1. Are there administrative powers retained by the grantor?
2. May the income or principal return to the grantor?
3. Is the income or principal of the trust used to discharge the grantor's legal obligations, including an obligation to support or maintain some dependent or other person?
4. Is the income or principal of the trust to be used for paying premiums on the grantor's life insurance policies?
5. If there is a power to control beneficial enjoyment, though no benefit may be conferred upon the settlor, is this power in the grantor, in a subordinate party, in an independent party, or in an adverse party?

6. If there is a power to control beneficial enjoyment, though no benefit may be conferred upon the grantor, does the power relate to income only, or to principal only, or to both income and principal?

7. If there is a power to control beneficial enjoyment, though no benefit may be conferred upon the grantor, is the power extensive or limited as to the variation in beneficial enjoyment?

When a grantor retains the above powers of dominion and control over trust property and income, he is considered to be the substantial owner of that property and is taxable on its income, rather than the trust and its beneficiaries. A typical power would be the right to revoke the trust. Such a trust is called a "grantor trust." The grantor need not actually receive any income in order to be taxed on it. If the grantor or some nonadverse party possesses a prohibited power over the trust's corpus or income, the grantor is taxed on the trust's income. However, very broad powers can be given to an independent trustee, such as a bank.

A Mallinckrodt trust is an extension of the grantor trust rules. A person other than the grantor can be treated as the owner of any portion of a trust where (1) the person has a power exercisable solely by himself to vest the corpus or income therefrom in himself, or (2) such person has previously partially released or otherwise modified such a power but after the release or modification still retains other powers prohibited to a grantor.

If a person in the capacity of trustee or cotrustee has the power to apply income to the support of an individual whom he is legally obligated to support, then such trustee or cotrustee is taxable upon income so applied but not on any additional sum.[15] This exception to the general applicability of the Mallinckrodt principle is a technical one. The power to use money to support dependents must be possessed by an individual in his/her capacity as trustee or cotrustee.

EXAMPLE 4. G creates a trust and names a local bank as sole trustee, but he gives his married daughter the power to appoint the income for the support and maintenance of her minor children. The daughter is taxable on all the income whether or not used for the support of her children.[16]

Suppose the daughter is a cotrustee with the bank and only in that capacity has the power to appoint the income. Now she is taxable only on the money actually used for the support of her children.[17]

Estate and gift tax benefits may result from a grantor lead trust. A grantor lead trust occurs when the income from property is paid to a grantor for a period of years and the remainder accrues to a younger-generation beneficiary, such as a child. Although the grantor retains the income interest, there is a complete gift as to the remainder. As long as the grantor does not die during the income term, any subsequent appreciation in the property goes to the younger-generation beneficiary free of estate and gift taxes. Where the grantor dies during the income term, Section 2036 would pull the property into the grantor's estate. Thus, the grantor should be young enough to be likely to outlive the income term.

In conclusion, caution is in order for anyone planning the use of trusts in estate arrangements. It is essential that strict compliance be made with the rules set forth in the Code in order to obtain the desired result of the planning effort. However, even though there is generally no federal tax advantage to the revocable trust, it is especially suited for people not financially able to part irrevocably with portions of their property during life.

Miscellaneous Types of Trusts

A reciprocal, or cross-trust, doctrine is a judicial concept that switches grantors of trusts in order to prevent tax avoidance. Suppose Baker creates a trust for the benefit of Carl, and Carl also sets up a trust of equal value for Baker. Under the terms of Baker's trust, any income is paid to Carl for life, with the remainder to Carl's children. Similarly, the trust created by Carl provides for income to Baker for life with the remainder to Baker's children. This strategy is not a valid tax-planning technique, even though technically neither grantor has retained a life estate. The courts use the reciprocal trust doctrine in order to switch the grantors of the trusts. Each grantor is treated as if he created a trust under which he retains a life interest, and thereby the trust assets are included in his gross estate under Section 2036 as a retained life estate.[18]

In one recent decision, however, a decedent and his spouse created two trusts. The spouse was given a special power of appointment over trust income and corpus of the trust created by the decedent for her benefit. The spouse's trust for the decedent's benefit did not grant him a power of appointment. Here the Tax Court held that the reciprocal trust doctrine did not apply because of the limited difference in the disposition patterns of the two trusts.[19]

The apocalypse trust is also meeting opposition from the IRS. Under such an arrangement a taxpayer transfers all assets to a trust and also assigns his/her lifetime services to the trust. For example, a doctor or dentist may transfer his/her place of business to a trust. The beneficiaries are generally the taxpayer's family, with the grantor retaining broad powers over the income and corpus of the trust. The trust collects all the taxpayer's income and deducts all the taxpayer's expenses. The purpose of this arrangement is to shift income to taxpayers in lower tax brackets as well as to avoid the estate tax. Four revenue rulings bar the use of these apocalypse trusts.[20]

USES OF TRUSTS IN ESTATE PLANNING

Although several uses and advantages of trusts were given in other parts of this chapter, this section illustrates a few specific examples where trusts can be put to good use in estate planning. Of course, anytime a trust is devised for any estate planning program, that trust must be tailored to meet the needs and circumstances applicable to the specific situation. The illustrations given here will be generalized situations, and therefore the trusts suggested are not designed to solve specific problems.

Generation Skipping

Estate owners often wish to avoid having to pay estate taxes on successive life estates. Many times the estate owner will be satisfied to skip the tax at the death of the primary beneficiary. Skipping the estate tax on the death of the primary beneficiary can be accomplished by the use of a trust. The estate owner simply leaves the estate in trust, with the income going to his/her spouse for life and the remainder to the children upon the death of the remaining spouse. There is no estate tax on the property in which the survivor merely held a life interest.

The Tax Reform Act of 1976 took away some of the estate tax advantages of a long-term trust. Specifically, the law imposes an estate tax on generation-skipping trusts. A generation-skipping trust is a trust in which the taxpayer passes property to a person at least two generations younger, but some control or benefits of the property first go to some individual of the in-between generation.

The generation-skipping tax is triggered when there is termination of the benefits to the in-between generation or when there is a distribution of trust corpus to the ultimate beneficiary. Even though this new generation-skipping tax is imposed on the trust corpus, it is computed as if the individual in the in-between generation owned the property outright. The applicable tax (sometimes called Chapter 13 tax) is essentially equivalent to the transfer tax that would have been imposed if the assets actually had been transferred outright to each successive generation that had beneficial enjoyment or control over the assets. Although the amount of the tax is calculated with reference to the "deemed transferor's" marginal tax rate, the actual tax is payable generally from the trust property and not from the property of the intermediate beneficiary's estate.

There is one important exclusion to the generation-skipping tax. This exclusion occurs in the very common case in which the taxpayer leaves the income of a trust to his/her children and the remainder to grandchildren. Such a generation-skipping transfer to the taxpayer's grandchildren receives an exclusion to the tax in the amount of $250,000 of trust corpus per child (not grandchild) of the taxpayer.

Notice that this exclusion is applied to the aggregate fair market value of the trust property upon the termination of the grantor-children's life income interest in the trust. Therefore, since the grantor is unable to predict the appreciation in the assets or an overall inflation level, tax planning is difficult in this area.

One way to avoid the generation-skipping tax is to layer gifts so as to completely skip the grantor's children by giving them some assets outright and placing approximately $250,000 per child in generation-skipping trusts. Another way is to place property in trusts for grandchildren without any life estate for children.

Although there is some activity in Congress to eliminate this tax, the generation-skipping tax must now be considered when dealing with most trust transfers. Certain transfers still avoid the generation-skipping tax. For example, a wife can transfer income-producing property to a trust, income to her husband for life, and at his death the corpus could be distributed as follows:

1. Equal shares can be distributed to the children.
2. If any child is not alive, such share goes to the child's surviving issue.
3. If such nonliving child has no surviving issue, the share goes to the settlor's surviving issue.

In any one of these three situations, there would be no generation-skipping tax.

Consider another example. An individual transfers income-producing property to a trust, income to his wife for life, and at her death the trust corpus is to be divided into equal shares for his children, each child to receive the income from his/her share for life, and at the child's death, the corpus to be distributed as follows:

1. Child's share at death is to be distributed to his/her surviving issue.
2. If the child has no surviving issue, his/her share is to be allocated among the individual's surviving issues.
   a. Any share of a child is to be added to his/her trust.
   b. That share of any other issue is to be distributed to him/her.

There is no generation-skipping tax at the death of the wife who possesses an income interest. However, when a child dies with a distribution of corpus to his/her children (or the children of his/her siblings) the so-called Chapter 13 tax would apply to the excess of the total value of the distributions over $250,000. There is no tax on the portion of the decedent's trust share added to the trust shares of the decedent's siblings.

Avoiding Probate

Many estate owners dislike the fact that the amount of their estate and the way in which they provide for their families become a public record. All property subject to probate or to court disposition becomes public record and thus is open to public scrutiny. The sure way to avoid this public scrutiny is to avoid probate.

In a smaller estate, probate can be avoided by holding property jointly between spouses. On the death of the first spouse, all of the property goes to the surviving spouse outside of probate. Administration expenses are reduced. Such jointly held property may be exempt from state inheritance taxes along with disclosure and reporting requirements.

Estate owners also can avoid probate by placing their properties in a revocable trust for the benefit of their survivors (so-called living trust). The trust becomes irrevocable upon the grantor's death. The fact is that property left in trust is not subject to probate; neither does it become part of the basis from which the executor's and attorney's fees are determined. Thus, by placing the property in trust, the estate owner avoids the public scrutiny and reduces the amount of the executor's fees that this estate would have to pay. Also, disgruntled relatives are more prone to attack the capacity of estate owners to make a will than the right of the estate owner to establish an *inter vivos* trust.

Also, lifetime giving is another way to avoid probate.

Continuance of Management

As pointed out earlier in this chapter, the trust is very advantageous where continuous, competent management of the trust property is necessary. In some cases, estate owners may be aging and may doubt their own future ability to make the proper decisions. Another situation where the trust is beneficial is where there is a need to achieve a continuing and unified management of the property so that it will be uninterrupted by the death of the estate owner. Such flexibility is especially important when the trust property is a going concern and the estate owner does not have survivors capable of or interested in taking over the business. Even if the trust property is not a going concern, the estate owner may wish to provide competent management of such property for the benefit of the heirs. All these types of situations can easily be handled with a properly drawn trust.

Certainly there are many cases in which the estate owner has a surviving spouse or other beneficiaries who have proved themselves to be incapable of properly managing financial affairs. In such a situation the estate owner may establish a trust to support such a beneficiary; the most common type of trust used for this purpose is the spendthrift trust. A spendthrift trust is one in which the beneficiary is unable to sell or give away the right to future income or principal, and the trust assets may not be reached by creditors.

Of course the estate owner may simply want to provide for the health, education, and other needs of a minor child. Support trusts, which were discussed earlier, are used to achieve these results.

Equally important is the need in many cases to withhold property from people who are legally unable to manage their own affairs. These include infants and persons who are mentally incompetent. The trust form is much better suited to practical administration in such cases than is a guardianship. For example, a nonmarital trust could be established for a handicapped child. The trust could be used to receive government benefits to which the handicapped may be entitled. Essentially, such a trust could cover the physical, social, and educational needs of the child.

The estate owner can also secure income tax benefits through the use of trusts. If the owner makes an irrevocable trust, then the income from the trust property is not included in gross income. If the estate owner cannot afford to part irrevocably with the property, it may be transferred into a revocable trust for a period greater than 10 years (the so-called Clifford trust), and the income from such trust will not be included in gross income.

POWERS OF APPOINTMENT

Powers of appointment may be useful estate planning tools when setting up trusts. There are two types of powers: A general power of appointment and a special power of appointment. People have a general power of appointment if they can appoint the property (1) to themselves, (2) to their estates, (3) to their creditors, or (4) to creditors of their estates. Any other power is considered to be a special power of appointment (that is, the power to appoint to anyone except in the preceding four categories).

People who have a general power of appointment are treated for estate and gift tax purposes as if they own the property. If they exercise the general power during their lifetime, they pay a gift tax. If they hold onto the power (die without exercising it), the property is included in their gross estate. As a general rule, one should not give a general power of appointment.

Assume that Mr. Devour gives property to a trust, giving his grandson income for life, with a power to appoint to anyone except himself, his estate, his creditors, or his estate's creditors. The grandson could be given the power "to invade corpus in order to survive, to maintain himself, or to support himself." By giving the grandson a special power of appointment, the grandson could defer the generation-skipping tax by exercising the special power to create a present interest in a beneficiary in the same generation as the grandson (such as the grandson's spouse). If a grandson had been given a general power of appointment, there would be a tax on the grandson's death.

The estate planning could go a step further. The grandson could be given the noncumulative power to invade corpus on December 31 of each year to the extent of $5,000 or 5 percent of the corpus (whichever is greater). This is called a *Crummey* power (which is a general power of appointment). Important, however, is that the gift is a present interest and qualifies for the annual exclusion. A lapse of a general power of appointment triggers estate and gift tax consequences. But a lapse is not treated as a release (i.e., taxable) unless the power exceeds in value, at the time of the lapse, the greater of $5,000 or 5 percent of the property. Therefore, this contingency distribution would not be included in the taxable estate or gift. To avoid income tax problems the beneficiary should be given about one month to disclaim the power.

Often, in a marital trust, the trustees have the discretionary power to invade principal in favor of the surviving spouse's well-being, maintenance, and health (that is, an ascertainable standard). Where the marital trust and the residuary trust are quite wealthy, it may be advisable to provide the surviving spouse with enough flexibility to invade the corpus of the marital trust in order to allow lifetime gifts to other family members. Remember that the principal of the marital trust is included in the surviving spouse's estate because of his/her testamentary power of appointment; thus, reduction of the value of the trust's principal through lifetime gifts may be wise.

There are an unlimited number of uses of trusts designed

to meet the needs of special situations. Of course, it is not feasible or even possible to list or discuss every one of these. The illustrations discussed above were presented to give the reader some insight into the many uses and advantages of trusts in estate planning.

CONCLUSION

The flexibility and benefits of both the *inter vivos* and testamentary trusts place them among the most effective tools of estate planning. A properly conceived trust, drawn with due regard for economic and family considerations as well as tax benefits, can insulate trust property from state tax and prevent unnecessary attribution of trust income.

When a trust is established, it is natural and proper that the settlor and his/her advisors plan it in such a way as to obtain the most favorable tax consequences. But the purpose of its establishment is ordinarily not just to save taxes; these savings are incidental, if they can be realized at all, to other elements in the process of carrying out the strong social and economic purposes of providing an orderly and sensible devolution of property.

Thus, there are many factors other than the tax advantages to consider before including a trust in the estate plan. Consideration must be given to the economic and social needs of the proposed beneficiaries of the trust, and it must be determined that the trust can reasonably satisfy these needs. The trust and the results of its operation must be evaluated in light of the overall objectives of the estate owner. If the trust is to be implemented, it must help rather than hinder the achievement of the estate owner's objectives. Also, an evaluation must be made of the management of the trust property; that is, the ability and accomplishments of the trustee must be considered.

NOTES

1. George C. Bogert and George T. Bogert, *The Law of Trusts and Trustees,* 2d ed. (St. Paul, Minn.: West Publishing, 1965), sec. 1.
2. American Law Institute, *Restatement of the Law, Second, Trusts,* 2d ed. (St. Paul, Minn.: American Law Institute Publishers, 1959), sec. 368.

3. George C. Bogert, *Handbook of the Law of Trusts,* 4th ed. (St. Paul, Minn.: West Publishing, 1963), p. 142.
4. *Richard I. Armantrout et al.,* 67 T.C. 996 (1977); Rev. Rul. 75-448, 1975-2 C.B. 55.
5. Section 2056(b)(7)(B)(ii).
6. Edwin H. Corbin, "Living Trusts in Action," *Trusts and Estates* 106 (July 1967), p. 625.
7. Ibid., p. 627.
8. A. James Casner, *Estate Planning,* vol. 1, 3d ed. (Boston: Little, Brown, 1961), p. 94.
9. *American Law Reports Annotated,* LXIV (Rochester, N.Y.: The Lawyers Co-Operative Publishing Company, 1929), p. 466; *American Law Reports Annotated Second Series,* XLIV (Rochester, N.Y.: The Lawyers Co-Operative Publishing Company, 1956), p. 521.
10. William Schwartz, *Future Interest and Estate Planning* (Cincinnati: The W. H. Anderson Company, 1965), pp. 86–87.
11. Section 677(b); see *Morrill* v. *U.S.,* 228 F. Suppl. 734(D. Me. 1964).
12. Section 673(c).
13. Gilbert Thomas Stephenson, *Estates and Trusts,* 4th ed. (New York: Appleton-Century-Crofts, 1965), pp. 102–3.
14. Ibid., p. 329.
15. Section 678(c).
16. Reg. 1.678(c)-1(b).
17. Reg. 1.678(c)-1(a).
18. *U.S.* v. *Grace,* 395 U.S. 316 (1969).
19. *Estate of Levy,* 43 T.C.M 910 (1983).
20. Rev. Rul. 75-257 through 75-260.

10

Philanthropy in Your Estate Plan

What always happens—what has happened in every nation that has ever set up a graduated income tax—is that the highest actual rates are paid by the middle class.

—from The April Game

Motivated by social or moral reasons, many people combine tax savings with philanthropy. Gifts to charitable organizations can be made during lifetime or at death through a will. This chapter is devoted exclusively to the restrictions on such contributions and to significant tax savings that can result from properly planned transactions. Any estate plan should consider the benefits of charitable giving.

HOW TO TREAT CONTRIBUTIONS

Lifetime contributions to certain qualified organizations are generally deductible from adjusted gross income (D from AGI) by taxpayers. Effective for contributions made after December 31, 1981, people who do not itemize their personal deductions are allowed to deduct a portion of their charitable contributions from gross income. This provision will expire in 1987 unless Congress passes a new law, but from 1982 through 1986 the amount of the deduction for nonitemizers is as follows:

1982	25 percent of first $100 (i.e., maximum is $25).
1983	25 percent of first $100 (i.e., maximum is $25).
1984	25 percent of first $300 (i.e., maximum is $75).
1985	50 percent of all contributions.
1986	100 percent of all contributions.

Since charitable contributions are generally D from AGI, taxpayers should make charitable contributions only in years in which they have enough itemized deductions to exceed their zero-bracket amount; otherwise, the contributions are useless as tax savings. Among charitable organizations generally qualified as recipients are a church or association of churches; a college or university; a hospital; governmental units; certain private foundations; a community chest, trust, fund, or foundation that is organized and operated exclusively for religious, charitable, scientific, literary, or educational purposes, or for the prevention of cruelty to children or animals; and other organizations that are exempted from taxation under Section 501(a) of the Internal Revenue Code.

Details of specific national nonprofit charities may be obtained by writing to the Solicitation Review Manager, Council of Better Business Bureaus, 1150 Seventeenth Street, N.W., Washington, D.C. 20036. For local charities, consult with the Chamber of Commerce or Better Business Bureau. Keep in mind that lifetime charitable gifts reduce one's estate, which in turn reduces the estate tax.

In order to appreciate the limitations on lifetime charitable contributions, one must understand that there are two types of charitable organizations: the public charity and the private charity. Gifts to public charities qualify for a 50 percent ceiling; that is, taxpayers can deduct up to 50 percent of their "contribution base." Those contributions in excess of this ceiling can be carried over for the next five tax years. A person's contribution base is his/her adjusted gross income, disregarding any net operating-loss carry-back. The charities qualifying for the 50 percent ceiling include most churches, American Red Cross, American Philatelic Society, American Numismatic Association, Boy Scouts, Girl Scouts, Ford Foundation, private operating foundations, and many other well-known charities. When in doubt, ask the potential charitable organizations if contributions to them qualify for a deduction.

All other qualified charities that are not 50 percent charities are 30 percent charities, such as private nonoperating foundations or organizations (for example, the Crumbley and Milam Foundation). Gifts to these charities are deductible up to the lesser of 30 percent of the taxpayer's contribution base or 50 percent of the contribution base minus contributions to 50 percent charities (including carryovers of such contributions and no reduction for the 30 percent ceiling on appreciated property). For example, if you contribute 38 percent of your contribution base to a 50 percent charity (say, a church) your contributions to 30 percent charities are deductible only up to 12 percent of your contribution base. You are allowed to carry over any excess gifts to 30 percent charities.

There are two types of private foundations: private operating foundations and private nonoperating foundations. A private operating foundation is actively engaged in the conduct of charitable activities, whereas a private nonoperating foundation has a principal activity of making grants to others for charitable, educational, or religious purposes. A private operating foundation has an overall 50 percent ceiling on contributions, and a nonoperating foundation has a 30 percent overall ceiling.

An individual whose business is operated as a corporate organization may also have the corporation make charitable gifts. A corporation is allowed to deduct charitable contributions up to 10 percent of its taxable income per year (5 percent before 1982). An excess contribution in any one year may be carried over and is deductible pro rata for each of the five succeeding tax years. If the corporation is in the 46 percent tax bracket, approximately one half of any contribution is, in effect, contributed by the federal government.

Ordinary Income-Type Property

Three sets of tax rules apply to all contributions of appreciated property (that is, all property that would give rise to any gain if sold, such as stocks, diamonds, rare coins or stamps, antiques, and jewelry):

1. Ordinary income-type property.
2. Tangible, personal, capital-gain property, and some contributions of capital-gain property to certain private nonoperating foundations.
3. Appreciated capital-gain property.

Property appreciation that would not be all long-term capital gain to the contributor if it were sold at its fair market value on the date it was contributed falls into this first category of ordinary income-type property. For a charitable contribution of any property that gives rise to an ordinary-income appreciation on disposition, the property's fair market value is reduced by the amount of the ordinary-income appreciation in order to determine the deductible amount.

EXAMPLE 1. L purchased a painting for $2,500 and contributed it to a museum four months later when it was worth $4,000. Since the $1,500 of appreciation is short-term gain, L's charitable deduction is only $2,500 ($4,000 − $1,500).

If a dealer gives assets from his/her inventory to a charity, such property falls within this first category. That is, if the assets are sold from inventory, any income would be ordinary income. The critical question is whether an individual is a dealer or a nondealer. A person who is not a dealer must take care to avoid this dealer "taint." Too many transactions may often cause an IRS agent to classify an individual as a dealer; then any gains on the contribution of property would be ordinary income rather than capital gain.

Obviously, an individual should avoid gifts of short-term and ordinary-income property to charities whenever possible. Such property should be donated to a charity in a will in order to obtain a full estate tax deduction. Or a person may wish to leave ordinary-income property in a will to his/her children, who will get a stepped-up basis for appreciation; they can then give the property to a charity and obtain a full income tax deduction.

Tangible Personal Capital-Gain Property

A second category of appreciated property involves the contribution of tangible, personal, capital-gain property. As a general rule, such property receives a full deduction. Capital-gain property is a capital asset and, if sold at the time contributed, will result in a long-term capital gain. A rare coin or stamp collection held by a collector or investor for at least six months and one day falls within this definition of capital-gain property (but not qualified appreciated stock). However, a coin or stamp collection in the inventory of a dealer would not fall within this definition but would be considered to be ordinary-income property.

Two exceptions apply to this second category. First, if the asset contributed is tangible personal property, then in order to qualify for the full deduction, its utilization by the charity must be directly related to the exempt function of the charity. If not directly related to the exempt function of the charity, then the deduction is limited to cost plus 60 percent of the appreciation.

EXAMPLE 2. Jerry purchases a stamp collection for $2,500, holds it for 18 months, and then contributes it to a church when it is worth $4,000. The church sells it. Since the stamps are not directly related to the exempt function of the church, the deduction would be limited to Jerry's cost of purchase plus 60 percent of the appreciation, $900—a total deduction of $3,400. However, if the stamps were donated to a museum to be used for display purposes, Jerry would be entitled to the larger $4,000 deduction.

Thus, whether a contribution is for an unrelated use or directly related use by a charity is very important to a taxpayer. The term *unrelated use* means a use unrelated to the purpose or function constituting the exemption tax basis of the charitable organization. For example, if a rare gem collection that has been contributed to an educational institution is used for educational purposes by placing it in a library for display and study by students, the use is not an unrelated use. But if the collection is sold and the proceeds are used by the organization for educational purposes, the use of the property is an unrelated use. If a gem collection is contributed to a charitable organization or governmental unit, the use of the collection is not an unrelated use if the donee sells or otherwise disposes of an insubstantial portion of the collection. Obviously, potential donors of appreciated tangible personal property must match the item of property to the appropriate charity. For example, rare coins should be given to the American Numismatic Association, rare stamps to the American Philatelic Society, and so forth.

Maintenance of Proof

What proof of use should taxpayers maintain? First, they may establish that the property is not in fact put to an unrelated use by the charity. Or, second, at the time of the contribution it is reasonable to anticipate that the property will not be put to an unrelated use by the charity. Taxpayers who give property to a museum, if the donated property is of a general type normally retained by the museum, may reasonably anticipate (unless they have actual knowledge to the contrary) that the property will not be put to an unrelated use, regardless of whether it is later sold or exchanged with another museum.

Taxpayers who make a charitable contribution of appreciated artistic articles (for example, antiques, etchings, furs, jewelry) and claim a deduction in excess of $200 must attach to their income tax return the following information:

1. Name and address of the organization to which the contribution was made.
2. The date of the actual contribution.
3. A detailed description of the property (such as coins or stamps) and its condition.
4. The manner of acquisition (by purchase, gift, inheritance, or other means).
5. The fair market value of the property along with the method utilized in determining the fair market value. (If there was an appraisal, a copy of the appraiser's signed report should be provided.)
6. The cost or adjusted basis of the property.
7. Where the deduction is reduced by any of the appreciation, the reduced amount.
8. Any agreement or understanding between the taxpayer and the charity.
9. The total amount claimed as a deduction for the tax year.

Any deduction for a charitable contribution must be substantiated, when required by the district director, by a statement from the organization to which the contribution was made. This statement should indicate whether the organization is a domestic organization, the name and address of the contributor, the amount of the contribution, the date of actual receipt of the contribution, and whatever additional information the district director may deem necessary. When the property has a fair market value in excess of $200 at the time of receipt, the statement should also indicate the location of each item, if it is retained by the organization, the amount received by the organization on any sale of the property, the date of sale, or, in case of disposition other than sale, the method of disposition. The statement should indicate the use of the property by the organization and whether or not it is used for a purpose or function constituting the basis for the charity's exemption from income tax under Internal Revenue Code Section 501 or, in the case of a governmental unit, whether or not it is used exclusively for public purposes.

The donee-charity must file an information return on disposition of charitable deduction property. This filing requirement is necessary where the property's value exceeds $5,000 and the donee sells it within two years of the date it was contributed. A $50 penalty is imposed for each failure to file such return.

Gifts to Private Foundations

A second type of transaction may cause a 40 percent reduction in the appreciation of the contributed property. If capital-gain property (other than qualified appreciated stock) is given to a private nonoperating foundation (which is not a private operating foundation or community foundation), and the donor does not make qualifying distributions equal to the amount of such contributions within two and one half months after the close of the year, then the deduction is limited to the property's fair market value minus 40 percent of the appreciation (28/46 in the case of a corporation).

Any contribution of "qualified appreciated stock" to a nonoperating foundation may be taken at fair market value (and not reduced by 40 percent of the appreciation). Qualified appreciated stock is stock held for more than six months for which market quotations are readily available.

EXAMPLE 3. Chuck has an adjusted gross income of $30,000 in 1985 and contributes $12,000 to a public charity and $9,000 to a private operating foundation. Chuck could deduct a total of $15,000 in 1985 (50% × $30,000), with a $6,000 carryover for up to five years.

Appreciated Capital-Gain Property

A third category of appreciated property involves the contribution of appreciated capital-gain property to a charity that is directly related to an exempt function. Capital-gain property is a capital asset and, if sold at the time contributed, gives rise only to long-term capital gain. Diamonds or gems, rare coins or stamps, antiques, and similar items qualify as capital assets, and if sold at the time contributed, give rise only to long-term capital gain. Such items qualify as capital-gain property. When a taxpayer contributes appreciated capital-gain property to a qualified charity, his/her deduction ceiling is reduced to 30 percent, rather than the normal 50 percent, unless the taxpayer makes a special election to reduce the amount of this contribution (the percentage is 20 percent for nonoperating foundations).

In other words, the total amount of contribution of capital-gain property considered for deduction purposes for any tax year cannot exceed 30 percent of the taxpayer's contribution base (generally, adjusted gross income). When an individual makes a special election, his/her deduction ceiling remains at 50 percent along with a 50 percent carryover, but the taxpayer may deduct only the basis of the capital-gain property plus 60 percent of any appreciation.

EXAMPLE 4. Chuck Charitable, who has a $10,000 adjusted gross income, makes a charitable contribution during 19X7 of part of his rare stamp collection to the American Philatelic Society for display purposes. The portion of the collection contributed has a basis of $2,000 but is valued at $10,000 on the date of contribution. Under the general rule, he has made a contribution of $10,000. During 19X7 Chuck may deduct $3,000 (30% × $10,000) and have a contribution carryover of $7,000 (but subject to the 30 percent carryover rule).

On the other hand, if Chuck so desires, he may elect to value his contribution at $6,800 ($2,000 basis plus 60 percent of $8,000 appreciation). In this case, he could deduct $5,000 during 19X7 (50% × $10,000) with a contribution carryover of $1,800 (subject to the 50 percent carryover rule). Taxpayers probably will not wish to elect the 50 percent rule when they make a contribution of highly appreciated property.

Of course, a taxpayer who owns property that is worth substantially less than its cost basis should sell it and then contribute the proceeds to the charity.

If a person contributes property to a charitable organization and pays an appraisal fee to a dealer in order to determine the fair market value of the property, the appraisal expenses are deductible from that person's adjusted gross income, provided he/she itemized deductions and does not use the standard deduction.

These rules are summarized in Table 6.

TABLE 6   Charitable Contribution Summary

	Overall Ceiling Limitation	Capital Gain Property	Carryover Period
Public charities	50%	30%	5 years
Private operating foundations	50	30	5 years
Private nonoperating foundations	30	20*	5 years

*Does not have to be reduced by 40 percent of the appreciation if qualified appreciated stock.

Written Appraisal Requirement

A written appraisal is required for charitable gift property (other than publicly traded securities) made after 1984 where the gift exceeds $5,000. A qualified appraisal summary must be attached to the return on which a deduction is claimed. If a taxpayer makes gifts of two or more similar items, they are added together in determining whether the $5,000 limit is exceeded. Examples of similar items are a group of stamps, coins, books, or lithographs.

Bargain Sale of Property

A bargain sale may be an excellent technique to minimize a donor's out-of-pocket cost. Before the law was changed in 1969, taxpayers could sell appreciated property at cost to a charity and end up with their investment back without any tax plus a charitable deduction for the appreciation. Now, however, they must allocate their cost basis between the part of the property that they sold and the part that is a gift. Presto, such taxpayers have a taxable gain on the bargain sale, but they still have minimized the out-of-pocket cost of their charitable gift. On the other hand, donors who wish to give the charity the largest benefit should make an ordinary gift to their selected charity.

EXAMPLE 5. Cherry Charitable sells her rare coin collection worth $10,000 (which has been held a number of years) to a museum for her cost of $4,000. She must allocate 60 percent of her cost ($2,400) to the portion given and 40 percent ($1,600) to the portion sold. If she is in the 50 percent tax bracket, her $6,000 gift ($10,000 − $4,000) saves her $3,000 in taxes, and she recovers her $4,000 investment—a nice total of $7,000. She will pay a tax of no more than $600 on her $2,400 ($4,000 − $1,600) long-term capital gain (25% × $2,400). Her net return is thus $6,400, and her favorite charity has $6,000 more in its coffers.

Suppose Cherry makes an outright gift of the coins to the museum. If the coins are directly related to the exempt function of the museum, the $10,000 gift saves her $5,000, and the museum gets the full $10,000 tax basis.

Contribution of Services

No deduction is allowed for the contribution of services. For example, suppose you donate your services to the nonprofit Girl Scouts organization. The cost of your time is not deductible. However, unreimbursed expenditures, such as transportation or lodging made incidental to the rendering of services to a qualified organization, are deductible as contributions. The standard mileage rate for computing the cost of operating an automobile in rendering this service is 12 cents per mile. Parking fees and tolls are deductible in addition to this mileage allowance.

Future Interest

A transfer of a future interest in property to a qualified charity may not be deducted as a charitable contribution until all intervening interest in and rights to the possession or enjoyment of the property have expired. Thus, except for a remainder interest in a residence or farm, and certain remainder interest in a trust, no deduction is allowed for a gift in the future. In order for a remainder interest in a trust to qualify for a charitable deduction, any transfer must be in the form of a charitable remainder annuity trust or charitable remainder unitrust (defined in Section 644) or a pooled-income fund [defined in Section 642(c)]. In order for an income or lead interest to charity to be deductible, the transfer must be in the form of an annuity or a unitrust interest [defined in Section 170(f)(2)(B)]. For more detail, see Chapter 6.

Suppose an individual conveys by deed of gift to a museum the title to a gem collection in 19X7, but reserves the right to the use, possession, and enjoyment of the collection during his/her lifetime. At the time of the gift, the value of the gem collection is $40,000. Since the contribution consists of a future interest in tangible personal property in which the taxpayer has retained an intervening interest, no contribution is considered to have been made in 19X7. Assume that the taxpayer relinquishes all right to the use, possession, and enjoyment of the gem collection and delivers it to the museum in 19X8, when the collection is worth $45,000. In this case the taxpayer is treated as having made a charitable contribution of $45,000 in 19X8.

Where a charitable gift exceeds $10,000 or is a future-interest gift, the transfer must eventually be reported on a gift tax return. But when the charitable gift is reported, the taxpayer is allowed a deduction on the gift tax return (that is, a "wash" effect). There is no percentage limitation as to the amount deductible on the gift tax return.

A deduction is allowed on the federal estate tax return for any bequests, legacies, devises, or transfers to a charitable organization or unit of government at the decedent's death. This deduction is more fully discussed in Chapter 6.

Disclaimers

A specific bequest to a charity coupled with a disclaimer in favor of a charity can be a valuable provision in a will. If the estate tax rate is less than the income tax rate of the heirs, a greater benefit would occur if the heir made the charitable contribution. Further, in a small estate the deduction is wasted on the estate tax return because the estate is less than the exemption equivalent.

To provide maximum flexibility, a taxpayer may wish to specifically bequeath to his/her children along with a provision that, if the children disclaim any amount given, such amount is to be distributed to the charity of the decedent's choice. This bequest/disclaimer provision allows the heirs to determine upon decedent's death what is more advantageous, an estate deduction or an individual income tax deduction. Keep in mind that the charitable bequest can be larger in the will since the child can reduce the amount going to the charity if the child's personal financial situation changes.

Charitable Gifts of Stock of Closely Held Corporation

A charitable gift of stock of a closely held corporation to a charity, followed by a corporate redemption of the stock from the charity, can be a valuable tax-planning strategy. The donor obtains a charitable contribution deduction for the fair market value of the stock and does not incur a dividend or capital gain tax, even though the funds that go to the charity come from the corporation. If the donor is the sole shareholder, no dilution of ownership occurs. The charity should not be legally obligated to go through with the redemption, and the donor should probably not contribute more than 10 percent of the stock of the corporation [see Section 170(e)(5)(c)].

11

Compensation and Estate Planning

Nothing is easier than the expenditure of public money. It doesn't appear to belong to anyone. The temptation is overwhelming to bestow it on somebody.

—*Calvin Coolidge*

Corporate executives are likely to be compensated in various ways. Compensation plans range from current salary to death-benefit-only plans. Since these various forms of executive compensation are significantly different, executives must evaluate not only the economic impact of their compensation plans but also the income and estate tax ramifications.

Before considering the estate tax consequences and estate planning avenues involving compensation, a brief review of the income tax considerations is necessary.

INCOME TAXATION OF COMPENSATION

Salaries, commissions, and bonuses are taxed to cash basis taxpayers in the year they receive such payment. Even though such types of compensation leave little room for tax planning, such earned income is taxed at a maximum rate of 50 percent. In many situations, this tax of 50 percent, along with a high rate of inflation, enhances the desirability of taking compensation in the form of current cash payments.

Retirement Plans

Since the enactment of the Employee Retirement Income Security Act of 1974 (ERISA) and all its many requirements, a large number of corporations have dropped their qualified retirement plans. These employers as well as many others have turned to nonqualified plans that can be discriminatory and do not have to meet any special statutory provisions. Nonqualified plans may take any number of forms. For instance, the plan may be funded or unfunded, an employee trust may or may not be set up, or the plan may simply state that payments will be made in the future. These payments or the amounts thereof may or may not be based on future events, continued service by the employee, or other conditions, and some nonqualified plans may be purely voluntary arrangements.

The income tax consequences of nonqualified plans depend on the nature, type, and conditions of the plan and are governed by Section 83. If the plan is funded and the employee is given immediate rights that are not subject to risks, the employee must include in gross income each year the amount of contributions made by the employer on his/her account. However, if the employee's rights are subject to a substantial risk of forfeiture (SRF), the employee has no immediate income or income tax, but in the year in which his/her rights become nonforfeitable (vested) or the SRF lapses, the entire value of his/her interest in the fund must be included in income for tax purposes. If the employee is required to perform future services as a condition of vesting, his/her rights are deemed to be subject to a substantial risk of forfeiture.

If the nonqualified plan is unfunded, the employee has no income for tax purposes until the year in which funds are actually or constructively received. Constructive receipt of funds, discussed later in this chapter, has been the downfall of many taxpayers. The taxpayer should carefully avoid the pitfalls of constructive receipt. Rev. Rul. 60-31 gives some insight into determining what types of deferred compensation will or will not be treated as constructively received.

Even with all the additional requirements and restrictions imposed by ERISA, qualified pension and profit-sharing plans continue to be two of the primary types of executive compensation. The popularity of these plans may be traced to their favored tax treatment. The employer gets an immediate tax deduction for contributions made to the plan, but the employee is not taxed until he/she actually receives the benefits. The tax treatment then depends on whether the employee elects to take the benefits in a lump sum or in an annuity.

Annuity distribution. If the employee elects to take the benefits in annuity form, the benefits received are taxed in accordance with Section 72.[1] Section 72 provides for the computation of an exclusion ratio. This exclusion ratio is applied to all benefits received by the employee, and the ratio determines the amount of the benefit that can be excluded from income for income tax purposes. The remainder of each payment must be included in the taxpayer's gross income. The exclusion ratio is determined by dividing the employee's cost (if any) by the employee's expected return under the annuity contract. The taxpayer's expected return is generally found by multiplying the amount of the annual payment under the contract by the proper multiple, which is determined by using the actuarial tables prescribed in Section 72 of the regulations. The multiple is basically the number of years in the person's estimated remaining life span. Once the exclusion ratio is computed, it remains constant regardless of the time period for which the payments are made.

There is one major exception to Section 72 rules. If the employee will receive all his/her cost in the plan within the first three years, no exclusion ratio is computed. Instead, the taxpayer excludes all benefits from gross income until he/she has fully recovered the cost. From that point, 100 percent of the additional benefits received are included in gross income. Of course, if the employee has made no contributions to the plan, 100 percent of all payments received are included in gross income for income tax purposes.

Profit-Sharing Plans

An employee who elects to receive a lump-sum distribution from a qualified plan has entirely different income tax consequences. The income taxation of lump-sum distribution was changed by the enactment of ERISA in 1973. Basically, the distribution is divided into two portions: a capital-gain portion and an ordinary-income portion. The capital-gain portion is attributable to pre-1974 contributions, and the ordinary-income portion is attributable to post-1973 contributions. The ordinary income portion is determined this way:

$$\text{Taxable amount of distribution} \times \frac{\begin{array}{c}\text{Calendar year of}\\ \text{participation after 1973}\end{array}}{\begin{array}{c}\text{Total calendar years}\\ \text{of participation}\end{array}}$$

The remainder of the distribution may be treated as a long-term capital gain. However, 60 percent of any long-term capital gain may be subjected to an alternative tax. In addition, ERISA provides a 10-year-forward averaging rule for the ordinary-income portion that can be elected for the entire distribution. The 10-year-forward averaging rule is quite complicated and beyond the scope of this book, but the authors strongly recommend that all executive employees seek competent professional advice in examining the tax consequences of lump-sum distributions versus annuities from qualified plans.

Lump sum refers to a distribution of the entire balance to the credit of the participant, calculated as of the date of payment, paid within one taxable year to the beneficiary on account of the participant's death. Thus, a taxpayer may pay tax currently or defer it under favorable rules:

1. The taxpayer may elect a 10-year averaging technique on part of the distribution and long-term capital gain on the remainder (the portion of the distribution related to the service of the participant prior to January 1, 1974).

2. The taxpayer may elect a 10-year averaging technique on the entire distribution, because in some instances ordinary-income treatment is more favorable than capital-gain treatment.

3. The taxpayer may roll the funds over into his next employer's retirement plan or into an individual retirement account (IRA). A later distribution from an IRA does not qualify for favorable lump-sum treatment, but does qualify for five-year income averaging. The major advantage of a rollover is that the entire sum compounds tax-free until the taxpayer withdraws it.

A taxpayer should pay the tax currently (i.e., under 1 or 2 above) if the tax liability is less than the present value of the expected future tax. Otherwise, the taxpayer should defer it under 3 above. At midcareer a rollover is probably best. Around age 65 the decision is not always clear-cut.

Employee-only contribution plans. Where substantially all (85 percent or more) of the contributions under a qualified plan are derived from employee contributions, any withdrawals (or loans) by the employee from the plan are taxable as income to the extent of the earnings in the employee's account. Thus, not only are the earnings ineligible for the 10-year averaging technique but also employee contributions have been withdrawn from the plan.

EXAMPLE 1. Taxpayer has contributed $4,000 a year for four years to a plan under which substantially all the benefits are derived from employee contributions. In December 1985, her account is valued at $17,100 when she withdraws $4,000. She realizes $1,100 in income ($17,100 − $16,000) and receives $2,900 as a return of capital, with $13,100 remaining in her account.

Stock Distributions

Another type of deferred compensation is payable in the form of restricted property, such as restricted stock. These restrictions are of various types, such as a requirement that the employee does not actually receive the stock or has to return the stock if an additional period of employment is not completed. Of course, these restrictions usually prohibit the employee from selling the stock during this time period. Normally, an employee is taxed on the excess of the fair market value of the property over cost (if any) of that property in the first tax year that the property is either transferable or is not subject to a substantial risk of forfeiture. By definition, there is a substantial risk of forfeiture if the employee's right to the property is conditional on performing substantial future services.[2]

Stock options are still another form of executive compensation. Stock options basically fall into two groups: statutory and nonqualified.

An incentive stock option (ISO) is a type of statutory stock option. There are no tax consequences when an ISO is granted to an employee or when it is exercised. The employee is generally taxed at capital-gain rates when the exercised stock is sold. In general, no business-expense deduction is allowed to the employer with respect to an ISO.

In order to receive ISO treatment, an employee must not dispose of the stock within two years after the option is granted and must hold the stock itself for at least one year. If all requirements are met other than the holding periods, any gain taxed on the sale date is ordinary income rather than capital gain, and the employer is allowed a business-expense deduction (assuming the employer has kept an accurate record of the early sale and is aware that a deduction is available). The spread (difference between the option price and the fair market value on the exercise date) is a tax-preference item.

When an employee receives a nonqualified stock option, it is necessary to determine whether the stock has a readily ascertainable value. A stock option is deemed to have such value if it is actively traded on an established market or meets other requirements specified in Reg. 1.421-6(c)(3). If the stock has a readily ascertainable value (that is, a warrant), the employee has taxable income to the extent of the difference in the value of the option and the amount (if any) paid for it.[3] If the option does not have a readily ascertainable value, the employee would realize no income upon receiving the option, but instead would have taxable income if the option is exercised. The amount of taxable income is the difference between the fair market value of the stock and the price paid for such stock.[4]

EXAMPLE 2. An executive is in the 50 percent tax bracket. He receives an ISO in 1982 with the following values:

	FMV
1982 (grant date)	$40,000
1983 (exercise date)	70,000
1985 (sales date)	90,000

His cash proceeds as compared to a nonqualified stock option are $40,000 versus $31,000 (see Table 7).

Here the employer receives a $30,000 deduction for a nonqualified stock option but no deduction for an ISO. If the employer is in the 46 percent tax bracket, the corporation would lose a $13,800 tax benefit (.46 × $30,000) in order to provide the executive with $9,000 more cash.

TABLE 7

	ISO	Nonqualified
Grant date income	–0–	–0–
Exercise date income	–0–	$30,000
Tax at 50 percent		– 15,000
		$15,000
Proceeds on sale	$90,000	90,000
Less basis	– 40,000	– 70,000
	50,000	20,000
Tax at 20 percent	– 10,000	– 4,000
Gain	40,000	16,000
Cash proceeds	$40,000	$31,000

If a company wishes to give more than $100,000 per year to any executive, it should give a $100,000 ISO plus separate nonqualified stock options.

Life insurance benefits. From a tax viewpoint, life insurance is a desirable fringe benefit. If the company provides the employee with group-term insurance, there is no income to the employee unless the face value of the policy exceeds $50,000. When the face value exceeds $50,000, the employee must include in his/her gross income an amount that represents the cost of the insurance in excess of $50,000. However, this amount is determined according to tables prescribed in Reg. 1.79-3. The rates in these schedules are quite low and do not in any way represent the actual cost of the insurance. For example, the amount included in income for a $250,000 group-term policy for a 46-year-old employee would be only $960.

Types of insurance other than group term provided for the employee by the employer generate taxable income to the employee in the amount of the cost of the insurance.

Another advantage to life insurance is that proceeds paid to a beneficiary by reason of death do not constitute income for income tax purposes. There is one exception to this rule, and that is where the proceeds are paid in installments. In such a situation, the interest part of the payment is deemed to be taxable income. However, if the beneficiary is the spouse of the insured, he/she may exclude the interest up to a maximum of $1,000 per year.[5]

Death-benefit-only plan. Another form of executive compensation that has been gaining in popularity is the death-benefit-only plan. Under such a plan, the corporation usually agrees to pay some amount to the deceased employee's heirs or estate. Generally, there are no income consequences to the employee because at no time are any benefits received. At the time of distribution, the beneficiary must include the payments in his/her gross income for income tax purposes. However, up to $5,000 may be excluded under Section 101(b). This exclusion applies only to amounts paid on account of the employee's death, and only if the employee had no vested rights in the payments before death. However the exclusion would still apply to vested benefits paid under a qualified plan if the benefits were paid to the employee's beneficiary by a lump-sum distribution within one tax year.[6]

ESTATE TAXATION OF COMPENSATION

With respect to estate tax, the major Code sections that deal with retirement benefits include the following:

Section 2033. Property in which the decedent had an interest.

Section 2035. Transactions in contemplation of death.

Section 2036. Transfers with retained life estate.

Section 2037. Transfers taking effect at death.

Section 2038. Revocable transfers.

Section 2039. Annuities

Therefore, in planning an estate, an employee must pay particular attention to these sections when making decisions concerning retirement plans and/or funds. The following pages outline some of the potential tax consequences and provide some tips for tax-planning devices.

Nonqualified Retirement Plans

If the executive-employee is covered by a nonqualified plan, it is quite difficult to generalize as to the tax consequences because of the many variations that could exist in the plans. However, deferred compensation payable to the employee's estate is generally included in the gross estate under Section

2033. If the deferred compensation is payable to any other beneficiary, it is normally included in the gross estate under Section 2039. Section 2039 deals with annuities that are receivable by a beneficiary as a result of the beneficiary's surviving the taxpayer (decedent).

In order for Section 2039 to apply, all four of the following conditions must exist:

1. The decedent was receiving or had the right to receive payment.

2. The right to such payment was for the decedent's life or for a period not ascertainable without reference to his/ her death.

3. The decedent contributed to the cost of the contract.

4. The beneficiary is entitled to the benefits by reason of surviving the decedent.[7]

In the case of a nonqualified plan, any contributions made to the plan by the employer are deemed to be contributed by the decedent-employee, and thus condition 3 is met.

Once it has been determined that an annuity is to be included in the gross estate, the value of the annuity is determined according to Section 2039(b). Basically, this value is calculated by multiplying the value of the annuity by a fraction in which the numerator is the amount of the purchase price contributed by the decedent and the denominator is the total cost of the annuity. Since the employer's contribution to a nonqualified annuity is attributable to the employee, usually this fraction is 100 percent. The value of the annuity is the fair market value of the annuity contract as of the date of the decedent's death, and it is usually determined by the actuarial tables found in Reg. 20.2031-8 and Reg. 20.2031-10.

Tax-planning tips for nonqualified plans. An employee may be able to avoid estate tax treatment for survivor death benefits if he/she has no right to lifetime payments and cannot change the beneficiaries. However, even here the IRS may attempt to use the gift tax to attach such benefits. This was the situation in Rev. Rul. 81-31.[8].

An employment agreement outlined in Rev. Rul. 81-31 provided that in consideration for future services to be rendered by employee E, the employer corporation had agreed to pay death benefits to E's surviving spouse if E was employed by the corporation at the date of his death. The benefits were twice E's annual salary at death. E had no right to lifetime payments, nor could he change the beneficiaries. Further, no amount was payable to E's estate in the event of the spouse's prior death. The ruling held that E had made a taxable gift equal to the survivor death benefits at the time of E's death. The unlimited marital deduction after 1981 should eliminate any resulting tax from this revenue ruling.

In planning for survivor death benefits, the employee should arrange to have no right to name or change beneficiaries nor to vary the amounts going to any beneficiary. The employee should not have the right to receive payments after employment has ended. Finally, the employee's estate should not be named as a contingent beneficiary.[9]

Qualified Retirement Plans

The law provides favored tax treatment to qualified retirement plans. As discussed earlier in this chapter, the employee is not taxed on the employer's contributions until the benefits are received. In addition, there are estate tax advantages in the form of an exclusion from the gross estate for a portion of the death benefits paid to a qualified beneficiary under a qualified plan (prior to 1985).

Qualification of named beneficiary. Prior to 1985, Section 2039(c) provided for an exclusion from the employee-decedent's gross estate of annuities or other payments (other than lump-sum distributions) that are made to a named beneficiary other than the decedent's estate or executor. This exclusion was limited to $100,000. In order to qualify, these benefits must be paid under a qualified plan or annuity contract purchased for an employee by a tax-exempt school, publicly supported charity, or retired serviceman's family-protection plan. This exclusion is limited to the portion of the benefits paid to a qualified beneficiary and which are attributable to the employer's contributions. The benefits attributable to the employee's contributions must be included in the estate. The Tax Reform Act of 1976 made a very important change in this exclusion. For employees dying after December 31, 1976, the benefits must be paid in some form other than a lump-sum distribution if the exclusion is to apply. Payments received by the beneficiary within one taxable year are deemed to be a lump-sum distribution.[10]

For decedents dying after December 31, 1984, the $100,000 exclusion in Section 2039(c) is repealed. Thus, there is no longer an exclusion for qualified plans, IRAs, tax-sheltered annuities, and military retirement plans. Estate plans may have to be changed where a credit shelter trust was the recipient of $100,000 worth of the proceeds. Otherwise, the credit shelter trust may be overfunded, which will cause the marital deduction amount to be underfunded—resulting in a greater estate tax.

After 1984, the only exclusion in Section 2039(c) involves a community-property interest. If a person has a community-property interest in his/her spouse's vested interest in a qualified retirement plan based solely on employer contributions to such plan (which were not treated as employee contributions) and such spouse dies before the covered employee, the deceased spouse's community interest is excluded from his/her gross estate. Contributions by the employer (or former employer) to a qualified retirement plan are not considered as being contributed by the decedent.

Distribution requirement. The entire interest of an employee must be distributed no later than the required commencement date for plan years beginning after 1984. Predeath distributions must begin by April 1 of the year following the year the participant turns 70½ or retires (whichever is later). As an alternative, the entire interest may be distributed in the form of an annuity, beginning no later than the required commencement date over either (1) the life of the employee, (2) the lives of the employee and a designated beneficiary, or (3) a period not extending beyond the life expectancy of the employee (and a designated beneficiary).

Where a participant is a 5 percent owner, the employee's entire interest must be distributed no later than April 1 of the calendar year following the plan year even though the employee has not retired.

Other rules apply to postdeath plan distributions. Where distributions have begun prior to the participant's death, the distributions must be made at least as rapidly as distributions that were begun before death. The beneficiary may elect to accelerate the distribution. For distributions beginning at death, the entire interest generally must be distributed within five years after the participant's death or within five years of the death of the surviving spouse. Payments must begin within 90 days of the death.

Rollover retirement or annuity withdrawals. If an employee's qualified plan is terminated, or if an employee elects a lump-sum withdrawal, taxation still can be avoided upon his/her withdrawal. This avoidance can be done by "rolling over" the employee's entire lump-sum withdrawal into an individual retirement account or annuity or into another qualified plan if the employee takes a new job. For such an election to qualify, it must be completed within 60 days of the distribution of the proceeds from the qualified plan. Such a rollover does have some limitations: the distributions from the IRA are not eligible for the 10-year-forward averaging rule or for capital-gain treatment.

If an employee decides on a lump-sum withdrawal but does not anticipate any future need for the proceeds, he/she should consider the creation of an irrevocable *inter vivos* trust for the benefit of children or grandchildren. If the proceeds from the qualified plan are transferred into such a trust, the transfer becomes a taxable gift. Since such taxable gifts are added back to the estate before applying the estate tax, it is doubtful that such a transfer would reduce estate taxes unless the value of the property appreciates after the gift. However, the trust relieves the employee of paying income tax on the investment income, and, of course, the estate will be reduced by the amount of the accumulated income.

Selection of annuity disbursement. If the employee elects to receive benefits in the form of an annuity, there are still several decisions to make: whether the annuity should be for life only, a period certain, or a joint and survivor annuity. In many cases this decision is an economic one rather than a tax-related decision. Of course, if the annuity is for life only, there are no benefits remaining to be included in the estate. If the employee outlives the period certain, there will be no remaining benefits. But if the employee dies before the end of the period, the remaining benefits are subject to estate tax unless they qualify for the limited exclusion under Section 2039(c).

Choice of beneficiary. The employee's choice of a beneficiary to the remaining benefits of his retirement plan has some important tax consequences. First, potential problems arise when the employee's benefits passing to a spouse do not qualify for the marital deduction because these proceeds were excluded from the gross estate. Second, the value of the proceeds would increase the size of the spouse's estate and, if he/ she already holds substantial assets, could create even greater estate tax problems. Unless the spouse remarries, there would be no marital deduction for his/her estate. To avoid such consequences, the employee could name a trust as the beneficiary and give the trustee the power to accumulate or distribute income (as well as a five or five percent power)* to the surviving spouse for life, with the remainder going to children or other heirs upon his/her death. Such action would prohibit the benefits from being taxed in the survivor's estate and would also qualify for the Section 2039(c) exclusion in the decedent's estate (prior to 1985).

Tax considerations. Another related problem in naming an irrevocable beneficiary in order to receive the benefits of a trust or survivorship of an annuity is that the employee is deemed to have made a taxable gift in the amount of the value of the survivorship rights. However, the amount of the taxable gift is limited to the portion of the value of the benefits attributable to the employee's contributions.[11] Thus, if all contributions to the plan have been made by the employer, there is not a taxable gift.

A non-tax-related problem concerning joint and survivor annuities is worth mentioning. It is quite possible that such a contract does not end when the employee divorces and remarries. The first spouse is more likely to receive the benefits upon the employee's death. Therefore, if an employee anticipates divorce, some other form of annuity contract probably should be selected.

If, at the time the annuity payments are to begin, the employee is still employed, or both spouses have substantial income from other sources, the employee should consider establishing a 10-year trust (the Clifford trust) for some member of the family (other than the spouse) who is in a lower income tax bracket. Of course the employee would be deemed to have made a taxable gift upon the creation of the trust. But the income from the trust would not be taxed to the employee

---

*The "five or five power" concept refers to the power of the beneficiary of a trust to withdraw annually $5,000 or 5 percent of the assets of the trust. See E. W. Turley, "The 'Five or Five Power': An Obscure Estate Planning Tool," *Washington and Lee Law Review* 33, no. 3, pp. 701–15.

because the income would go to the designated family member and would not become a part of the employee's gross estate; therefore, indirectly, this would save estate tax.

Stock options. There are no provisions in the Code or regulations that grant special concessions to stock options. Therefore, all stock options (incentive and nonqualified) owned by the employee at death are included in gross estate under Section 2033. The options would be valued at their fair market value on the date of death for estate tax purposes.

Since, under the terms of an incentive stock option, the employee cannot transfer such options, only a few things can be done in the way of estate planning. However, in the case of a nonqualified stock option, the employee might consider making a gift of the option. A gift of a stock option does have some disadvantages. First, when the transferee exercises the option, the employee must include in personal income for income tax purposes the difference between the fair market value of the stock on the date of exercise and the price paid for such stock. Second, under current law, the amount of any taxable gifts is added to the estate before applying the estate tax rates. However, any appreciation in value between the date of the gift and the date of the employee's death is successfully removed from the estate.

The making of a gift of stock options should be considered only in connection with the overall estate plan. Such gifts should not be undertaken without prior professional advice.

Life insurance. Section 2042 controls the estate taxation of life insurance. This section provides that the gross estate shall include the value of all proceeds from life insurance (1) that is payable to the decedent's estate or for the benefit of his/her executor or estate or (2) that is payable to any other beneficiary if the decedent possessed at death any incidents of ownership exercisable either alone or in conjunction with any other person. Therefore, it is apparent that any insurance in which the corporate employee owns an interest is included in gross estate. In addition, the proceeds will be taxed in the estate if they are payable to the estate or to the executor or for the benefit of the estate, regardless of who owns the policy. Inclusion in the estate often occurs when least expected.

One problem area is the inclusion of the proceeds in the estate when they are paid to a named beneficiary but are made available for the benefit of the estate. This inclusion often happens when the beneficiary is required to pay some of the debts or obligations, such as funeral expenses of the estate. Another problem area is where the insurance has been used as collateral for the decedent's debts; such use would automatically throw the proceeds into the decedent's estate.

Incidents of ownership. If the proceeds of the life insurance policy are payable to a named beneficiary other than the estate, the employee-decedent must make sure that no incident of ownership is retained if the proceeds are to be excluded from the gross estate. Incidents of ownership are not limited to ownership in a strict legal sense but also include the right to economic benefits of the insurance policy. Therefore, incidents of ownership include the right (1) to name or change the beneficiary, (2) to surrender or cancel the policy, and (3) to assign the policy for a loan or to borrow against the cash-surrender value. Also, incidents of ownership include any reversionary interest, whether arising by the terms of the policy, a contract, or operation of law in the policy or the proceeds of the policy, but only if the employee-decedent's reversionary interest immediately before death exceeds 5 percent of the value of the policy.

Insurance in trust. If a life insurance policy is held in trust and under the terms of the policy or trust the employee-decedent (either alone or in conjunction with someone else) has the right to change the beneficial interest in the proceeds or policy, such person is deemed to have an incident of ownership. Where the employee-decedent is the sole or controlling stockholder (control means more than 50 percent of voting power) and the corporation retains some economic benefits (such as the right to change the beneficiary), then if the proceeds are payable to anyone other than for the benefit of the corporation, the employee-decedent is deemed to have retained some incidents of ownership and the proceeds are included in gross estate. If the corporation is directly or indirectly the beneficiary, and therefore the net worth of the corporation is increased, the decedent is not deemed to have retained incidents of ownership. In addition to the types of incidents of ownership mentioned above, one must evaluate the applicable state laws, especially in community-property states, to ensure that these laws do not convey incidents of ownership to the decedent.[12] In one case, the court decided that if the taxpayer's consent was needed to change a beneficiary, the taxpayer had incidents of ownership.[13].

Prior to Rev. Rul. 72-307 an employee was deemed to have retained some incidents of ownership of group-term insurance simply because he/she could terminate employment and the insurance would be canceled. Under current law an employee can give away all incidents of ownership in group-term insurance if he/she can assign ownership of the policy and if (1) he/she has a right to convert the policy to ordinary insurance, (2) he/she has assigned all rights, including the right to convert, and (3) state law allows such an assignment.[14]

Estate-planning tips for life insurance plans. An employee can reduce his/her gross estate, and thus taxable estate, by prohibiting the inclusion of life insurance proceeds in the estate. This exclusion may be accomplished by naming a beneficiary other than the taxpayer's estate or executor, and by retaining no incidents of ownership. The taxpayer may make a completed gift of the life insurance policy to another family member. Under current law the value of such a taxable gift is added back to the gross estate. However, in most cases, the value of a life insurance policy during the taxpayer's life is much less than the proceeds paid upon death. Therefore, the value of the gift after the $10,000 annual exclusion might be very small. Remember, though, that the donor must live at least three more years in order to avoid the rule about gifts in contemplation of death.

All estate owners should have a competent professional review of their entire estate plan before making such a beneficiary transfer. This review is important for many reasons. One is that in many situations the entire purpose of buying life insurance is either to help build the estate or to provide liquidity for the estate. The proceeds from the insurance are to be used to help pay funeral expenses, administration expenses, or death taxes. Without these proceeds, many estates would have to sell other assets to meet obligations. Another warning is appropriate. If the estate owner transfers the policy but requires the beneficiary to pay some of the debts or other obligations of the estate, the proceeds will be included in the estate. Thus, a gift tax is paid on the transfer and an estate tax on the proceeds.

Another problem in irrevocable assignments of life insurance is that conditions and relationships change. For instance, an executive might irrevocably assign her spouse a life insurance policy, but years later the couple divorces. Then there is the case of secondary beneficiaries. A policy is assigned to the employee's spouse, and the spouse dies first. This situation may cause two problems. First, if the spouse's will leaves the insurance to the employee, the proceeds will have to be included again in the employee's estate. Second, the spouse might leave the insurance policy to minor children. Normally, in such a situation the proceeds cannot be borrowed by the estate; therefore, these funds would not be available to the estate in any manner.

If, after careful investigation and analysis, it is determined that the employee-taxpayer should reduce the gross estate by irrevocably transferring life insurance, there are several avenues for such transfers. The transfer can be in the form of an outright gift, or the transfer may be in the form of a trust. If the transfer is in trust, extreme caution must be used in drafting the trust instrument and the naming of the trustee so as to ensure that the taxpayer does not retain any incidents of ownership. Expert counsel should be sought for these transfers.

The employee might transfer ordinary life insurance, split-dollar insurance, or group-life insurance. Each of these types presents special problems, but usually it is easier to completely and irrevocably transfer ordinary life insurance.

The IRS has provided means of assigning group-life policies. If the group policy is an optional policy that the employee can buy, the employee could allow an "applicant owner" (a specified relative such as a husband or wife) to obtain the coverage as the person insured. If the relative pays the premiums out of his/her separate funds, the proceeds are excluded from the employee's gross estate because neither the employee nor the estate had any incidents of ownership.[15]

If the group-term policy is paid for by the employee, there are more problems in its transfer. An IRS ruling indicates the tax consequences of transferring such a policy to a trust. According to the ruling, if the policy had been in effect for five years and had been transferred to an irrevocable trust, the proceeds would be paid to named beneficiaries. The ruling implied that there was no taxable gift at the time of the transfer because the employee's interest in such a policy had no ascertainable value. Any future premium payments made by the employer would be additional compensation (even if not taxable) to the employee, and thus the insured person would be making a gift of such compensation to the assignee. This gift would be treated as a gift of present interest and therefore would be eligible for the $10,000 annual exclusion.[16]

Obviously, there are many tax consequences to life insurance and the transfer of such policies. Life insurance should be considered in all estate plans if for no other reason than to provide liquidity. However, the authors recommend that careful study of the entire estate plan be made before making transfers of such policies.

Death-Benefit-Only Plans

If providing for the employee's spouse after death is one of the primary concerns (and it should be) in the estate planning, then the executive should consider the nonqualified death-benefit-only type of plan. A death-benefit-only plan provides for the corporate employer to pay a death benefit or a salary continuation to a named beneficiary or beneficiaries of the employee after his/her death. If such a plan is properly constructed, the employee can successfully have the proceeds excluded from the estate. This plan also provides benefits to heirs at no income tax cost to the employee.

For the proceeds to be excluded, several factors must be considered. First, the employee cannot be participating or entitled to participate in any other retirement or deferred-compensation plan, because the IRS will treat the separate plans as one. Therefore, the employee is entitled to benefits and must include the entire proceeds in the estate as an annuity under Section 2039.[17]

A second factor or condition is that the employee may not retain the right to change the beneficiary, because this right provides him/her with the power to alter, amend, revoke, or terminate the benefits, thereby making those benefits includable in gross estate under Section 2038.[18]

A third factor pertains to a legally enforceable contract between the corporation and the employee in which the corporation is required to make such payments. In such a contract, the employee-decedent is probably deemed to have made a transfer to the beneficiary during his/her lifetime.[19] Under such circumstances the proceeds of the plan are not included in the gross estate, but the value of the transfer at the time of the transfer is added back to the estate before computing the estate tax.

Still another factor to be considered is the possession of a reversionary interest in the proceeds by the employee. Such reversionary interest might exist in a clause such as "benefits payable to my spouse if she is living, otherwise to my estate."[20] Or if a secondary beneficiary is not named, such an interest might be determined under the 5 percent rule of Section 2037.

In addition to the factors mentioned above, the law states that the benefits are pulled back into the employee's estate if the plan is entered into within three years of death (under Section 2035, gifts in contemplation of death).[21]

Tax-planning tips with death-benefit-only plans. Certain death-benefit-only plans should be used only in those cases where the employee has substantial retirement funds other than those from the corporate employer. This type of plan is used only to provide benefits to heirs after the employee's death. However, if such a plan is feasible, it can provide substantial estate tax savings because its benefits are excluded from the gross estate. Because the costs (giving up rights to other retirement plans of the employer) are so significant, the authors recommend that careful consideration be given to the entire estate plan and other assets available for retirement before entering into such a contract.

To ensure that the proceeds of a death-benefit-only plan are excluded from the gross estate, the following conditions should be carefully observed:

1. The employee cannot receive *any* nonqualified deferred compensation or retirement benefits from the same employer.

2. The employer *cannot* retain the right to change the beneficiary.

3. The employee *cannot* retain a reversionary interest, that is, name secondary beneficiaries other than the estate.

4. The employee must not have died within three years of entering into the agreement.[22]

However, if there is no enforceable contract (the corporation is authorized only to make payment, or the corporation voluntarily makes payment) the three-years-of-death rule is not important.

CONCLUSION

There are many types and combinations of compensation packages. Only a few of the many types of compensation have been discussed in this chapter. However, from this limited discussion, it is apparent that each type of compensation has both income tax and estate tax consequences. In some instances, the employee must forgo income tax advantages to provide estate tax benefits, and vice versa. To the extent that the employee can control the type or types of compensation to which he/she is entitled, the authors recommend that a determined effort be made to integrate the income tax and estate tax consequences with the pure economics of the individual's situation in order to devise a comprehensive estate plan.

NOTES

1. Section 402(a).
2. Section 83(a) and (c).
3. Reg. 1.421-6.
4. Reg. 1.421-6(d)(1).
5. Section 101(d)(1)(B).
6. Section 101(b)
7. Section 2039(a).
8. 1981-4 IRB 30.
9. H. M. Esterces, "Analysis of Gift and Estate Tax Consequences of Death Benefits under Nonqualified Plans," *Journal of Taxation,* February 1981, p. 103.
10. Section 402(e)(4)(A).
11. Section 2517.
12. Reg. 20.2042-1(c)(2)-(6).
13. *Eleanor M. Schwager,* 64 T.C. 75 (1975).
14. Rev. Rul. 69-54, 1969-1 C.B. 221 and 72-307, 1972-1 C.B. 397.
15. Rev. Rul. 76-421, 1976-2 C.B. 300.
16. Rev. Rul. 76-490, 1976-2 C.B. 300.
17. *Estate of Bahen,* 305 F.2d 827, 62-2 USTC 12091 (Ct. Cls. 1962).
18. Rev. Rul. 76-304, 1976-2 C.B. 269.
19. *Estate of Bogley,* 514 F.2d 1027, 75-1 USTC 13068 (Ct. Cls. 1975).
20. *Estate of Fried,* 54 T.C. 78 (1970).
21. *Estate of Porter,* 54 T.C. 103 (1970).
22. Nell Margulis, "Death-Benefit-Only Plans Create Estate Planning Opportunities for High-Tax Bracket Executives," *Estate Planning,* July 1977, p. 284.

12

Specific Estate Planning Techniques

Another difference between death and taxes is that death is
frequently painless.

—*Anonymous*

Everyone should have a will. In your will a person called an
executor (or executrix) should be designated to settle your affairs upon your death. There should be an inventory of most of
your assets available to the executor.

If you do not have a will, it would be wise to contact an
attorney and have one drawn. This advice applies equally for
men and women, married or single. Also, if your will was
drawn before 1982, a new will may be necessary due to the
many changes in the Economic Recovery Tax Act of 1981.

If your assets exceed the $400,000 estate tax level, obtain
further information about estate planning from an attorney or
certified public accountant so that possible savings can be obtained by avoiding the estate tax.

If you die without a will, the state will appoint someone to
settle your estate. This settlement process will be very expensive and time consuming. There may be very little of your
estate left for any heirs.

Everyone needs a will—rich or poor, young or old. A copy of
the will should be kept outside of your safe deposit box.

Common disaster clause. A major problem is who shall get the custody of minor children in a common disaster. A car accident or plane crash can eliminate a husband and wife instantly. Or a widow or widower can die with minor children.

A married couple should make a decision and put it in writing in the form of a custody agreement designating who will rear any children in case of a common disaster. The parents of one of the spouses, a brother or sister, or an older child should be asked to serve as the custodian of the children. This choice should be reviewed periodically. In case of a divorced person, this decision can be very important.

Obviously any estate plan should be designed to support and educate the children until they are adults. Often people do not consider their most important assets—their children. A custody agreement is extremely important for the life and happiness of the entire family unit.

GENERAL GUIDELINES

No exact quantitative guideline figures may be given over the next several years due to the gradual increase in the unified credit and the decrease in the federal estate tax rates.

Married couples with small estates may wish to have a simple "I love you will." Here each spouse leaves all of his/her assets to the surviving spouse. Be sure that arrangement is made for the assets to be left in a trust for any minor children in case both parties die simultaneously (such as in a car accident).

As the estate becomes larger, an individual must decide whether to pay now or to pay later. In other words, with the unlimited marital deduction, a spouse can leave an estate of any size to the surviving spouse and pay no estate tax now. However, the surviving spouse may be pushed into a higher estate tax bracket. Whether a deferral strategy is best depends to a certain extent on how much longer the surviving spouse lives. The longer the surviving spouse lives, the better a deferral strategy becomes. For example, the deferred estate taxes may be reinvested by the surviving spouse and may far exceed any extra tax due when the surviving spouse dies many years later. Also, the surviving spouse's estate can be reduced gradually by a program of $10,000 gifts per donee each year.

The two alternatives may be outlined as follows, assuming that the husband dies first.

Pay tax now: Husband dies and does not use the unlimited marital deduction. Instead his assets are placed in a bypass trust, with income to his wife for life and the remainder to their children. When the wife dies, these assets will not be taxed again to her.

Pay tax later: Husband dies and leaves all his assets to his wife. No estate tax is due because of the unlimited marital deduction. If the wife still has these assets at her death, they may be taxed at a higher rate. Even here the husband should place the exemption equivalent into a bypass trust with income to wife for life, because the amount placed in the bypass trust avoids the estate tax at both the husband's and wife's deaths.

The reason for avoiding the marital deduction for the exemption equivalent amount is to keep the property from being taxed in the surviving spouse's estate. In a medium-sized estate, however, there is a danger in automatically placing the exemption equivalent in a bypass trust. Since the exemption equivalent is increasing so rapidly over the next several years, most of the decedent's assets may be placed in the bypass trust with little protection for the surviving spouse. Thus, a minimum pecuniary amount of property may be directed to the surviving spouse, with the remainder placed in the bypass trust.

Some general rules may be established to maximize the amount going to the beneficiaries:[1]

1. A complete transfer to the surviving spouse is advantageous when the spouse needs all of the earnings from both estates for consumption, and the surviving spouse's remaining life is at least 19 years.

2. When the spouse needs only the income from the original estate for consumption, the best alternative is to transfer nothing. Instead use the unlimited gift tax deduction to equalize the two estates.

3. When the surviving spouse needs a percentage of earnings from both estates for consumption, the longer the expected remaining life and the greater the disparity between the two estates, the larger the transfer needed in order to maximize the amount going to the beneficiaries.

TWO-PART AND THREE-PART WILLS

Briefly summarized in the following paragraphs are two kinds of wills designed to provide adequately for surviving spouse and children, while paying as little in estate taxes as possible (again, assume that the husband dies first).

In a two-part will, some assets pass directly to the surviving wife, with a minimum pecuniary amount specified (e.g., a will might state that no less than $300,000 is to go directly to the wife). She controls these assets. The remaining assets, up to the exemption equivalent, go into a bypass trust, so that they are not taxed in the wife's estate either. If there are still assets left over beyond the exemption equivalent amount, they go directly to the wife (and qualify for the unlimited marital deduction).

In a three-part will, some assets go directly to the surviving wife, who controls them. Again, a minimum pecuniary amount may be specified. Also, as in the two-part will, some property goes directly to a bypass trust, up to the exemption equivalent. The remaining property passes to a QTIP trust, with income to wife for life, and property going to children at wife's death.

Of course, the kind of will that is best for a given person depends on the individual situation and may change as the person's circumstances change. Appendixes C and D provide information about simple wills.

CONCLUSION

After reading this book, you should have a better idea of the many factors that must be carefully considered before drawing a will or making an estate plan. Competent, professional advice is, of course, essential. The authors hope that the terms and concepts introduced here will help you understand more clearly the suggestions of your estate planning team, so that all of you, working together, can do a better job. *Remember:* Review your estate plans frequently!

NOTE

1. E. Schnee and P. Wiehrs, "Using the Marital Deduction: A Simulation," *The Tax Adviser,* February 1984, pp. 76–84.

Personal Financial Statement for Estate Planning

This form is taken from Bruce McDowell's Investment Newsletter and is used by permission. It is included here as a guideline to help you gather relevant information in a format that will be useful when you meet with your estate-planning team. The form can be adapted to suit individual needs.

Date _____

Part 1: Present Income and Assets
(1) Cash on hand $_____
(2) Amount in checking accounts $_____
    (2a) Annual interest from (2) $_____
(3) Amount in savings deposits $_____
    (3a) Annual interest from (3) $_____
(4) Amount in money market funds $_____
    (4a) Annual interest from (4) $_____
(5) Amount in certificates of deposit $_____
    (5a) Annual interest from (5) $_____
(6) Amount in treasury bills $_____
    (6a) Annual interest from (6) $_____
(7) Amount in other debt instruments $_____
    (7a) Annual interest from (7) $_____
(8) Cash value of life insurance policies $_____
(9) Cash value of annuities or retirement
    funds $_____

(10) Value of securities (as detailed on last page)

(10a) Bonds $_____

(10b) Common or preferred stocks $_____

(10c) Notes held $_____

(10d) Mortgages held $_____

(10e) Tangibles owned $_____

(10f) Silver coins or bullion $_____

(10g) Gold coins or bullion $_____

(10h) Annual income from (10) $_____

(11) Value of stock holdings or partnership in personal businesses $_____

(11a) Annual income from personal business or from employment $_____

(12) Value of personal home $_____

(13) Value of furniture, fixtures, and contents $_____

(14) Value of personal equipment for business or profession $_____

(15) Value of automobiles $_____

(16) Value of rental real estate $_____

(16a) Annual rental income $_____

(17) Value of other real estate $_____

(17a) Annual income from (17) $_____

(18) Present income from all forms of insurance $_____

(19) Present income from social insurance $_____

(20) Present income from pensions or retirement contracts $_____

(21) Value of all other assets $_____

(21a) Annual income from (21) $_____

TOTAL ANNUAL INCOME $_____

TOTAL NET WORTH $_____

Part 2: Probable Future Income and Assets

(1) Estimated bonus $_____

(2) Estimated social insurance $_____

(3) Estimated pension income $_____

(4) Health and accident insurance $_____

(5) Life insurance $_____

(6) Cash from inheritance $_____

(7) Real estate from inheritance $_____

(8) Securities from inheritance $_____

(9) All other $_____

TOTAL EXPECTANCY $_____

Part 3: Present Liabilities
(1) Demand obligations (bank loans,
notes, IOUs, etc.) $_____
(2) Unsecured notes payable $_____
(3) Secured notes payable
    (3a) Mortages $_____ *(Balance outstanding)*

    (3b) Automobiles $_____ *(Balance outstanding)*

    (3c) Securities $_____ *(Balance outstanding)*

    (3d) Life insurance $_____ *(Balance owed)*

    (3e) Real estate $_____
    (3f) All other $_____ *(Balance outstanding)*

(4) Accounts payable
    (4a) Charge accounts $_____
    (4b) Medical expenses $_____
    (4c) All other $_____
(5) Annual expenses to date
    (5a) Property insurance $_____ *(Outstanding)*
    (5b) All other insurance $_____ *(Outstanding)*
    (5c) Property taxes $_____ *(Outstanding)*
    (5d) Estimated income taxes $_____ *(Outstanding)*
    (5e) All other taxes $_____ *(Outstanding)*
    (5f) Utilities $_____ *(Outstanding)*
    (5g) Maintenance $_____ *(Outstanding)*
    (5h) Clothing expenses $_____ *(Outstanding)*
    (5i) Family food expenses $_____ *(Outstanding)*
    (5j) Educational expenses $_____ *(Outstanding)*
    (5k) Contributions to charity $_____ *(Committed and outstanding)*

    (5l) All other $_____ *(Outstanding)*
(6) Other personal obligations $_____ *(Outstanding)*
(7) Estimated possible emergencies $_____
TOTAL LIABILITIES $_____

Part 4: Adjusted Net Worth
Total annual income (from Part 1) $_____
Total net worth (from Part 1) $_____
Total liabilities (from Part 3) $_____
Total adjusted net worth (subtract total
liabilities from total net worth) $_____

Part 5: Detailed Worksheet for Determining Capital Gains

For each category below that applies to you, set up a table using one column for each of the items listed here.

(1) *Securities:* Serial or certificate number, par value of bonds or number of shares of stocks, company, details of bond issues or type of stocks, date of purchase, original cost, and current value.

(2) *Silver and gold coins and bullion:* Face value of coins or troy ounces of bullion, type of coins or bullion, details of mintage or purity, date of purchase, original cost, and current value.

(3) *Life insurance and annuities:* Face value of policy, company, type of policy, premium, total amount paid in, and age when taken out.

Considerations for Estate Planning

Estate inheritance taxes
Annual expenses of immediate family
Annual income (or lump sum) for immediate family
Payment of all obligations
Burial and final expenses
Capital fund for children and their education
Possible emergencies in remaining family
Trust funds to avoid double taxation

APPENDIX B

Transfer Tax Rates

The following tables are taken from the Instructions for Form 706, United States Estate Tax Return (revised as of January 1984). The complete instruction booklet may be obtained from the Department of the Treasury, Internal Revenue Service. Although the 1977 rates continue to apply, the maximum estate and gift tax rates are being reduced from 70 percent to 50 percent over a seven-year period in 5 percent increments, as follows:

Year	Maximum Rate
1981	70%
1982	65
1983	60
1984–87	55
1988 and after	50

In 1988, the rates will range between 37 percent and 50 percent, with the 50 percent rate applying to taxable gifts and bequests in excess of $2.5 million.

TABLE A Unified Rate Schedule

Column A	Column B	Column C	Column D
			Rate of Tax on
Taxable	Taxable	Tax on	Excess over
Amount	Amount	Amount in	Amount in
over	not over	Column A	Column A
			(Percent)
$ 0	$ 10,000	$ 0	18
10,000	20,000	1,800	20
20,000	40,000	3,800	22
40,000	60,000	8,200	24
60,000	80,000	13,000	26
80,000	100,000	18,200	28
100,000	150,000	23,800	30
150,000	250,000	38,800	32
250,000	500,000	70,800	34
500,000	750,000	155,800	37
750,000	1,000,000	248,300	39
1,000,000	1,250,000	345,800	41
1,250,000	1,500,000	448,300	43
1,500,000	2,000,000	555,800	45
2,000,000	2,500,000	780,800	49
2,500,000	See Table A(1) for year of decedent's death.		

TABLE A(1) Decedents Dying in 1982

Column A	Column B	Column C	Column D
			Rate of Tax on
Taxable	Taxable	Tax on	Excess over
Amount	Amount	Amount in	Amount in
over	not over	Column A	Column A
			(Percent)
$2,500,000	$3,000,000	$1,025,800	53
3,000,000	3,500,000	1,290,800	57
3,500,000	4,000,000	1,575,800	61
4,000,000	—	1,880,800	65

TABLE A(1)   Decedents Dying in 1983

Column A Taxable Amount over	Column B Taxable Amount not over	Column C Tax on Amount in Column A	Column D Rate of Tax on Excess over Amount in Column A (Percent)
$2,500,000	$3,000,000	$1,025,800	53
3,000,000	3,500,000	1,290,800	57
3,500,000	—	1,575,800	60

TABLE A(1)   Decedents Dying in 1984

Column A Taxable Amount over	Column B Taxable Amount not over	Column C Tax on Amount in Column A	Column D Rate of Tax on Excess over Amount in Column A (Percent)
$2,500,000	$3,000,000	$1,025,800	53
3,000,000	—	1,290,800	55

TABLE B   Maximum Unified Credit against Estate Tax

For Decedents Dying—	The Credit Is—
1981 and earlier	Use the November 1981 revision of Form 706
1982	$62,800
1983	79,300
1984	96,300

TABLE C Computation of Maximum Credit for State Death Taxes (Based on Federal Adjusted Taxable Estate Which Is the Federal Taxable Estate Reduced by $60,000)

Adjusted Taxable Estate Equal to or More than— (1)	Adjusted Taxable Estate Less than— (2)	Credit on Amount in Column (1) (3)	Rate of Credit on Excess over Amount in Column (1) (4)
			(Percent)
$ 0	$ 40,000	$ 0	None
40,000	90,000	0	0.8
90,000	140,000	400	1.6
140,000	240,000	1,200	2.4
240,000	440,000	3,600	3.2
440,000	640,000	10,000	4.0
640,000	840,000	18,000	4.8
840,000	1,040,000	27,600	5.6
1,040,000	1,540,000	38,800	6.4
1,540,000	2,040,000	70,800	7.2
2,040,000	2,540,000	106,800	8.0
2,540,000	3,040,000	146,800	8.8
3,040,000	3,540,000	190,800	9.6
3,540,000	4,040,000	238,800	10.4
4,040,000	5,040,000	290,800	11.2
5,040,000	6,040,000	402,800	12.0
6,040,000	7,040,000	522,800	12.8
7,040,000	8,040,000	650,800	13.6
8,040,000	9,040,000	786,800	14.4
9,040,000	10,040,000	930,800	15.2
10,040,000	—	1,082,800	16.0

———————————— APPENDIX C ————————————

Drafting a Truly "Simple Will" that Can Effectively Communicate to Both Client and Court

Lynn B. Squires and Robert S. Mucklestone,
Attorney, Seattle, Washington

A will can be both sophisticated in substance and simple in form. The lawyer's substantive task—to provide a legally valid instrument disposing of the testator's property—is not especially difficult given the many adequate forms available. The task of simplifying the form—to provide a self-explanatory memorandum that the testator can understand—is more difficult. A will is a highly personal document. Not only should the testator understand it, but he or she should also be able to explain its contents to others, especially family members.

Basic Principles

To draft a simplified will form in which every word is comprehensible to a client, the authors have relied on three fundamental principles of legal drafting: consistency, clear organization, and normal usage.

Reprinted by permission from *Estate Planning,* March 1983, published by Warren, Gorham & Lamont, Inc., 1633 Broadway, New York, N.Y. 10019. Copyright 1983, Estate Planning Research Group, Ltd.

When specialized legal terms must be used, these terms are defined in everyday language to permit a lay reader's understanding. Customary boilerplate has been eliminated; technical language such as "per stirpes" and difficult concepts such as "marital deduction" have been avoided.

While observing these fundamental principles of drafting, the first concern must be the integrity of the substance of the will. No sacrifice of substantive content or of refinement of concept has been made for the sake of readability. Both audiences—the client and the court—are addressed in this form. The rationale for boilerplate provisions and redundant, archaic language was, of course, to ensure the success of the will in court. Neither boilerplate nor redundant language guarantees a successful document, however, and may, in themselves, create problems of interpretation. Drafting for simplicity, consistency, clarity, and good order should always result in improved substance.

The simple will form that follows is intended for a married person with children whose total estate is valued at less than the unified credit exemption equivalent, which for 1983 is $275,000. The following form is worded for a married man; the obvious pronoun and noun changes should be made if the will is for a woman. Although this form was drafted primarily for use by Washington residents, no unique provisions regarding community property are included that would limit its use in non-community property jurisdictions.

Several techniques were useful in drafting the form. In organizing any will, consider what the client or other reader would want to know first and what the reader would look for next. For example, in the form the "players" are identified on the first page so that the reader will not have to hunt through the document.

A particularly useful structure is the "If. . . then" sentence, consisting of an initial condition or clause followed by a consequence or result. Parallel structure should be consistently used. Short sentences should be favored over long ones. Sentences should be limited to one idea whenever possible.

Over-precision should be avoided because it often raises unnecessary questions. Vagueness also should be avoided, and statements should be general.

Given that the narrowest term will govern if there are questions of interpretation, overly narrow modifications or descriptions should not be used, nor should vague archaic terms such as "herein," "hereinafter," "said," "aforesaid," "hereafter," and "hereby." These terms give the appearance of precision without specifying the place or time referred to.

Simple Will Form

The following form reflects the authors' belief that a will can be plainly written so that those who sign it and those who are bound by it may understand it fully. The drafting decisions reflected by the form are discussed in the paragraphs that follow each section.

WILL OF [NAME]

I, [name], declare this to be my Will and revoke all prior Wills and Codicils.

ARTICLE 1. FAMILY; GUARDIAN

My immediate family now consists of my wife [name] ("my wife"), and our [   ] children, [names], all of whom reside with me at [address]. The provisions of this Will shall apply not only to my [   ] children named above and their issue, but also to all children who may hereafter be born to or adopted by me and to their issue.

Naming of testator. Wording that typically appears in the first sentence of a will has been simplified here. The phrase "make, publish, and declare" has been shortened to "declare" in order to avoid both wordiness and overprecision. "Will and testament" has been reduced to "Will." The customary statement "I hereby expressly revoke and cancel any and all other wills, codicils, and testamentary dispositions heretofore at any time made by me" has been reduced to the single word "revoke." The phrase "any and all wills previously made by me" has been shortened to "all prior Wills."

Family. The immediate family is identified, and provision is made for afterborn children. If a child is not named or provided for (a "pretermitted" child), the testator will be deemed to have died intestate as to that child, and the child will be entitled to that portion of the estate that the child would have received had the testator died without a will. For this reason, it may be important to define children as including afterborn and adopted.

"Immediate family." Since a notice of appointment must be sent to each "heir" (those that would be entitled to a portion of the estate if the testator dies without a will), it is helpful to have names and addresses which were current when the will was signed.

"Wife." "Wife" and "husband" are used rather than "spouse" because clients think of themselves as wives and husbands rather than as spouses, and thus identify more immediately and comfortably with the situations described in the will.

"All of whom reside with me." The authors prefer "reside" rather than the less familiar term "domicile," which has a more

precise legal meaning. An individual's residence is, in nearly every instance, his or her domicile. For almost every client, "domicile" used as a noun or otherwise ("domiciled") will be unnecessarily perplexing. In instances where the residence is not the domicile, an explanatory statement such as the following should be added: "My present domicile is in the State of Washington. Although I presently reside in Washington, D.C., it is my intention that the State of Washington continue as my domicile."

"Issue." "Issue" is used rather than "descendants," "children," or "heirs" because "issue" includes all the lawful lineal descendants of the ancestor and all lawfully adopted children. In most states, "lawfully adopted child" is not an "heir" of his or her natural parents.

"All." For brevity, "all" has been used consistently, rather than "any and all."

"Hereafter be born." This phrase is used to avoid a pretermitted child in the event that any children might be born or adopted after the date of the will. The length of this sentence is offset by the internal parallelism provided by the "not only . . . but also" structure. When sentences are necessarily longer than 25 words, internal parallel structures increase readability.

> If my wife does not survive me and it becomes necessary to appoint a guardian for any child of mine, I appoint [name] Guardian of the person and estate of each such child. If [name] at any time declines to act, fails to act, or is unable to act as Guardian, I appoint [name] as a Guardian of the person and estate.

The guardian is then appointed, as being next in importance to the testator. Most parents want to exercise their legal right to appoint a guardian for any minor child.

"Guardian of the person and estate." This nomenclature is used rather than "guardian of the person and property" because state statutes provide for these appointments. While an individual may be appointed as guardian of both the person and the estate of a minor or incompetent, a corporate trustee (a bank with trust powers) cannot act as guardian of the person.

ARTICLE 2. EXECUTOR

2.1 Designation. I appoint my wife, (name), as my Executor. If she at any time declines, fails, or is unable to act as my Executor, I appoint [name] as my Executor. If both my wife and [name] at any time decline, fail or are unable to act as my Executor, I appoint [corporate name and address], and its successors, to act as my Executor.

Appointment and powers of the executor appear on the first or second page for easy identification.

The sequence of two "if...then" sentences serves to simplify and clarify possible outcomes, beginning with the most likely outcome and continuing in logical order: (1) my wife will be executor; (2) if she is unable, then X will do it; (3) if neither she nor X is able, then Y will do it. This clear, logical progression is easier for a client to understand than the convoluted explanations often found in a single extra-long sentence.

2.2 Bond waiver; powers. No bond, surety, or other security shall be required of my Executor in any jurisdiction for any purpose. My Executor shall have unrestricted nonintervention powers to settle my estate in the manner set forth in this Will. Furthermore, my Executor shall have full power, authority, and discretion to do all that my Executor thinks necessary or desirable in administering my estate, including the authority to:

(a) Make interim distributions of principal and income to those who are to receive the principal and the income;

(b) Sell, lease, exchange, mortgage, pledge, or assign all or any part of the property of my estate for any purpose which my Executor thinks is in the best interests of my estate, whether or not it is necessary in order to pay debts, taxes, or expenses of administration;

(c) Invest and reinvest property that is not specifically given, in any form of investment that my Executor thinks advisable; and

(d) Continue to operate any business or business properties in which I have an interest at the time of my death and, in so doing, delegate discretionary as well as administrative powers.

The powers of the executor are separated visually from the designation so that the reader may quickly locate one or the other. The powers are also easy to locate by tabulation and by indentation. Each of the four categories begins with a verb so as to clearly link each category with the introductory phrase "including the authority to." In the typical Will, powers of the executor are frequently set forth in a single seemingly endless sentence.

"Unrestricted nonintervention powers." Because some state stat utes may give the court the authority to "restrict" the powers of the personal representative, the use of "unrestricted" is an attempt by the testator to indicate to the court that he or she does not want such a restriction.

The second and third sentences in section 2.2 and in subsection (a) have parallel structures for clarity and ease of reading. By repeating words and arrangements of words at the beginning of successive sentences, sentences are easier to limit to a single idea, rendering them more comprehensible to the client.

"Full power." The combination of the phrase "full power" and the word "including" provides ample breadth to the executor's powers. There is no need for such modifiers as "without limitation" or "in addition to any other powers granted by this will or by law." The word "including" is the key, indicating a partial rather than complete list.

"Thinks." The authors use "thinks" rather than the more common word "deems," preferring to leave "deeming" to the courts and "thinking" to the testator. Clients are unlikely to describe any action they might take as "deeming."

"Those who are to receive the principal and the income." This clause illustrates the drafter's occasional need to lengthen in order to clarify. The term commonly used instead is "remainder beneficiaries," which may be incomprehensible to a client. Such a reader can, however, easily understand "those who are to receive the principal and the income."

"Specifically given." "Specifically given" refers to a specific gift, such as a home, as opposed to a residuary gift. Because it is more common, "given" is consistently used rather than the archaic "bequeathed," which adds no futher meaning.

"Continue." "Continue" is the last of four parallel active verbs beginning with "Make," "Sell," and "Invest." Active verbs are easier to understand and more vivid than forms of "to be" or other weak verbs; here they receive emphasis because they are the first words in indented and tabulated series.

> *2.3 Taxes from residue.* I direct that all estate, inheritance, and other taxes imposed by reason of my death, and interest or penalties on those taxes, shall be paid by my executor out of the residue of my estate. This direction shall apply to all such taxes attributable to all property of my estate even though some property does not pass under my Will or is not part of the residue of my estate.

Taxes from residue. This section is placed in Article 2 because it directs the executor and so fits logically after the designation and powers of the executor. This section could also be placed as a separate article after Article 2.

Debts and administrative expenses have been omitted from this form because these are required by statute to be paid from the estate. If creditors do not file a claim within the statutory period, then creditors might argue that they should be paid anyway if a direction appears in the will.

"On those taxes." The repetition of "on those taxes" is preferred to the use of the vague "therein" ("interest or penalties therein"). Repetition of words normally presents no obstacle to the reader; in fact, once the reader has comprehended a word, the second appearance of that word speeds up the reading because it need not be "processed" again. If, however, a word like "therein," "herein," or "aforementioned" is used in place of a word or idea, then the reader must either translate "therein" or read back over earlier material to find what the "there" refers to.

"This direction." The two sentences in section 2.3 are designed to be comprehended as a conceptual unit: the first describes the executor's responsibility; the second modifies the first. Rather than fit both ideas into one long sentence, two sentences have been constructed with "matching" subjects: "I direct that" and "This direction shall...."

ARTICLE 3. DISPOSITION OF PROPERTY

3.1 Home; tangible personal property. If my wife survives me by thirty days, I give her all of my interest in

(a) the residence property which we occupy as a home at the time of my death, together with all rights associated with the property, and

(b) tangible personal property of every kind, for example, motor vehicles, boats, furniture, furnishings, books, objects of art, sporting equipment, jewelry, clothing, and other property of a household or personal kind.

If my wife does not survive me by thirty days, I give to those of my children who survive me by thirty days the tangible personal property described in (b) of the preceding paragraph (except motor vehicles and boats). This property, if two or more of them survive me by thirty days, shall be divided among them by my Executor, in as nearly equal shares as may be practicable, having due regard for their personal preferences. My Executor may sell any of such property and distribute the proceeds to equalize the shares. My Executor shall be discharged in distributing tangible personal property so given to any minor child when the child or any adult having custody of the child delivers a written receipt to my Executor.

All of the property is disposed of in one article rather than in several separate ones. This extremely important section should be self-contained. That is, the reader should find out in one place how all of the property will be disposed of rather than having to read through the entire will to perceive a complete picture of the property disposition. The article is divided into two subsections. The first part of section 3.1 defines tangible personal property, and the second part explains what is to be done with it if the wife (or husband) does not survive the testator by 30 days.

"Tangible personal property" is used to distinguish between intangible personal property, such as shares of stock or bank accounts, and tangible items, such as those listed in subsection 3.1(b). (See, *e.g., Estate of Dodge,* 6 Cal.3d 311, 491 P.2d 385, 98 Cal. Rptr. 801 (1971).)

"Give." The archaic "bequeath" and "devise" are replaced by the more common "give."

Parallel structure, tabulation, and indentation are used to emphasize the items given to the wife (or husband). The parallel nouns "the residence property" and "tangible personal property" both follow logically from the introductory phrase "all of my interest in."

"All rights associated with the property." This general and inclusive phrase is preferable to a more detailed statement of such rights, for example, this overprecise description: "appurtenances, including easements, rights of way and other tangible or intangible rights associated with the use of such property."

"For example." This phrase is used to indicate that what follows is an illustration only, not a complete list.

Section 3.1, beginning with the clause "If my wife survives me by thirty days" is echoed in the clause "if my wife does not survive me by thirty days." The repetition of the earlier structure draws attention to the conceptual link.

A provision for order of deaths in case of simultaneous death might be necessary if one spouse has substantial separate property. Otherwise such a provision is unnecessary because survivorship periods of 30 days and four months also cover simultaneous death.

3.2 Residue. If my wife survives me by four months, I give her the residue of my estate. If my wife does not survive me by four months, I give the residue of my estate in equal shares
> one to each of my children who survives me by four months and
> one by right of representation to surviving issue of each
of my children who does not survive me by four months but who leaves issue surviving me by four months.

If neither my wife nor any of my issue survive me by four months, I give the residue of my estate
> one-half as if I had died on the last day of the four-month period without a Will and
> one-half as if it were my wife's estate and she had died
on the last day of the four-month period without a Will, according to the [state] laws of descent and distribution.

* * * *

I have initialed for identification purposes all pages of this my Will and have executed the entire instrument by signing this page on [date], at [place].

[Signature]

Section 3.2 is arranged in a pattern of parallel structures to simplify its complex substance. The largest parallel structures occur at the beginning of each of the two paragraphs. Within the first paragraph, the second sentence is parallel to the first and follows logically from it: "If my wife survives me. . . . If my wife does not survive me. . . ." Within the last sentence, internal parallelism helps to order ideas and increase readability: "one to each. . . and one by right. . . ." For simplicity and clarity, the phrase "by four months" is repeated and such phrases as "prior to the time of the later death" are omitted as being nearly incomprehensible to any reader.

The second paragraph parallels and repeats the beginning of the first: "If neither my wife nor any of my issue survive me by four months. . . ." The division of residue is clarified by indentation and parallelism within that first sentence: "one-half as if I had. . . one-half as if it were. . . ." This form avoids the redundant wording customary in residuary clauses.

STATEMENT OF WITNESSES

Each of the undersigned declares under penalty of perjury under the laws of the state of [_____], on this [_____] day of [_____) at [place] that the following is true and correct:

(1) I am over the age of twenty-one years and competent to be a witness to the Will of [name] (the "testator").

(2) The testator in my presence and in the presence of the other witness whose signature appears below
  (a) Declared the foregoing instrument to be his Will;
  (b) Requested me and the other witness to act as witnesses to his Will and to make this statement; and
  (c) Signed such instrument.

(3) I believe the testator to be of sound mind, and that in so declaring and signing he was not acting under any duress, menace, fraud, or undue influence.

(4) The other witness and I in the presence of the testator and of each other now affix our signatures as witnesses to the Will and make this statement.

[Signature]_____

[Address]

[Signature]_____

[Address]

A will must be signed by the testator and in most states attested by two or more competent witnesses, "subscribing their names to the will in the presence of the testator by his direction or request. . . ." The witnesses may, at the request of the testator, make an affidavit on the will "stating such facts as they would be required to testify in court" to prove the will. In some states, whenever any matter in a proceeding is required to be established or proved by a person's affidavit, the matter may be proved by an unsworn statement which:

1. Recites that it is certified or declared by the person to be true under penalty of perjury.
2. Is subscribed by the person.
3. States the date and place of its execution.
4. States that it is so certified or declared under the laws of the state.

"Signatures." No state now requires that witnesses set their seals upon a will. Thus the customary wording "In witness whereof I have hereunder set my hand and seal" may be eschewed both in form and substance.

Conclusion

A will should clearly communicate a testator's wishes, both to the court and to the testator when the testator reads it outside the lawyer's office. The substance of a will is ordinarily easier to draft than, for example, the substance of a contract. As a personal document, however, a will presents a different kind of challenge: lawyers must bridge the distance between their specialized knowledge and a client's general knowledge.

This challenge can be met by following the principles of drafting: consistency, clear organization, and normal usage. As a final step in preparing a will, the drafter should check consistency of word use by reviewing the will as a whole to check each use of key words and to eliminate synonyms or other inconsistencies. The will should be reviewed as a whole for impractical organization and for terms that may be unfamiliar to a lay reader. When lawyers use forms provided by their law offices or by banks, they should tailor the forms to suit their clients' needs, especially their need to understand completely their own will. Client appreciation for the lawyer's effort to simplify should make that effort well worth the time.

APPENDIX D

"Simple Will" Can Be Simplified Further to Produce a More Concise but Effective Document

Leon Fieldman, Attorney, Chicago, Illinois

The trend in recent years to improve the use of the English language by lawyers has not bypassed the field of estate planning. "Plain English" drafting of wills and trusts is advocated by some and debated by others. A will both sophisticated in substance and simple in form was recommended in Squires and Mucklestone, *Drafting a truly "simple will" that can effectively communicate to both client and court,* 10 EP 80 (March 1983). The provisions suggested there can be simplified even more—rigorous editing can substantially shorten that will, without changing its substance. Clients, secretaries, and file clerks alike will be pleased with the compressed version. It will be easier to understand, less apt to have errors, faster to prepare and less bulky.

Sample Provisions Compared

What follows is the simple will proposed by Squires and Mucklestone, followed by an abbreviated version using the same substance and organization. For ease of comparison, each revised section is identified as "Fieldman" at the start.

Reprinted by permission from *Estate Planning,* September 1983, published by Warren, Gorham & Lamont, Inc., 1633 Broadway, New York, N.Y. 10019. Copyright 1983, Estate Planning Research Group, Ltd.

WILL OF [NAME]

I, [name], declare this to be my Will and revoke all prior Wills and Codicils.

ARTICLE 1. FAMILY; GUARDIAN

My immediate family now consists of my wife, [name] ("my wife"), and our [   ] children, [names], all of whom reside with me at [address]. The provisions of this Will shall apply not only to my [   ] children named above and their issue, but also to all children who may hereafter be born to or adopted by me and to their issue.

WILL OF [NAME]

Fieldman

I, [name], declare this to be my will and revoke all prior wills and codicils.

FIRST: FAMILY AND GUARDIAN

My wife, [name] ("my wife"), and our [   ] children, [names], comprise my immediate family. All reside with me at [address]. This will applies to all my children, including any hereafter born or adopted, and to their issue.

If my wife does not survive me and it becomes necessary to appoint a guardian for any child of mine, I appoint [name] Guardian of the person and estate of each such child. If [name] at any time declines to act, fails to act, or is unable to act as Guardian, I appoint [name] as Guardian of the person and estate.

Fieldman.

If my wife does not survive me, I appoint [name] guardian of the person and estate of each minor child of mine. If for any reason [name] does not act as guardian, I appoint [name] as guardian of the person and estate.

ARTICLE 2. EXECUTOR

2.1 Designation. I appoint my wife, [name], as my Executor. If she at any time declines, fails, or is unable to act as my Executor, I appoint [name] as my Executor. If both my wife and [name] at any time decline, fail or are unable to act as my Executor, I appoint (corporate name and address), and its successors, to act as my Executor.

SECOND: EXECUTOR

Fieldman   **A.** *Designation.*

I appoint my wife my executor. If for any reason she does not act as executor, I appoint [name] my executor. If for any reason neither my wife, nor [name] acts as executor, I appoint [corporate name and address] my executor.

2.2   Bond waiver; powers.   No bond, surety, or other security shall be required of my Executor in any jurisdiction for any purpose. My Executor shall have unrestricted nonintervention powers to settle my estate in the manner set forth in this Will. Furthermore, my Executor shall have full power, authority, and discretion to do all that my Executor thinks necessary or desirable in administering my estate, including the authority to:

(a) Make interim distributions of principal and income to those who are to receive the principal and the income;

(b) Sell, lease, exchange, mortgage, pledge, or assign all or any part of the property of my estate for any purpose which my Executor thinks is in the best interests of my estate, whether or not it is necessary in order to pay debts, taxes, or expenses or administration;

(c) Invest and reinvest property that is not specifically given, in any form of investment that my Executor thinks advisable; and

(d) Continue to operate any business or business properties in which I have an interest at the time of my death and, in so doing, delegate discretionary as well as administrative powers.

Fieldman   **B.** *Bond waiver and powers.*

My executor shall not be required to give bond, surety, or other security. My executor shall have power, without court order, to settle my estate as this will provides and to do all my executor thinks necessary or desirable to administer my estate, including power to:

1. distribute principal and income on an interim basis to those entitled to it;

2. sell, lease, exchange, mortgage, pledge, or assign all or part of my estate's property, whether or not necessary to pay debts, taxes, or administration expenses;

3. invest and reinvest property not specifically given; and

4. continue to operate any business or business properties in which I have an interest at my death and, in so doing, delegate powers.

2.3 Taxes from residue. I direct that all estate, inheritance, and other taxes imposed by reason of my death, and interest or penalties on those taxes, shall be paid by my Executor out of the residue of my estate. This direction shall apply to all such taxes attributable to all property of my estate even though some property does not pass under my Will or is not part of the residue of my estate.

Fieldman **C. Taxes from residue.**

My executor shall pay from the residue of my estate all death taxes imposed because of my death and interest and penalties on those taxes, whether on property passing under this will or otherwise.

ARTICLE 3. DISPOSITION OF PROPERTY

3.1 Home; tangible personal property. If my wife survives me by thirty days, I give her all of my interest in

(a) the residence property which we occupy as a home at the time of my death, together with all rights associated with the property, and

(b) tangible personal property of every kind, for example, motor vehicles, boats, furniture, furnishings, books, objects of art, sporting equipment, jewelry, clothing, and other property of a household or personal kind.

If my wife does not survive me by thirty days, I give to those of my children who survive me by thirty days the tangible personal property described in (b) of the preceding paragraph (except motor vehicles and boats). This property, if two or more of them survive me by thirty days, shall be divided among them by my Executor, in as nearly equal shares as may be practicable, having due regard for their personal preferences. My Executor may sell any of such property and distribute the proceeds to equalize the shares. My Executor shall be discharged in distributing tangible personal property so given to any minor child when the child or any adult having custody of the child delivers a written receipt to my Executor.

THIRD: DISPOSITION OF PROPERTY

Fieldman **A. Home and tangible personal propert**

If my wife survives me by thirty days, I give her all of my interest in

1. the residence property which we occupy as a home at my death, and all rights associated with it, and

2. all tangible personal property, for example, vehicles, boats, furniture, furnishings, books, art objects, sporting equipment, jewelry, and clothing.

If my wife does not survive me by thirty days, I give my tangible personal property (except vehicles and boats) in equal shares to my children who survive me by thirty days, but my executor shall consider their personal preferences in making that division. My executor may sell any of that property and distribute the proceeds to equalize the shares. My executor shall be discharged for tangible personal property so given to any minor child if the child or an adult having the child's custody gives a written receipt to my executor.

3.2 Residue. If my wife survives me by four months, I give her the residue of my estate. If my wife does not survive me by four months, I give the residue of my estate in equal shares

one to each of my children who survives me by four months and
one by right of representation to surviving issue of each of my children who does not survive me by four months but who leaves issue surviving me by four months.

If neither my wife nor any of my issue survive me by four months, I give the residue of my estate

one-half as if I had died on the last day of the four-month period without a Will and
one-half as if it were my wife's estate and she had died on the last day of the four-month period without a Will,

according to the [state] laws of descent and distribution.

* * * *

I have initialed for identification purposes all pages of this my Will and have executed the entire instrument by signing this page on [date], at [place].

[Signature]

Fieldman **B.** *Residue.*

If my wife survives me by four months, I give her the residue of my estate. If my wife does not survive me by four months, I give the residue in equal shares: one to each of my children who survives me by four months and one to the descendants *per stirpes* who survive me by four months of each of my children who does not so survive me.

If neither my wife nor any of my descendants survive me by four months, I give the residue of my estate according to [state] laws of descent and distribution, one-half as if I had died with no will on the last day of that four-month period and one-half as if it were my wife's estate and she had died with no will on that last day.

I have initialed all pages of this will and have signed it on [date], at [place].

[Signature]

STATEMENT OF WITNESSES

Each of the undersigned declares under penalty of perjury under the laws of the state of [_____], on this [_____] day of [_____] at [place] that the following is true and correct:

(1) I am over the age of twenty-one years and competent to be a witness to the Will of [name] (the "testator").

(2) The testator in my presence and in the presence of the other witness whose signature appears below
   (a) Declared the foregoing instrument to be his Will;
   (b) Requested me and the other witness to act as witnesses to his Will and to make this statement; and
   (c) Signed such instrument.

(3) I believe the testator to be of sound mind, and that in so declaring and signing he was not acting under any duress, menace, fraud, or undue influence.

(4) The other witness and I in the presence of the testator and of each other now affix our signatures as witnesses to the Will and make this statement.

[Signature]_____

[Address]

[Signature]_____

[Address]

STATEMENT OF WITNESSES

Fieldman

Each of the undersigned declares under penalty of perjury under [state] law, on _____, 19 __, that the following is true:

A. I am over age twenty-one and competent to witness this will.

B. The testator in my presence and in the presence of the other undersigned witness
   1. declared the foregoing document to be his will;
   2. asked me to act as a witness to his will and to make this statement; and
   3. signed his will.

C. I believe that the testator is of sound mind and did not act under duress, fraud, or undue influence in so declaring and signing.

D. In the presence of the testator and of the other witness I sign as witness to this will.

[Signature]

[Address]

[Signature]

[Address]

Comments and Analysis

Why capitalize "Will," "Codicil," "Guardian" or "Executor"? In everyday writing, those words would be in lower case. Lawyers should use everyday writing if they want to help clients understand legal documents.

The use of "Article" to identify parts of a will is surplusage. Call the parts "First," "Second" and "Third" or "One," "Two" and "Three."

In a simple will, the use of a decimal system to identify paragraphs seems ponderous. Perhaps that system is appropriate for a long contract with many subparagraphs, but for a simple will with few subparagraphs a better and more consistent method of identification is the classical outline system that has been used above.

The following points relate to specific provisions of the two wills.

1. In the first part (family and guardian), Squires and Mucklestone prefer "issue" to "descendants." I have adopted their view here for consistency. However, be sure that under local law "issue" includes adopted descendants, if that is what the client wants.

In most states an "appointment" of a guardian in a will is no more than the testator's nomination of a guardian. The court actually appoints the guardian upon petition. If a guardian is not necessary, there will be no petition. Therefore, the phrase, "if. . . it becomes necessary to appoint a guardian for any child of mine" is surplusage. "Declines to act, fails to act, or is unable to act" is an example of the wordy overprecision to be avoided. "If for any reason" is simpler and broader.

2. In the second part (executor), the phrase "declines, fails, or is unable" appears twice. Its elimination is a double shortening. The reference to the corporate executor's "successor" is unnecessary in many states, where statutes provide for automatic succession.

"Full power, authority and discretion" is redundant language to eliminate. The simple use of "power" does that.

Squires and Mucklestone's executor's powers can be made much more taut. Because of the language in paragraph 2.2 that the executor can do all he or she "thinks necessary or desirable in administering my estate," these phrases are redundant: (1) "for any purpose which my Executor thinks is in the best interests of my estate" in subparagraph (b); and (2) "in any form of investment that my Executor thinks advisable" in subparagraph (c).

In contrast to "discretionary as well as administrative powers" in subparagraph (d), I use "powers," which is just as broad and avoids overprecision.

3. In the third part (disposition of property), more precise than "survives me by thirty days" would be "is living on the thirtieth day succeeding the date of my death."

As to "jewelry," I would normally add "watches," especially where a bequest of "jewelry" is made to one person and the balance of the tangible personal property goes to another.

If state law provides that bequests lapse in the event that the wife does not survive by 30 days, it would be clearer to the client if the will says so.

In the disposition of the residue, I have opted for "descendants *per stirpes*" rather than "by right of representation to surviving issue." Either phrase probably will require explanation to the client, but "descendants *per stirpes*" is shorter.

The statement that all pages are initialed is sufficient. To recite that the initialing was "for identification purposes" adds nothing.

As to the sentence before the testator's signature: "executed the entire instrument" is pure legalese. "Signed it" says the same thing.

4. In the statement of witnesses portion, Squires and Mucklestone use "true and correct." I use "true." They use "over the age of twenty-one years." I use "over age twenty-one." "Instrument" is their word; I prefer "document" or "will." Their "duress, menace," I shorten to "duress." "Affix our signatures," I condense to "sign."

A much shorter attestation clause would be as follows:

"We, the undersigned, certify that in our presence the foregoing document was, on the date thereof, signed and declared by the testator as his will, and that we, in his presence and in the presence of each other and at his request, then on that date signed our names as witnesses to it, believing the testator to be of sound mind and memory at the time of signing."

Conclusion

The simple will of Squires and Mucklestone is a good job, free of many of the lazy usages to which lawyers seem addicted. But, further close editing (always easier than producing the original will) can result in an even tighter and more readable document.

Index